Towards a Praxis Model of Social Work

A Reflexive Account of 'Praxis Intervention' with the Adivasis of Attappady

Madhu Prabakaran

2005

DEDICATION

Dedicated to the Adivasis of Attappady, and fellow native tribes of the world.

CONTENTS

ACKNOWLEDGMENTS

I thank profusely my teachers at School of Social Sciences, Mahatma Gandhi University, Kottayam who introduced me to the world of social theory. I could never have imagined the possibility of "Praxis Intervention" without the theoretical orientation I received from my teachers at the School.

I am grateful to my teachers at Tata Institute of Social Sciences, Mumbai for introducing me to the social work practice and theory.

I Thank Dr. Ponna Wignaraja for the 'deep immersion' training in 'Participatory Action Research' I received from him. It is from Dr. Ponna Wignaraja I learnt the technique of phased training method.

I am indebted to the adivasi participants of the praxis intervention for their complete involvement in the project. I also thank the hamlet residents of Attappady for their dedicated participation in the project.

I thank all the resource persons and team members of the praxis intervention project for their dedicated association with the project. I am very much indebted to the kind support I received from Mr. Jose peter, Mr. Gopala Krishnan, Mr. Brahma Putran and KT Thomas in running the Praxis intervention project.

Words would not be sufficient to thank my guide Prof. Nizar Ahmed. A few among the scholars can get a guide who could be so much learned, sincere, caring and loving.

I thank Dr. Rina Francis and Anjali Menon for proof reading the thesis. I adore the sincerity with which they read the thesis and corrected the language errors.

I thank Prof. Rajan Gurukkal, Prof. Bruce Kapferer, Dr. S. Raju, Prof. Damodharan Nampoothiri, Prof. M. Raghavan, Prof. J. Raghaviah, Dr. Sathish Chandran Nair, Prof. Kunjaman, Prof. Reghu Nandanan, Mr S. Mohanakumar, Ms. Radhika, Mr. Sanal Mohan, Dr. Devika, Mr Dinesan V., Mr. C.K. Raju, Ms.P.V.Shobha, Dr. P.K. Sasidharan, Dr. P.V. Narayanan, Ms.T.V. Geetha, Dr. T.V. Madhu, Prof. John. M. Itty, Mr. Amrut, Mr. Roy Mathew, and for their valuable comments.

Dinesan V. was accompanying me through out the project and also while writing this thesis. Dinesan is in fact very much part of all my academic endeavours. It would be a little odd to thank a person who is very much part of my academic self. He is not an 'other' for me. All the academic achievements in this thesis, if any, are his achievement too.

I am thankful to Dr. A.K Ramakrishnan, Dr. Raghava Varrior, Adv. PG. Padbanapan, Adv. Vijayamma, Dr. Prabudas, Dr. Raviraman, Dr. Sunny George, Dr. CU Thressia and Ms. Binitha Thampi for their participation in the Praxis intervention project.

I thank the library staff of School of Social Sciences; KILA, Thrissur and Centre for Development studies, Thiruvanathapuram.

I thank KILA, Thrissur for infrastructural and administrative support provided for the praxis intervention project. I place my special thanks to the directors of Kila: Dr. Michael Tharakan, Mr. T.O Sooraj and Dr. Balan for giving their unhindered support to the project.

Mr. Satyan of Kensoft, Kuttippuram was always offering helping hand whenever my computer stopped functioning. His help was valuable.

I thank Mr. Shibu and Mr. Unni of Minitek, Athirampuzha for their dedicated support in word processing, formatting and bringing out the final product of the thesis.

I thank all the administrative and clerical staff of the School of Social Sciences and The Mahatma Gandhi University for their support in the matters related to the university bureaucracy.

I also profusely thank my family members for their full-hearted support. My brother Dr. Ravikumar was always kind and helpful. I thank him for helping me financially when I required it. Similarly, Dinesan also was kind enough to provide financial assistance when I needed it the most. I place my special thanks to my wife Deepa, my daughter Maitreyi, my parents, my brothers and my in-laws. It was Deepa and my mother who had to bear all the economic and social costs of my academic endeavour expecting nothing in return. I honour their selfless love.

1 INTRODUCTION

This thesis introduces and theoretically explores the idea of '*praxis* intervention' and tries to support it with the help of a practical experiment carried out with the *adivasis (indigenous people, tribes)* of Attappady (Kerala, India). It problematises professional social work practice and suggests alternative model of social work drawing lessons from the experiment.

Adivasis are called 'tribals' in the government documents[1]. Attappady is a hilly terrain in the district of Palakkad found between Coimbatore of Tamilnadu in the east and Mannarkad of the Kerala state in the west. (The famous silent valley is located at Attappady). Irulas, Mudugas and Kurumbas are the *adivasi* communities of Attappady. Attappady has 183 *adivasi* hamlets of which representatives from 30 hamlets spreading the entire geographical area of Attappady, participated in this research project. The *adivasis* are

---

[1] The term '*adivasi*' is used instead of 'tribal' or 'tribe' this thesis because *adivasis* of Attappady proudly call themselves '*adivasis*' as the term means the 'prime inhabitants' or 'indigenous people' or people who belong to the place from very early times. The term is used in contrast to the term '*vandavasi*' meaning, people who occupied the *adivasi* land later. For *adivasis* the term has political significance. It reminds that the *vandavasis* are those who came late and settled there or a kind of colonisers. The term 'tribal' is not usually preferred as the term is a settler coinage that represents them as 'primitive'.

classified in the government documents as 'persistently poor.' Attappady is a hot spot of continuously failing developmentalism and a well known area for its depleted ecology because of human intervention. The place is also known for 'hunger deaths' (the deaths caused by starvation) and human misery.

The work is primarily methodological, since among its concerns developing a model of *praxis* intervention theory and practice figures first and foremost. By methodology is meant a system of principles and general ways of organising and structuring theoretical and practical activity and theory of this system [Spirkin 1983]. It is method adopted in relation to broader logical and theoretical considerations. The research design of the thesis considers the researcher too as a variable [Sjoberg and Nett 1992: 2-5]. Theory is treated in this exercise as the living territory of contemplation on the move. The recognition that the researcher herself/himself has an impact on the research design and outcome brings the ethics in scientific investigation to the central concern [Merton 1957 esp. chapters 2 and 3].

The thesis takes an interdisciplinary approach to social work. The thesis problematises professional social work practice and suggests alternative model of social work drawing lessons from an experimental *'praxis* intervention' research which was undertaken with the *adivasis* of Attappady. The thesis attempts to develop a model of *praxis* intervention theory and practice. The *praxis* model assumes that the prime concern of the social work profession in most of its work situation is to invoke the *'praxis* potential' of its 'clientele' and that of the social worker herself/himself. In this thesis, *praxis* intervention is understood as the method with which human potential to be sensuous (to make sense, to be sensible) is realised in unsettling the settled mentalities, especially where the settled mindsets prevalent in the social world seem to have contributed to their marginality.

The Praxis Intervention Project

The preparation for *praxis* intervention took four months and the actual project was of the duration of six and a half month. The preparation period included planning, pre-*praxis* fieldwork and workshops with the experts in the field and consultation with the elected representatives belonging to *adivasi* communities in the state of Kerala.

The objective of the project was to promote informed action and reflexion on the conditions of the social life around and the mindsets involved. The project had components of classroom sessions, workshops, fieldwork sessions and documentation.

It was a project of intermittent classroom and fieldwork sessions. Each classroom session was of one week's duration and each fieldwork session was of one month's duration approximately. The classroom sessions and fieldwork phases were arranged intermittently to facilitate fieldwork assessment in the classroom and for horizontal discussion among the participants. The classroom sessions were used for fieldwork guidance as well. Between the classroom sessions and fieldwork sessions there were workshops for planning and discussion. In addition, there were workshops held at the field location to review the field activity and learning. The literate among the participants were encouraged to write field journals. It was an action research project in which the participants were expected to explore their life-world and act on it. The classroom sessions introduced research questions, research methods and provided information for further research.

The *adivasi* participants selected one hamlet each for their fieldwork. The *adivasi* researchers, and through them hamlet residents were guided to explore the realities of their life-world and reflexively carry out action on their material condition, mind-sets with its external social coordinates. The research was guided by a team of participants with an academic or professional background in social work, sociology, anthropology, history, economics, gender studies, agriculture science, environmental science, philosophy and other related fields. Some of the participants of the project team were themselves activists. Among *adivasis* there were 30 regular participants, of whom 15 were elected representatives of the local bodies. Of all, 13 were women. The research team had the project undertakers, *adivasi* participants and external experts. They explored jointly the history of *adivasis*, the *adivasi* life-world, gender relation among *adivasis*, and the *adivasi* mythologies. They also explored their relationship with the mainstream population settled there at Attappady, health condition, nutrition and other issues step-by-step. The project of *praxis* intervention had phases arranged in tune with the spontaneity of the participant's learning. The learning had elements of discussions, debates, arguments, games, songs, dances, role-plays, writing charts, viewing movies, listening to lectures, fieldwork assignments, self-evaluations, tours etc. The research on their life-world in fact resulted in collective action for maintaining better nutritional status, better water availability and against alcohol menace.

The practice of *praxis* intervention could produce, 127 chart sheets consisting bullet points of classroom discussions or presentations, 27 fieldwork journals, six songs compiled, 30 evaluation sheets, 21 days of classroom sessions, six months of fieldwork, eight workshops among the project undertakers and external experts and four workshops with the *adivasi* participants at the field location.

Methods adopted in organising data

The project could generate documents in the forms of chart sheets, fieldwork journals, songs, evaluation sheets and the workshop proceedings, everything totalling about 1000 pages. There were also 30 hours of audio recordings of the project. Most of the documents were in the *adivasi* and Malayalam language. They were translated into English with a conscious attempt to keep their meaning intact. The statements in the document were separately catalogued. Later on they were arranged chronologically and based on their subject matter. The project undertakers held six workshops posterior to the project and discussed their understanding of the documents at hand. The excerpts from the catalogued documents are used as the qualitative data, informing of the internal transformation that the project could achieve within a short span of time.

Thesis Organisation

The thesis is broadly divided into four parts. Each part is presented as a chapter. The first part presents a theoretical argument. The second introduces Attappady and its people, the third reflexively interprets the *praxis* intervention exercise and the fourth problematises   the theory and practice of social work and locates *praxis* intervention within the varieties of social work schema.

The first chapter of the thesis discusses the theoretical aspects of *praxis*, *praxis* intervention, and the basic premise of the *praxis* intervention project. The chapter provides a theoretical model of *praxis* intervention. In this chapter 'routine *praxis*' is differentiated from the 'creative' or 'transformative *praxis*' and the theoretical possibility of unsettling the marginalizing mentality with 'creative *praxis*' is discussed.

The second chapter familiarises Attappady and the *adivasi* communities living there. The location of Attappady, its geographical features, its ecological condition, the changing demographic pattern, the cultural practices of *adivasis,* socio economic conditions of *adivasis* and the development profile of Attappady are described in the chapter. The chapter also shares some information collected as a part of pre *praxis* survey at Attappady.

The third chapter provides a reflexive account of the *praxis* intervention experiment. It contains relevant sections of the *praxis* intervention fieldwork reports and classroom accounts of the project. The data generated in the field, the classroom discussions and the contents of the participants' field journals are discussed in this chapter. The chapter traces out the method by which the 'transformative *praxis* potential' of the participants invoked by the project. The chapter also attempts theoretical interpretation of the data collected from the field. Here, an example is set in integrating social theory with the social work practice. Towards the end of the chapter, the researcher critically looks back into the biases (academic biases and biases emerging from the personal coordinates like the gender or class *habitus* of the researcher) that misinform him in his social work practice.

The fourth chapter provides a critique of the professional social work practice. The chapter places *praxis* intervention within the contemporary social work thoughts. The chapter critically looks at various definitions given to the social work practice. The discussion of the definitions is followed by an exploration of social work concerns and its mode of practices. The critique of social work practice from the social work field and also from the social sciences is explored in a section. The chapter also provides an alternative perspective of social work and places *praxis* intervention among the alternative perspectives available. The feasibility and limitations of *praxis* intervention are discussed in it. The chapter ends with a discussion on the methodological relevance of *praxis* intervention both in social work and social sciences.

2 PRAXIS MODEL

Understanding Praxis

The word *praxis* was in use in the early Greek philosophy, but with a different connotation from its present usage. Aristotle used the word referring to various biological life activities [Bottomore, et al: 2000]; for him the word suggested also the sciences and arts that deal with the freeman's ethical and political life. At times, he contrasts *'praxis'* (in the sense of practical activity) with *'polis'* (in the sense of productive activity) to distinguish performing or doing an activity from the *telos* or the end. *'Poesis'* is an activity with a particular end, performed with the knowledge of *'techne'* [2][Heidegger 1999:16] (technical knowledge in producing a house, table, etc.). *Praxis* for him is the practical activity that has to do with the conduct of everyday life as a member of a society. It is doing a right thing well in interaction with the fellow human beings. To perform practical activity (*praxis*), the knowledge of *phronesis* is required. *Phronesis* is the practical knowledge of life and living within a society (*polis*). It is neither technical nor cognitive ability that one has at one's disposal, but it is bound up with the kind of person that one is and is becoming. To him,

---

2   Heidegger observes that 'The meaning of *physis* is further restricted by contrast with *techne* – which denotes neither art nor technology but a knowledge, the ability to plan and organise freely, to master institutions. *Techne* is creating, building in the sense of a deliberate "pro-ducing."

the *'eupraxia'* is performing an activity well; similarly, the *'dypraxia'* is misfortune or bad activity. In the Greek tradition, *Praxis* (practical knowledge) is also contrasted with *'theoria'* (contemplative wisdom) [Schwandt 2001:205-208]. For Francis Bacon, the word meant applied practical or useful knowledge[3] in contrast to theoretical knowledge. He held that *praxis* is the fruit of pure knowledge [Bottomore 2000:435-6]. The term *praxis,* as Marx interpreted it, is probably from Cieszkowski's [Bernstein 1999: xv] coinage of the word to refer the "practical philosophy or rather a philosophy of practical activity" exercising a direct influence on social life and developing the future in the realm of concrete activity.

The term *praxis* occupies a central position in Marxism, existentialism, pragmatism and hermeneutics [Schwandt 2001: 205-209]. In this thesis, we use the word to capture the domain of human activity that falls between practice and theorisation. Here, by practice, we mean the habituated everyday practice, and by theory, the living territories of contemplation, constantly on the move [Pile and Thrift 1996: 24]. *Praxis,* like practice, is part of our existence of every moment, and like theorisation has the living territory of contemplation from the everyday life. In other words, praxis is synchronic of the practice, which is part of our existence of every moment, and the theorisation is the living territory of contemplation from the everyday life. It is being mindful of our existence and of everything we witness. For Feuerbach, *praxis* is the species character of human beings with which they make sense, think and weave their social world. Feuerbach identified praxis with the material forces inherent in the masses. In a letter to Ruge, dated 1843, he wrote:

---

3   As theoretical geometry can be distinguished from applied geometry.

> What is theory, what is practice? Wherein lies their difference? Theoretical is that which is hidden in my head only, practical is that which is spooking in many heads. What unites many heads creates a mass, extends itself and this finds its place in the world. If it is possible to create a new organ for the new principle, then this is *praxis*, which should never be missed.[4]

For Marx, it is a term that 'refers in general to action, activity; and in Marx's sense to the free, universal and self-creative activity through which man creates and changes his historical, human world and himself; an activity specific to man, through which he is basically differentiated from all other beings' [Easton and Guddat 1967:400-402]. Marx finds *praxis* in the social that is in the making. For him, human *praxis* is a specific dialectical tension between being and becoming, necessity and contingency, things and human activities [Woznicki 2004]. Andrew Woznicki points out that in Marx *praxis* is conceived as something which is done can be done or has the readiness to be done. (This is similar to the Heidegger notion of *praxis* as *Vorhandensein* and *Zuhandensein*) in the order of being. He further adds, in the objective sense, *praxis* is expressed in the form of a result obtained by man's activities and presents itself linguistically as a noun, namely as `deed' and `product.' *Praxis*, however, understood as a `deed' or `product' presupposes a subject, which makes *praxis* to be *praxis*. Expanding his argument, Woznicki states, "in the order of becoming then, *praxis* is the very condition of developing the productive forces of things by the human creative activity which is contained in the process as such and reveals itself linguistically as a verb: `to act' or `to work'. Consequently, in the dialectical tension between

---

[4]   Quoted in Chakravarthy 2004

being and becoming, the *praxis* of nature is interrelated with that of human activity" [ibid].

Marx's emphasis on *praxis* was intended to fix a critical standpoint from which he could

oppose the neglect of human agency by the German Idealism, on the one hand, and the

"dislike of human beings" into which previous materialism had fallen[5] on the other. For

Feuerbach, '*praxis*' is a divine endowment; for Marx it is a direct bridge to his materialist

conception of history. For Marx, what he called the revolutionary *praxis* is the sensuous

human activity in struggle with the dominant 'theses.' In other words, it is the sensuous

moment of dialectic struggle. *Praxis* is conceptualised in its reflexive as well as non-reflexive

variety in Marx [Gouldner 1980:32, 33]. The reflexive *praxis* is understood as the moment in

the dialectic change, and the non-reflexive one as the routinising mechanism operating

within the ideologies as a reproductive or status quo maintaining. It is, for him, the non-

reflexive habituating *praxis,* which leads to the false consciousness and alienation.

For Cornelius Castoriadis,

> *praxis* is a conscious activity and can only exist as a lucid activity, but it is
> different from the application of prior knowledge and cannot be justified by
> calling upon knowledge like this (which does not mean that it cannot justify
> itself). It is based on knowledge, but this knowledge is always fragmentary
> and provisional. It is fragmentary because there can be no exhaustive theory
> of humanity and of history; it is provisional because *praxis* itself constantly
> gives rise to new knowledge for it makes a language that is at once singular
> and universal. This is why the relations of *praxis* to theory, true theory
> correctly conceived, are infinitely tighter and more profound than those of

---

5   Marx: The chief defect of all previous materialism (including Feuerbach's) is the object, actuality, sensuousness is conceived only in the form of the object or perception [Anschauung], but not as a sensuous human activity, practice [*praxis*], nor subjectively. (Marx's first theses on Feuerbach.)

any 'strictly rational' technique or practice; for the latter, theory is only a code of lifeless prescriptions which can never, in its manipulations, encounter meaning" [1987:76].

To Markoviç, moments of *praxis* include

creativity instead of sameness, autonomy instead of subordination, sociality instead of massification, rationality instead of blind reaction and intentionality rather than compliance [1974:64].

Praxis according to him is the moment of self-determination (in contrast to coercion), intentionality (in contrast to blind reaction), sociality (in contrast to privatised nihilism), creativity (in contrast to sameness) and rationality (in contrast to blind chance) [1974: 64-69].

Invoking *praxis* potential becomes reasonable where the passive obedience to 'revealed' truths or succumbing to 'revered' knowledge claims to 'nominal' truths is 'immorality' [Kant 1991: 247-8], the naturalised neutrality is violence [Barthes 1975: 131; Cook 2001: 154], the socially existing collective conscience – the 'ties of ideas' -- is a product of individual human activities [Durkheim 2001: 292], value systems of the actors in social action constitute the social reality [Weber 1975: 75], the meaning of social text is decided by the 'art of [its] interpretation,'[6] and "because the wreckage of the *narcissist home* [Adamczewski 1995: 56, 58] has let us *homeless*, yet creative" [Adamczewski 1995:62].

The re-creative *praxis* is understood to be anthropologically valuable, essentially human, involving 'fabrication of meaning' that is 'more important than the meanings

---

[6]   Dilthey 1992; Gadamar 1979: xxiv, 350-1,359-60, Heidegger 1999:10; Mukherji 2000:25

themselves' [Bannet 1989:66]. A preparation for a re-creative *praxis* is primarily self-reflexivity, understanding [Bourdieu 1998] and a 'penetrative perception' of the structure (as a 'topological and geological survey of the battlefield') to 'topple the present order of things' [Foucault 1980:62]. A reflexive *praxis* is the counter to the mental process that is 'an imaginative rehearsal,' crystallising into more or less stabilised 'self conception' –a *homo clauses*[7]. It is an activity of suspending the perceived normality of the socially structured routine[8].

The interactionist tradition of social thinking has not only led one to ask new questions on the construction of selves from the social interactions, but also it has given the opportunity to realise the human potential of reflexive monitoring. Reflexivity is the characteristic of *praxis* potential. Besides explaining the fundamental humaneness, the idea of *praxis* throws light into the political possibility of undoing the harms that the sedimented rationality had done to the human sociality. With the *praxis* potential, one realises *life power*[9] and looks at one's sociality afresh. The life power emanating from the *praxis* possibility and

---

[7] Mead 1934:269-72; Goffman 1961:168; Goffman 2001; Goffman, 1986:13-14; Collins 2002:73,75; Elias 1994: 204

[8] Schutz 1962: 14; Garfinkel 1963:188; Garfinkel 1984:37-38].

[9] Hans Joas in his assessment of symbolic interactionism writes, "Marxism, is incomprehensible, at least in its origin, without its foundation in its own theory of action, in the 'expressionistic' concept of work according to which work effects the embodiment of the worker's labour power and skills in the product of his work. However many of those who contributed to the development of this tradition as a theory of society and history disregarded this foundation of Marxism. There has been hardly any elaboration of the notions of '*praxis*,' of 'activity' and of 'labour' (or 'work') nor relating of them to the problems addressed by the sociological theory of action.

Even, the most creative new approach to the sociological theory of action, which transcends utilitarianism, the normativist critique of utilitarianism and traditional Marxism [For example, Jürgen Habermas's theory of communicative action], does not achieve a comprehensive revision of sociological theory of action. The opposition of a communicative concept of rationality to the deficiencies of an instrumentalist understanding of rationality has the effect of excluding many dimensions of action, which can be found in the history of social thought. The unresolved problem in this connection is how the sociological theory of action can be integrated with the theoretical fecundity of pragmatism and the traditions of the philosophy of *praxis*, and with the expressionistic notion of work. For solution of this problem, pragmatism continues to be of central importance. For it has prepared the way not simply to take as a model for sociological theory of action the purposively action individual who has mastery over his own body and is autonomous in relation to his fellow human beings and to the environment but instead to explain the conditions of possibility of this type of 'actor.' For this clarification, the literature of symbolic interactionism supplies a wealth of material" Hans Joas [1987:110].

praxis potential is the 'active aspect' of being [Nizar Ahmed Undated, Typed Manuscript][10]. The idea of *Praxis* that had been left unelaborated in the everyday life situation had found a subtle inference in the micro social understanding of the interaction theorists. Despite a breakthrough in conceptualising self as an emergent from the social interaction (interactional *praxis*), the early interactionists could not empirically reason *how* participation in the structure of society shaped the individual conduct and vice versa [Turner 1995:318].

With Goffman and Garfinkel, the process of social interaction constituting the micro social structure is explained with more rigour and empirical evidence. With their analysis, the ways and means of *praxis* being routinised are better understood. Goffman's portrayal of the human reasoning and intentionality within the rituals and dramas of the presentations of selves and Garfinkel's exploration of the 'method of sense making' (ethnomethodology) assuming priority over its contents within the indexical settings [Turner 1995:395] explain the factors constraining human *praxis* emerging substantially creative. Improbability, though not the impossibility of the non-routine-creative *praxis* within human interaction and its structural properties, in fact alarms the action oriented social thinkers over the hectic labour required in reinvigorating the creative *praxis* from within the socially structurated infertility. Without invoking the creative *praxis* and the reflexive potential, it may not be possible to make political or social justice. The creative

---

[10]   Nizar Ahmed: Being for humans, is thus a sense of being which realises itself through this active aspect or power, by trans-substancing itself. By trans-substancing itself it transforms the interactive patterns, in turn is trans-substanced by the later. In this way human actions and power can be linked up and the notion of power can be de-linked from that of domination [Nizar Ahmed. <u>Aspects of Reflexivity in Social Theorising</u>. Unpublished Manuscript. Calicut: Documentation Centre, Institute for Social and Ecological Studies, Undated].

reflexivity being limited, it would be the formalities and the conventions forming the process of human consciousness. The available resources[11] within the historical facticities, interaction settings, and structural properties of the sociality when available only to further deepening the riverbeds of established patterns of reasoning and structurations, they cannot be jubilantly held as resources. If the 'resources' are available only to bury oneself, one cannot celebrate their existence.

Goffman is a critique of the overwhelming ritualistic[12] and routine[13] *praxis* that commonly occurs in the 'process and structures specific to the interaction order[14]' [2001: 274-5]. Goffman observes that within the routine *praxis* people exhibit smartness in *presenting*[15] themselves before the others in the interaction setting, while playing their roles[16].

---

11   Giddens observes, "Structure refers not only to rules implicated in the production and reproduction of social systems but also to resources." He argues further that the structure is internal to actors enabling them towards the structurational social *praxis* through their 'practical consciousness'. If the actors' practical consciousness is ethnomethodological, dramaturgical or mimetic one cannot find solace in its resourcefulness. Giddens holds that with the 'authoritative resources' (authoritative resources' in Gidden's terminology refers to non material resources involved in the generation of power, deriving from the capability of harnessing the activities of human beings) one can break with the present dominant episteme. However, Giddens acknowledges its low probability.

For Giddens structuration is the structuring of social relations across time and space, in virtue of the duality of structure. By duality of structure he means structure being the medium and outcome of the conduct it recursively organises. For him the structural properties of social systems do not exist outside of action but are chronically implicated in its production and reproduction. Given the doxic nature of self, and the utilisation of 'resources' for 'presentation' purpose in the Goffmanian sense, one may not over emphasis the power the agent has on the structural properties.

The structurational argument reifying the agency power could only be useful in blaming the victims for structural defects (could we say that the socially or economically poor communities too are responsible for the structural reality of the globalisation on par with the global commercial interest and their political arm? Similarly, what is that we would be meaning when we say the structure of global order is a 'resource' for the affected group? Is there anything more than a naming ritual in calling this forced compulsion as 'resource'?)

The duality of structure (some kind of synchronic Hegelianism?) argument leads one to the conclusion that the dominance and violence present in the structural properties of the sociality as cumulative unintended consequence of which everybody is equally responsible (is there any way out to be a 'non-agent'?). With this argument, the intentionality of the powerful in the social order is diluted. Thus, the argument becomes doubly status quoist, blaming the oppressed, and salvaging the oppressing. The argument is an invitation to everyone into the existing dynamics of *praxis* and its routine. [1986: 23, 25, 258-62, 374, 376].

12   Randall Collins commenting on Goffman's observation of 'ritually stratified social structure' writes that his work indicates that the entire structure of society, both work and private sociability, is upheld by rituals [Collins 2002:71; Goffman 1967:4].

13   The pre-established pattern of action which is unfolded during a performance and which may be presented or played through on other occasions may be called a 'part' or 'routine [Goffman 1959: 27].

14   Goffman defines interaction as the reciprocal influence of individuals upon one another's action when in one another's immediate physical presence [1959:26].

He understands the routine *praxis* as the convenient submission [2001:278-9] to rituals of interactions. Their compliance to the ritual order is possible despite the participants find nothing intrinsically just in it [2001:279]. Individuals go along with interaction arrangements for a wide variety of reasons.[17] From their apparent tacit support, we cannot conclude that a change in the present interaction order would be resisted or resented. He also notes that non-compliance to certain rituals of the interaction order does not mean the individuals broke away from the routine ritual *praxis*; one can be very much dependent on the logic of the interaction order and violate them as guided by a mix of motives. Goffman's exploration of self[18] and its entangled nature within the interactional structure offers a critique of the self in its deep slumber[19] within the interactional setting. He in fact implies that to be awake is to combat the heteronomous interaction order. Goffman's understanding that the heteronomy imposed on

---

15   Presentation for him is something like performance in a staged drama. With no audience, there will be no performance [Goffman 1986:125; Goffman 1959:240].

16   It should be noted that for Goffman, the individuals who act out roles

are not and cannot be just like individuals who act at roles. While enacting roles, the actors demonstrate at least a dual role, a stage actor (who seeks help from the prompter, cooperation from the members of the cast, response from the audience) and a staged character [Giddens 1987:119; Goffman 1986: 129].

17   He observes, 'Very often, behind community and consensus are mixed motive games' [Goffman 2001:279; Goffman 1986:222].

18   Goffman: 'The self… can be seen as something that resides in the arrangements prevailing in a social system for its members. The self in this sense is not a property of the persons to whom it is attributed, but dwells rather in the pattern of social control that is exerted in connection with the person by himself and those around him. This special kind of institutional arrangement does not so much support the self as constituted it.' [1961:168]. '…the proper study of interaction is not the individual and his psychology, but rather the syntactical relations among acts of different persons mutually present to one another…not, then, men (sic) and their moments. Rather, moments and their men' [Goffman 2001].

Randall Collins observes, " For Goffman, the self is not so much a private, individual attribute as a public reality, created by and having its primary existence in public interaction….The self is not something that the individuals negotiate out of social interactions: it is rather, the archetypal modern myth. We are compelled to have an individual self, not because we actually have one but because social interaction requires us to act as if we do. It is society that forces people to present a certain image of themselves, to appear to be truthful, self-consistent and honourable. However, the same social system, because it forces us to switch back and fort between many complicated roles, is also making us always somewhat untruthful, inconsistent and dishonourable. The requirements of staging roles make us actors rather than spontaneously the roles that we appear to beat any single moment. The self is real only as a symbol, a linguistic concept that we use to account for what we and other people do It is an ideology of everyday life, used to attribute causality and moral responsibility in our society, just as societies with denser (e.g. tribal) structure, moral responsibility is not placed with the individual but attributed to Spirits or Gods [2002:73, 75].

19   Goffman: 'I can only suggest that he who would combat false consciousness and awaken people to their true interests has much to do, because the sleep is very deep. And I do not intend here to provide a lullaby but merely to sneak and watch the way the people snore.' [1986:14.]

the individual agents by the interactional order agrees with Geertz'[20] conceptualisation that the common sense is anti-reflexive.

The method by which the members create, assemble, produce and reproduce the social structure is the object of analysis for the ethnomethodologists. In other words, the method of routine *praxis* and its reproduction in a given setting, the properties of commonsense knowledge and consequent action are the matters of interest for the ethnomethodologists. What interested Garfinkel, the founder of ethnomethodology is not just 'perceived behaviours, feelings, motives or relationships but 'the perceived normality[21] of these events' [1963:188], that is senselessly taken for granted and socially structured into routine practices. Garfinkel established that the *senseless* 'perceived normality' of social events could be investigated from 'outside' by experimental manipulations of sequences of actions,[22] which he termed 'breaching experiments[23]. ' Purposefully breaching the taken for granted interaction rules invite bewilderment from the victim of the experiment. He could experimentally prove that the taken for granted rules in the interaction setting make the participants senselessly automated and lead everyone in the interaction setting into the 'deep slumber' [Goffman 1986:13]. Garfinkel

---

20 Geertz: 'Common sense represents matters…as being what they are by the simple nature of the case. An air of "of-courseness," a sense of "it figures" is cast over things… They are depicted as being inherent in the situation, intrinsic aspects of the situation, the way things go' [1983: 139].

21 Perceived normality is 'the perceived formal features that environing events for the perceiver as instances of class events (typicality), Their chances of occurrence (likelihood), their comparability with past or future events, the condition of their occurrences; their compatibility with the past and or future events; the condition of their occurrences) causal texts.

22 Garfinkel: 'the operations that one would have to perform in order to multiply the senseless features of perceived environment; to produce and sustain bewilderment, consternation and confusion; to produced socially structured affects of anxiety, shame, guilt and indignation should tell us something about how the structures of everyday activities are ordinarily and routinely produced and manipulated' [Garfinkel 1984:37-38].

23 Breaching experiment is deliberately breeching the understood, but unspoken, rules of everyday encounters for experimental and research purposes. Garfinkel gives examples of breaching experiments from the ones his students carried out. For example, for the taken for granted formal question, "how are you?" the experimenter asks "How am I in regard to what? My health, my finances, my schoolwork, my peace of mind, my…?" to breach the taken for granted routine answer. The reply the student got is an angry face is " Look! I was just trying to be polite. Frankly, I don't give a damn how you are" [Garfinkel 1984:44].

watches and ridicules the non-sensuous automated indexically[24] determined human reflexivity in the interaction setting through his breaching experiments. Garfinkel addresses the entire process by which the commonly shared 'background knowledge' is used as the resource from which 'taken for granted' meanings are generated within 'common culture[25]' as the 'documentary method of interpretation'[26]. The focal point of Garfinkel's analysis is the social actors making sense of the things and events around them drawing the resource from the background knowledge they acquired biographically. Garfinkel locates (alienated) *praxis* in the situation of action, internalised rules and norms and in the unconscious reproduction of the normative frameworks. The process by which the human consciousness is reduced as 'the typifying medium *par excellence*' and a 'treasure house of ready made pre-constituted types' [Schutz 1962a: 14] is the subject matter of analysis in Garfinkel. We find descriptions [Heritage 1987:231] and explorations into indexically imprisoned human *praxis* in his ethnomethodological studies. As Goffman observes, these studies need not be a lullaby to the deep indexical sleep. The sleep is unrecognised as a sleep because within the sleep situation, everybody is highly active in their

---

24   Indexicality is the immediate context of social interaction. With the term it is implied that all human interpretive work draws resource from the context in which it occurs. For example, the "reality" of deviance will be conceived very differently, depending on whether it is viewed from a police patrol car or from the back seat of a vehicle full of partying teenagers.

25   Garfinkel: 'Common culture' refers to the socially sanctioned grounds of inference and action that people use in their everyday affairs and which they assume that others use in the same way [Garfinkel 1984:76].

26   This term was used by Karl Mannheim (1893-1947) and Alfred Schutz (1899-1959), but its current meaning derives from Harold Garfinkel, the founder of Ethnomethodology. The documentary method describes the process through which immediately given information (documents); appearance, police reports, past records, and typifications, are used to infer meaning and motive in the behaviour of others. The unproblematic commonsense is problematised in this method. The method consists of treating an actual experience as its "Document of," as "pointing to" as standing on behalf a presupposed underlying pattern, that has been biographically (historico-prospective unfolding of events) acquired. Individual documentary evidences, in their turn, are interpreted on the basis of "what is known" about the underlying pattern. It is a method to understand the objective world in a mirror of subjective prejudice. It is to reveal the Schutzian premise that a person assumes, assumes the other person assumes as well, and assumes it of the other person, the other person assumes it of him, that a relationship of undoubted correspondence is the sanctioned relationship between the actual appearances of an object and the intended object that appears in a particular way. Garfinkel's experiment with his students, in which he used a fake counsellor with prefixed random yes/no answers to answer the problems the students, is an example of the use of the method. Despite the yes/no answers being prefixed the students could extract meaning from the conversation using their background knowledge [Garfinkel 1984:70-94].

ethnomethodological and dramaturgical action, interaction and presentation. As the sleep is an epistemic sleep, it is only with an epistemic break that we can wake up. We need not have to be concerned of the epistemic sleep, had it been such that it inflicts no pain upon anybody or anything. Within the world of deep slumber, because there is unquestioned violence, undoubted privileges, and acute 'unnatural' inequality, it seems to set things right one has to wake up. Without being conscious of the deep sleep, one may not wake up. The interactionist tradition of social thought has informed the social sciences the awareness of the deep epistemic sleep people ordinarily undergo.

From the historical and structuralist standpoints, we get that the structured mindscape against which we invoke the *praxis* potential is far deep-seated, requiring careful preparation. The theorists of geographical praxis explore the geographical dialectics by which the structured mindscape spreads horizontally[27]. Their elucidations inform the spatial spread of dominant mentalities with its own reproductive schemata. The interactionist and micro-structural theorists portray the ritual means by which persons interactionally maintain the structurally provided mindscapes. The structuration theory explores, of course with a sense of reification, the process of structure and agent 'non-dually' united in the process of 'structuration' [Giddens 1986].

For Bourdieu, the mindscape (*habitus*) or its schema of reproduction is not somewhere out there, but it is very much within ones' constitution and internal disposition. To explain the habituated nature of our internality and that being well grid into its

---

[27]   Foucault 1986: 23; Foucault 1980; Lefebvre 1976b: 21, 70, 106; Lefebvre 1971: 46, 50, 59, 65, 195; Lefebvre 1976a: 33; Lefebvre 1979: 285; Lefebvre 1991: 214, 232; Lefebvre 1994; Soja 1997: 237-40, 246-9; Held 2002.

misrecognitions with almost little scope for its unsettlement, Bourdieu invents the expressions such as '*habitus*[28]', field[29], practice, positions, interest, misrecognition, bias, participant objectivation' and so on. One among the most impressive metaphors he brought in explaining social practice is that of the game where playing a game is not just the understanding its rules alone. To be a participant of the game, one has to have the 'sense' of the game with which one becomes constantly aware of the field as a whole, one's opponents, ones' team-mates, strategies[30] and techniques. Playing a game requires 'interests[31]'

---

[28] *Habitus* is the meeting point between institutions and bodies, that which enables the institutions to attain full realisation. That is, each person as a biological being connects with the socio-cultural order in such a way that the various games of life keep their meaning, keep being played in the basic way. It is the 'durably installed generative principle of regulated improvisations' that which in a practical sense 'reactivates the sense objectified in institutions' [Bourdieu 1990:57].

[29] Bourdieu conceptualises 'field' [Bourdieu and Wacquant 1992:92] as the one that which destines the internal disposition of the *habitus*, as the magnetic field could effect the disposition of iron particles within its domain. Field is a space within which the effect of the field is exercised [Ibid: 100]. Unlike the relationship between iron particles and magnetic field, in social fields he understands there are socially perpetuated values and capitals. The fields of law, literature, academics, and politics are examples for social fields. Capital (worthiness or social valuation within a social relation) of a disposition is determined by the rules peculiar to each field. With this, he challenges identification of capital only with the economic capital and reduction of human beings as *homo economicus*. With the conceptualisation of field, capital and their relatedness, Bourdieu presents the complex ways in which the objective/subjective structural/agency dimensions are deeply intrigued with one another.

[30] By strategy, Bourdieu means not the purposive and pre-planned pursuit of calculated goals as Coleman does, but the active deployment of objectively oriented "lines of action" that obey regularities and form coherent and socially intelligible patterns, even though they do not follow conscious rules or aim at the premeditated goals posited by a strategist [Bourdieu and Wacquant 1992:25].

[31] Swedberg observes that according to Bourdieu, "interest is 'to be there', to participate, to admit that the game is worth playing and that the stakes created in and through the fact are worth pursuing; it is to recognize the game and to recognize its stakes The opposite of interest (or "illusio") is indifference (or "ataraxia"). Each field has its own interest, even if its masquerades as disinterestedness. Bourdieu criticizes the economists' version of interest for being ahistorical - "far from being an anthropological invariant, interest is a historical arbitrary The economists are also in his opinion wrong in thinking that "economic interest" is what drives everything; "anthropology and comparative history show that the properly social magic of institutions can constitute just about anything as an interest [Swedberg 2003; Bourdieu 1998a. 75-91; Bourdieu and Wacquant 1992:116, 117].

Wacquant observes, 'With the concept of interest- a notion he has of late increasingly come to replace by that of illusio and, more recently still, by that of libido – Bourdieu seeks to do two things. First, to break with the "enchanted" vision of social action that clings to the artificial frontier between instrumental and expressive or normative behaviour and refuses to acknowledge the various forms of hidden, normative profits that guide agents who appear "disinterested." Secondly, he wants to convey the idea that the people are motivated, driven by, torn from a state of in-difference and moved by the stimuli sent by certain fields – and not others. For each field fills the empty bottle of interest with different wine. A middle class academic who has never been in ghetto gym the pugilistic interest (libido pugilistica) that leads sub-proletarian youngsters to value and wilfully enter into the self-destructive occupation of boxing. Conversely, a high-school dropout from the inner city cannot apprehend the reason behind the intellectual's investment in the arcane of debates in social theory, or his passion for the latest and it has the 'consistent style' of the players 'internalised[32]' from the experiences in the game and the same 'externalised' while playing. The habituated consistent style of the player being improvised at each moment of the game is '*habitus*' for Bourdieu [Calhoun 2000]. *Habitus* is not something people are born with, but it is that which we acquire through repetition, like a habit.

Bourdieu's learning was shaped by his fieldwork assignments; of which, the one he undertook with Algerian Kabyle peasants had a lasting impact on him. The traditional self-righteous Kabyle peasants, encountering the modern economy, gradually transformed into sub-proletariat underclass due to their *habitus*[33]-*clash*[34] with the modern *habitus* and structural transformation[35] induced by the French Colonialism in Algeria was the focus of the study. (Methodologically, Bourdieu always tried to combine intimate knowledge of practical

---

innovations in conceptual art, because he has not been socialised to give them value. People are "pre-occupied" by certain future outcomes inscribed in the present they encounter only to the extent that their *habitus* sensitises and mobilises them to perceive and pursue them. And these outcomes can be thoroughly "disinterested" in the common sense of the term, as can readily be seen in the fields of cultural production, this "economic world reversed" [Bourdieu and Wacquant 1992:25-26].

32   Bourdieu: 'In order to escape the realism of the structure, which hypostatises systems of objective relations by converting them into totalities already constituted outside of individual history and group history, it is necessary to pass from the opus operatum to the modus operandi, from statistical regularity or algebraic structure to the principle of the production of this observed order, and to construct the theory of practice, or, more precisely, the theory of the mode of generation of practices, which is the precondition for establishing an experimental science of the dialectic of the internalisation of externality and the externalisation of internality, or, more simply, of incorporation and objectification' [Bourdieu. 1977: 77].

33   The *Habitus* is the system of durable, transposable dispositions, which function as the generative basis of structured, objectively unified practices [Bourdieu 1979: vii, footnote].

34   Here I am using the phrase '*habitus* clash' to mean what Bourdieu explained 'the economic system imported by colonisation – the objectified heritage of another civilisation, a legacy of accumulated experiences, techniques of payment or marketing, methods of accountancy, calculation and organisation – has the necessity of a "cosmos" s (as Weber puts it) into which the workers find themselves cast and whose rules they must learn in order to survive.' 'the dramatic confrontation between economic cosmos imposing itself and economic agents whom nothing has prepared to grasp its deep intention, one is forced to reflect on the conditions for existence and functioning of the capitalist system, i.e. on the economic dispositions which it both favours and demands' [Bourdieu. 1979: 3, 6.]

35   Bourdieu: It was not by chance that the relationship between structure and *habitus* was constituted as the theoretical problem in relation to a historical situation in which that problem was in a sense presented by reality itself, in the form of permanent discrepancy between the agent's economic dispositions and the economic world in which they had to act [Bourdieu 1979: vii].

activity with more abstract knowledge of objective patterns, with awareness that there can always be misrecognition[36] of the objective patterns of social reality from the social actors who are thoroughly inside the action and the outside observer who are thoroughly outside it). [37]

According to Bourdieu, the characteristic set of dispositions biographically acquired limits the conscious choice of the social actors in their interactions. The internal disposition that contributes to the nonconscious, taken-for-granted social interaction is *habitus*[38] in his terminology. *Habitus* is the meeting point between institutions and bodies, that which enables the institutions to attain full realisation. That is, each person as a biological being connects with the socio-cultural order in such a way that the various games of life keep their meaning, keep being played in the basic way. It is the 'durably installed generative principle of regulated improvisations' that which in a practical sense 'reactivates the sense objectified in institutions' [Bourdieu, 1990:57; Bourdieu 1979]. *Habitus* is 'Produced by the work of

---

36   Misrecognition is not simply error; indeed, in a practical mode of engagement every recognition is also misrecognition. The practical sense for him is the 'social necessity turned into nature, converted into motor schemes and body automatisms, what causes practices, in and through what makes them obscure to the eyes of their producers, to be sensible, that is, informed by a common sense. It is because agents never know completely what they are doing that what do has more sense than they know' [Bourdieu 1990:69].

37   For example, in an activity as simple as the gift giving, it may be possible that both the actors themselves and the outside researcher may be unaware of the strategies practically enacted through that act, despite it can be better understood by a reflexive probing. The gift giving which is understood as disinterested, voluntary and not subject to equivalence, may be actually a strategic act of symbolic dominance than the actors themselves are aware.

38   Roy Nash [Nash 2001] points out that Bourdieu's concept of *habitus* has been often mistaken as 'deficit theory.' For example, Branson & Miller argued that with his concept of class *habitus*, Bourdieu pictured the working class as 'trapped in their *habitus* through cultural impoverishment and cultural difference' [Branson and Miller 1991:42]. Mehan et al. sharply criticised Bourdieu for his "dark', 'determinist', and 'immutable formulation immutable formulation' [Mehan et al. 1996 :296]. The criticism has come from the ground that Bourdieu, like deficit theorists of 1950s 'blaming the victim.' An in-depth reading of Bourdieu would reveal that this criticism is misplaced. Throughout his career, Bourdieu is a critique of the structural properties over determining the agents irrespective of their class status. (For example Bourdieu writes, 'one cannot, at the same time, denounce the inhuman social conditions imposed upon proletarians … and credit the people placed in such situations with the full accomplishment of their human potentialities' [Bourdieu 1998b :136]. Bourdieu was not blaming the victim, rather he was deeply worried about the corrupt structure deeply percolated into subjectivity leaving no space for an Archimedean point from where action can be initiated. Bourdieu was in fact too much involved in creating such an Archimedean point despite its rare probability. He is religious in his activism who realised that the church of activism is deeply corrupt. As he wrote in Homo Academicus, his effort was 'to gain rational control over the disappointment felt by an 'oblate' [a religious devotee] faced with the annihilation of the truths and values to which he was destined and dedicated, rather than take refuge in feelings of self-destructive resentment' [Bourdieu 1988: xxvi].

inculcation and appropriation that is needed in order for objective structures, the products of collective history, to be reproduced in the form of the durable, adjusted dispositions that are the condition of their functioning' [Ibid]. It is constituted in the course through which agents partake of the history objectified in institutions. The partaking makes it possible to inhabit institutions, to appropriate them practically, and so to keep them in activity, continuously pulling them from the state of dead letters, reviving the sense reposited in them. At the same time, the agents impose revisions and transformations to their internalised dispositions[39]. '*Habitus* is the product of *modus operandi* of which the producer has no conscious mastery. It contains the 'objective intention' flowing from the *modus operandi* '*outrunning conscious intentions*' of the actor. The 'strategies' of the actors in practical situations generate from these preconscious 'objective intentions.' Bourdieu uses the notion of *habitus* to break with the cognitivist view that the actors just follow cultural rules, static cognitivism of structuralism and the existential understanding of subjectivity[40]. He further explains that the *habitus* is not just an internalised set of characteristics of the individual, but also the collective 'orchestration established among dispositions that are objectively coordinated' [Ibid: 59] which is the 'subjective but non-individualised system of internalised structures, common schemes of perception, conception and action' [Ibid: 60] exemplified by class *habitus*, in which 'the singular *habitus* of members of the same class are united in a relationship of homology, that is, diversity within homogeneity reflecting the homogeneity

---

[39]   Ibid

[40]   For example, a person playing football is not just guided by the rules of the game, but with the internalised experiences too. Similarly, while playing the players do not consciously apply the laws of motion in physics; rather they unconsciously use them in fraction of seconds from the competence gained from their experiences. For Bourdieu, social competence too is internally dispositional as that of the competence in sports or music.

characteristic of their social conditions of production' [Ibid]. The *habitus*, as defined by Bourdieu is:

> systems of durable, transposable dispositions, structured structures predisposed to function as structuring structures, that is, as principles which generate and organise practices and representations that can be objectively adapted to their outcomes without presupposing a conscious aiming at ends or an express mastery of the operations necessary in order to attain them.[41]

In Bourdieu it is not just subjectivity/ objectivity, theory/ practice, but also methodology/ theory, researcher/ research dichotomies are disfavoured with his conceptualisation of the 'participant objectivation.' Participatory objectivation is 'objectifying the act of objectification.' By 'objectifying the objectification' it is meant the researcher, while observing and objectifying, taking a similar critical distance towards the objectification itself. It is being sensitive to the immensely possible biases from the researcher's social coordinates, field and intellectual orientation and self-critically problematising them to reduce the impact of the biases [Bourdieu 2003]. According to Bourdieu, within the sociological analysis, the participant objectivation is the essential but difficult exercise of all because it requires the break with the deepest and most conscious adherence and adhesions, those quite often give the object its very "interest" for those who study it- i.e., everything about their relation to the object they try to know that they least want to know [Bourdieu and Wacquant 1992:253]. It is through the participant objectivation the practical relation to practice is substituted with the observer's relation to practice [Bourdieu 1990:34]. Through

---

[41]   Ibid: 53.

the practice of participant objectivation, Bourdieu aims to make the critical and political activity of social research the *'solvent of doxa'*[42].

With Bourdieu, sociology takes a deeply ethical and action turn[43] that could be contrasted with the 'linguistic turn' of the postmodernists. With the 'action turn', there is a re-vision of our view of the nature, purpose and method of social enquiry. Bourdieu has raised the status of 'action research' from participatory observation to the participant objectivation and thereby given it a radical shift without losing objectivity, wherein the social research is made possible to meet the requirement of contribution to the abstract body of knowledge and practical knowing embodied in the moment to moment action [Heron 1996:34] of the social life situation. Action, from the perspective of Bourdieu, is not limited to transforming the objective conditions alone, but also implies the *transformation of the subjective conditions through which the objective conditions are perpetuated.* Bourdieu with his 'sociological action' opens up a new opportunity for social work practice that is well founded within the social theory.

Bourdieu is cautious[44] in conceptualising the social action for social transformation, as it is difficult to find a convenient 'Archimedean Point' from where the transformative action could be initiated. He held that the actions encouraged by naïve-over-optimism or a

---

42   By bringing the hidden doxa into light and public debate.

43   According to Calhoun, 'Science—including sociology and anthropology—was for Bourdieu a practical enterprise, an active, ongoing practice of research and analysis (modus operandi), not simply a body of scholastic principles (opus operatum). It was no accident that he titled his book of epistemological and methodological preliminaries The Craft of Sociology' [Calhoun 2002:23; Reason and Torbert 2001].

44   Calhoun observes, 'Bourdieu called for an objective analysis of the conditions of creativity, and the pressures that resisted it, rather than an idealization of it as a purely subjective phenomenon. He demanded that social scientists pay scrupulous attention to the conditions and hence limitations of their own gaze and work—starting with the very unequal social distribution of leisure to devote to intellectual projects—and continually objectify their own efforts to produce objective knowledge of the social world' [Calhoun 2002:11].

social action that has no space for the activist's or researcher's non-narcissistic yet self-objectivation, would not only just be a setback to the claims of the social action but also aggravate the same set of conditions that demand the social action [Calhoun 2002].

Bourdieu finds that both academics (Social Science) and politics are guilty [Bourdieu et al. 1999: 629] of their *nonassistance to persons in danger';* politics in failing to take the full advantage of the possibilities of action (minimal though they may be) and social science in its unwillingness to uncover *doxa* and its mythologies and advocate politics to gain the reflexive astuteness of academics, and science to gain the political rigour of standing with the persons in danger.

Bourdieu's message in The Weight of the World is, *"Do not deplore, do not laugh, do not hate – understand'* [Ibid: 1]. For Bourdieu, *'understanding is explanation*[45]. Understanding, Bourdieu holds, is *'a reflex reflexivity based on a craft, on sociological "feel" or "eye"* [Ibid: 608]. Sociology or social action, he held, can be adequately scientific only with the 'understanding,' without which, it would be merely 'scientistic' [Ibid: 607]. Understanding, for Bourdieu, occurs 'on the spot' of the interaction. For Bourdieu the act of understanding constitutes 'democratisation of the hermeneutic posture' [Hamel 1998] and 'active and methodical listening[46].' It is an act of 'intellectual love' [Bourdieu et al. 1999: 614], facilitation of

---

45   For Bourdieu what he calls 'generic and genetic comprehension' is understanding. For him is explanation too. Where the generic comprehension is understanding the interviewee as necessarily they are by mentally putting ourselves in their place and genetic comprehension is grasping the social conditions of which they are products. He writes, 'Against the old distinction made by William Dilthey, we must posit that understanding and explaining are one.' [Bourdieu et al. 1999 :613]

46   Active methodological listening is accompanied by the researcher's mentally putting themselves in the place of the researched. It is attempting to situate oneself in the place the interviewees occupy in the social space in order to understand them as necessarily what they are, by questioning them from that point on, and to some degree to take their part. Bourdieu distinguishes this practice from the phenomenological enquiry, within which, the phenomenologists projecting themselves into the other [Bourdieu et al. 1999 :609,613]

'joy in expression' [Ibid: 615], 'induced and accompanied self-analysis' [Ibid], 'a sort of spiritual exercise that, through forgetfulness of self, aims at a true conversion of the way we look at other people in ordinary *circumstances of life*' and should be devoid of the 'symbolic violence' [Ibid: 608-9]. Understanding for Bourdieu is the 'on the spot' action with the 'sociological feel' [Ibid: 618]. For him, 'understanding' is not just understanding the 'other', but also working to 'gain knowledge of our own presuppositions.' [Ibid: 608]

Bourdieu's 'on the spot' sociological understanding is a silent but rigorous action programme, wherein the persons with the sociological skill and the participants of a sociological interview undergo a 'spiritual revolution' of understanding; where the sociologists pose questions to the social actors and to themselves with which they could jointly 'access the core principles of the discontent and malaise' [Ibid: 620] and 'bring to light' 'the real bases of discontent and dissatisfaction' that are found 'buried deep within the people who experience them' [Ibid :621] in a spontaneous dialogue with no aura of artificial intellectualism. By the sociological action, Bourdieu aspires, 'like a midwife, the sociologist can help them [social actors] in this [emancipatory] work provided the sociologist has a deeper understanding both of the conditions of existence of which they are product and of social effect that can be exercised by the research relationship' [Ibid: 621]. On the spot sociological intervention for Bourdieu is a 'craft' different from the research within the microcosm of academics, which is abstract and purely intellectual way of knowing. This 'craft', Bourdieu claims 'is a real "*disposition to pursue truth*", which disposes one to improvise on the spot, in the urgency of the interview [or social action]; strategies of self-presentation and adaptive responses; encouragement and opportune questions, etc., so as to help respondents deliver truth or, rather to be delivered of it.'

From Bourdieu's perspective, it can be derived that the capital accumulation or marginalisation, though constitutes the real experience of our social living, is built on a flimsy foundation of socially ingrained belief systems within the existing mode of understanding. The critical force of the concepts like 'misrecognition' and 'symbolic domination' in his works imply the status or the exchange-value of any form of capital that can indeed be unrelated to the worth with which they are identified [Sayer 2002]. The plot of the socially constructed mythology thickens as it has the corollary social positions, interests, fields and structures. Whether the challenge to habituated and habituating *praxis* could be made possible through reflexive re-look into one's own biases, whether the deeply ingrained misrecognitions could be recognised by various means such as repositioning roles, relocating fields, inventing new interests and by unsettling existing mode of thinking are the questions to be explored.

The premise of praxis intervention

The premise of *praxis* intervention is largely taken from Bourdieu's position on understanding of the 'on the spot sociological action' and the 'participant objectivation.' The object of *praxis* intervention social work is not just its client community and their physical or material conditions alone, but also the mindscape of the social worker, as well as that of her 'clients' or 'client communities' [Bourdieu and Wacquant 1992:38]. Though the practice of reflexive participant objectivation, the practitioner re-looks the taken for granted assumptions in order to wake up from her epistemic sleep and helps her clients too to help them to wake up from theirs. The *Praxis* intervention aims at altering the discriminatory mentalities and their structural extensions (social mindscapes) through *habitus praxis*. The approach of this study deviates from Bourdieu in conceptualising the *habitus praxis*. For Bourdieu the actor or agency is *the habitus* well intertwined in the practices and not a human being capable of rising above the constrain of the habitus[47] [Archer 2000b: 150-1, 166-7; Sayer 1999: 59-62; Sayer 2002]. For us, *praxis* potential is trans-historical, trans-subjective, trans-rational species character of human beings, capable of unsettling the settled logic. One of the sources of invoking *praxis* potential is the moral resistance people could display at the injustice of the arbitrary allocation of capital within a given mode of social misrecognitions. The moral resistance emerges from people's capability to be critically sensuous of the social reality they are placed in. Unfortunately, as Axel Honneth observes:

> ... within academic sociology, the internal connection that often holds between the emergence of social movements and the moral experience of disrespect has, to a larger extent, been theoretically severed at the start. The motives for rebellion, protest, and resistance have been transformed into categories of 'interest', and these interests are supposed to emerge from the objective inequalities in the distribution of material opportunities without ever being linked, in any way, to the everyday web of moral feelings [Honneth 1995: 161].

The human species potential of sensuousness, the non-fixity of meanings[48] and the diversity of indexicalities available [Wittgenstein 1976: section 154; Garfinkel 1984] together make humans

---

[47] For Bourdieu *Habitus* is a biographical, positional, historical construct internalised as a second nature and so forgotten as history, [Bourdieu 1990:56] functions as a generative apparatus predisposed to function structuring structures of internal logic of structures and agents [Ibid: 53]. Andrew Sayer observes, in the early works of Bourdieu the moral sentiments and judgements is either ignored or reduced to an emanation of their *habitus*. Either he further states that by discounting actors' moral judgements - by ignoring them or reducing them to emanations of their *habitus* and position in the social field - and by implicitly prioritising interest as the basis of social struggle [Sayer 2002].

[48] Wittgenstein: What is essential is to see that the same thing can come before our minds when we hear the word and the application still be different. Has it the *same* meaning both times? I think we say not [Wittgenstein 1976: section 140] (emphasis original).

into *praxis beings* rather than just leaving them to be sedimented *habitués*. It is only with the *praxis* potential that one can hope for the unsettlement of the social misrecognitions and the subsequent internality through a reflexive probing. Unsettling or suspending the *habitus* with the *praxis* potential is what we term the *'habitus praxis'*. *Habitus praxis* could suspend the generative logic of the social networking and its figurations get them and reinvigorated from their nodal points of pressure [Elias 1994: 288, 343].

Praxis intervention as a social action Project

The *Praxis* Intervention is a social action project sensitive to the human conditions of plurality [Arendt 1958: 7]. It is a political project, wherein the *life politics* of the people facing the historically endowed facticities[49] assumes the paramount importance [Ferguson 2001]. It is an action research[50] practice with a special emphasis on invigorating the sensuousness of the people involved.

Wide ranges of activities are called 'action research' so that the term is almost clichéd to mean anything, like the bureaucratic rituals of the 'participatory projects, 'tool-kit based instant 'participatory' events,[51] or a critical social work practice. The advocates of the philosophy of action

---

[49] The degree to which a given social event is real. Facticity is thus not a mere "matter of fact" in the manner of seventeenth- and eighteenth- century philosophy; it is rather a lived or existential fact, a disclosed or phenomenological fact [Marcuse 1964: 170-203; Habermas 1996:132-3].

[50] The idea of action research in the West is associated with the science in education movement in the late nineteenth century [McKernan 1991:8]. The term was first coined by Kurt Lewin in 1940s to describe a particular kind of research that united the experimental approach of social science with programmes of social action to address social problems [Reason and Bradbury 2001: .2; Lewin 1947] and with interlocking cycles of planning, acting, observing and reflecting [Kemmis and Mc Taggert 1990:8]. The philosophical ideas of John Dewey, the group dynamics movement in social psychology of 1940s, and the Teacher-Researcher movement of UK are cited for the existence of action research philosophy and practice, before it has been well formulated by Lewin [McKernan 1996:8-11; Haron 1971]. In 1970s, the method of action research is popularised in Latin America by Orlando Fals Borda and by DeSilva and his colleagues in South Asia [Fridres 1992; Borda 1998; DeSilva et al. 1998; Borda. 2001].

[51] Tool kit approaches to action research are popular with Non Governmental organisations. The tool kit approaches are variably named as 'Participatory Rural Appraisal (PRA),' 'Rapid Rural Appraisal (RRA),' and so on. The tool kit approaches of instant participatory techniques originated from the objective of collecting reliable data from the masses cost effectively for the purpose of governance and market research. The philosophy of action research has its origin in the critical

research hold that it shares its epistemological base with Marxian Humanism [Reason and Bradbury 2001: 3], Gandhian non-violent civil resistance, Gadamer's critical hermeneutics, Gramscian concept of political *praxis* and organic intellectualism, Thoreau's ethical economics, Feyerabend's resistance to the monopoly of 'scientific' methods[52], Kuhn's notion of 'paradigm shift,'[53] Agnes Heller's 'systemic reciprocity' [Heller 1989:304-5], Paulo Frieire's 'dialogical conscientisation,' Samir Amin's 'critique of imperialism,' the argument of subaltern philosophy, feminism, pro-labour concerns, and so on [Borda 2001: 27-36]. The method brought up questions concerning the spectatorship of the 'scientific society[54]' and that of the 'development experts.' It has been noted that there has always been a stream of 'hidden curriculum' [Eikeland 2001:145-6] of practical considerations organising the content and method of 'spectatorship.' In practice, action research rejects the artificially created mutually exclusive dualisms between the social action and the social theory, social researcher and the researched, 'experts' and their 'clients.' Action research is a life process of knowing[55], understanding and *interpreting* the existing construct of the social and systematically challenging the political injustice in it. John Heron describes the 'cooperative inquiry' of action research as the process of 'transpersonal empowerment' that helps people give birth to rich and subtle

streams of social thoughts.

52 Feyerabend in his famous manifesto of 'Against Method' states his basic theme as follows, "No set of rules can ever be found to guide the scientist in his choice of theories, and to imagine there is such a set is to impede progress. The only principle that does impede progress is anything goes" [Feyerabend 1970].

53 Kuhn showed that it is a myth to consider that the science progresses building upon established truth in a linear path. And also established that scientific research, however objective, takes place within a taken for granted framework (paradigm) and from time to time with the emergence of scientific communities with different interests, the paradigms themselves are shifted to a new direction [Kuhn 1962].

54 It refers to an outlook, in which the science has emerged as the authority to define everything rather than a humble systematic learning.

55 Shotter observes that knowing is not a thing to be discovered or created and stored up in journals, rather it is that arises in the process of living and present in the voices of ordinary people in conversations [Shotter 1993:7].

phenomenologies, thus liberating themselves from the age-old authoritarianism of schools and institutions of spiritual, secular or academic kinds [Heron 2001: 333-335]. According to Reason and Bradbury, the primary purpose of action research is to produce practical knowledge that is useful to the [disadvantaged] people in the everyday conduct of their lives. A wider purpose of action research is to contribute through this practical knowledge to the increased well being–economic, political, psychological, spiritual– of human persons and communities, and to a more equitable and sustainable relationship with the wider ecology of the planet of which we are an intrinsic part [Reason and Bradbury 2001:2]. However, the 'action' intended by the action researchers is the 'activity of the self in which our capacities are employed,' [Mac Murray 1957: 86] bringing people together around shared topical concerns, problems and issues…in a way that will permit people to achieve mutual understanding and consensus about what to do, [Kemmis and Mc Taggart 1990: 100] generating knowledge of the world in the course of bringing about material changes. Action in these understandings is the acting on the external world and learning from that action. Within the *praxis* intervention approach, the objective of action is primarily to enhance reflexive monitoring of the 'self'. The object of the *praxis* intervention action is the *habitus* (internality). Action here would mean reflexive interpretation of one's *habitus* and the sociality around. Interpretation can be interpreted as action. Wittgenstein says

> Do I really see something different each time, or do I only interpret what I
> see in a different way? I am inclined to say the former. But why? – *To*
> *interpret is to think, to do something; seeing is a state*[56]. [Wittgenstein: 1976: 212]

The action to bring about the material changes should flow from the *reflexive self-monitoring*, unsettled internality and the reverberation the unsettled internalities could produce in the figurational process[57] [Giddens 1986; Bourdieu 1993; Elias 1994]. The *praxis* intervention is a project of non-violent action against the taken for granted mind-sets of the statues quo.

---

[56]   Emphasis added.

[57]   By figuration Elias represents the process by which what appears as the 'social thing' or 'habitués' brew up. For him the sociality is a process located within the web of human relationships with mobility and directions influenced by the relational pressures and *habitués'* response [Elias 1994: 288, 343]. The relational pressures are conceptualised as power in Elias. He conceptualises power in terms of power relations, ratios and balances between individual and collective *habitués*. [Elias 1984: 251]. By the term figuration, he stresses the temporal and relational aspect of sociality along with habitational dimension. *Habitus* for Elias is, 'a mediating mechanism between social webs and the actual practices performed by individual actors' [Sheffy 1997: 37] located in a temporality. With the idea of figuration, Elias resists *habitus* as *homo-clauses*, misrecognised as the little world of individuals existing quite independently of the world outside [Elias 1994:204] and also against conceptualising social life in terms of states, objects or things [Elias 1978:103, 104; Elias 1994:214]. Elias explains what he means by the term figuration using the metaphor of play as 'the changing pattern created by the players as a whole – not only by their intellects but by their whole social selves, the totality of their dealings in their relationships with each other. It can be seen that this figuration forms a flexible latticework of tensions. The interdependence of the players, which is a prerequisite of their forming a figuration, may be an interdependence of allies or of opponents" [Burkitt 1991:164].

3 A BRIEF PROFILE OF ATTAPPADY AND ITS ADIVASIS

Location and Landscape

The field location of the *Praxis* intervention project is Attappady (10° 55' to 11° 15' N Latitude, 76° 45' E Longitude). Attappady is an approximately 750 Sq km east slopping plateau in the north-western corner of Mannarkad *taluk* in the Palakkad district of Kerala. To its north is the Nilgiris district and the east the Coimbatore of Tamilnadu. To the southwest and northwest, the Palakkad district of Kerala borders Attappady. Attappady is essentially a plateau at an approximate elevation of 500 m above the sea level, which is dissected by Bhavani, *Siruvani* and *Kodungarapallam* in to a series of valleys. [Nair 2002].

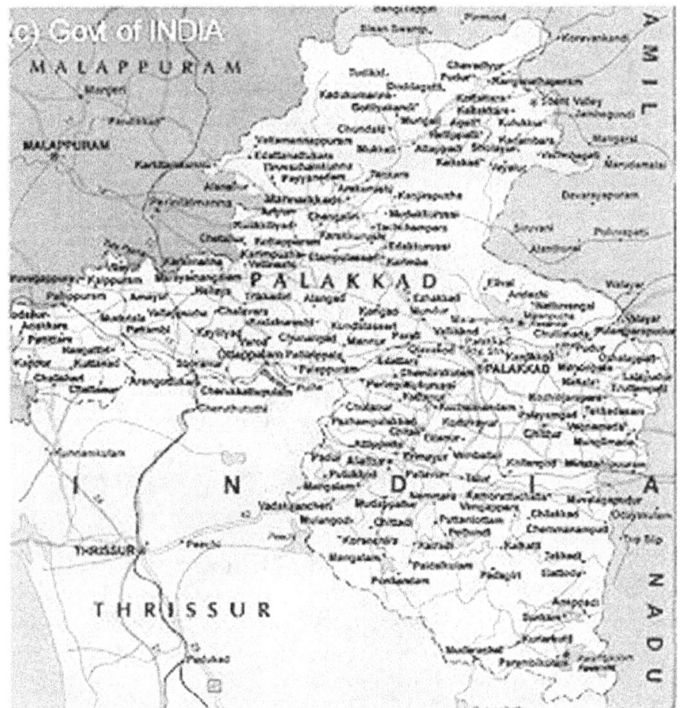

Fig. 1 Palakkad District

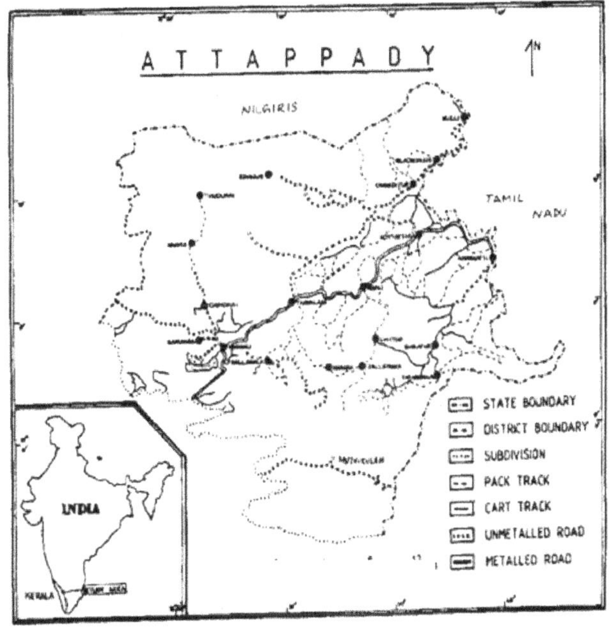

Fig.2 Attappady

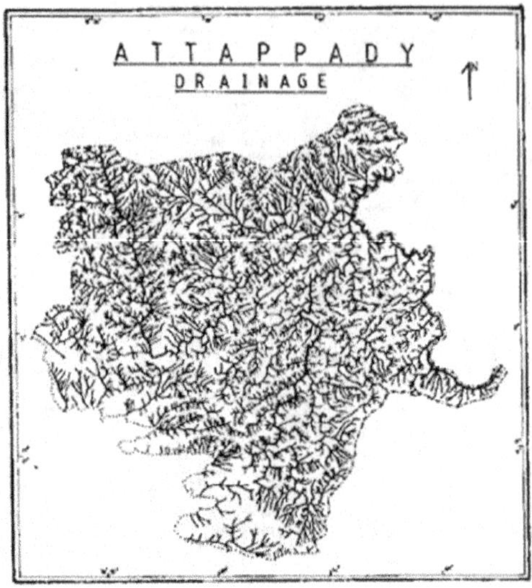

Fig. 3 Attappady Drainage

The area called Attappady is the east-slopping, deeply dissected valley of the Bhavani River located at an average elevation of 500 m above mean sea level. The *Kunda* and *Kovakunda* ranges of the Nilgiris rising up to more than 2000 m form its northern boundary. The Siruvani, Palamala and the Varadimala ridges form its south-western, southern and south-eastern border. Though there are occasionally higher peaks, the ridges are on an average 1500 m high. A low saddle open out on the western part of Attappady and this is the Thenkara - Mukkali access into Attappady from the west. On either side of this saddle, high north-south ridges link the Nilgiris with the Siruvani hills. All along to the west of this ridge is the Palakkad plains. On the eastern side of Attappady, between the Nilgiris and the Varadimala ranges, there are a series of low east-west ridges through which Bhavani river exits from the Attappady plateau.

Fig. 4 Attappady- Relief

The road-link from Anakkatty in Attappady continues on to Thadakam and further east to the Coimbatore plains. A number of spur hills run down from the high Nilgiris to the valley of Bhavani in the northern half of Attappady plateau. Similarly, a series of ridges run out towards the north-west and north-east from the Siruvani and Varadimala ridges on the southern half of Attappady. Bhavani originating in the Nilgiris and smaller tributaries such as the West and East Varagar draining the southern slopes of the Nilgiris receives the Siruvani River flowing from the south-western part of Attappady. Kodungarapallam draining in Varadimala ridge flows north along the south-eastern edge of Attappady and joins Bhavani at Koodappatty. The Kuntha River flowing south from the Nilgiris forms the north-eastern border of Attappady for a short distance and joins Bhavani further to the east in Tamilnadu. Attappady was a heavily forested humid tropical eastern slope of the Western Ghats with flora and fauna, typical of the heavy rainfall southern part of the Western Ghats in peninsular India.

SL No	Slope of land / speciality	Area hectares	%
1	Plains	432.5	0.5
2	Slope of 5 - 10 degrees	1147.5	1.54
3	Slope of 10 - 15 degrees	3055	4.10
4	Slope of 15 - 35 degrees	26040	34.95
5	Steep slope	42752	57.39
6	Streams, rivulets	875	1.17
7	Ponds	197.5	0,27

Table-1 Area and slope of land in Attappady

Fig. 5 Attappady Average Slope

Climate, Rainfall and natural vegetation

Attappady has essentially a humid tropical climate. The Crestline of the Nilgiris and peaks elsewhere reaching above 1800m have a sub-temperate climate with winter night temperatures going below 12°C. Frost is not uncommon. Topographical heterogeneity, proximity of the high Nilgiris, location close to the Palakkad Gap, its position as an east slopping mid-elevation plateau, all create a wide range of climatic conditions within the compact area that we call Attappady. The western part and the southern part of Attappady get most of its rain from the south-west monsoon. On the other hand, the eastern portion receives most of its rain during the north-east monsoon. The higher Nilgiri ridges and the Siruvani hills get plentiful rainfall from both the monsoons. Because of the position of high ridges intersecting rain-bearing clouds within Attappady, even nearby locations have very different microclimates. Extensive denudation and the repeated failure of the north-east monsoon have contributed to accelerating desertification of Attappady.

Fig. 6 Attappady- Rainfall Distribution

The altitudinal, climatic and topographic peculiarities have contributed to a wide range of forest vegetation types occurring in Attappady. Repeated human incursions over many millennia and its impact on the ecology have added a spectrum of degradative or successional phases to the original forest vegetation. The recent extensive and intensive human manipulations have accelerated the degradative change in plant communities. All the higher ridges have sub-temperate montane evergreen forests and wet temperate grasslands above 1600m. Extensive grasslands with small patches of montane evergreen forests are called shola Grassland vegetation. Extensive reaches of the Nilgiris and peaks in Siruvani hills have this forest type. Below 1600m until about 900m above mean sea level and in sheltered valleys receiving more than 1800 mm of rainfall annually, typical evergreen forests, which are also called rainforests, occur. Silent Valley and Attappady reserve forest have extensive areas of this type of forest. Most of the remaining areas of Attappady used to be covered by semi evergreen forests. Areas with less moisture retaining soils and abandoned 'gloom' areas with regenerating vegetation had moist deciduous forests. Excepting in the government Reserved Forests, most of the uncultivated, but previously forested areas of Attappady retain only scrub vegetation at present. Some ridge tops subjected to regular annual fires have savanna vegetation.

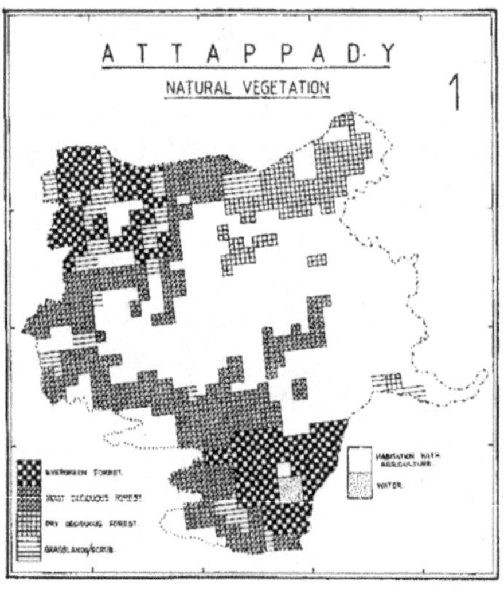

Fig. 7 Attappady Natural Vegetation

History and Demography

According to the known history, Attappady was the province of Zamorin of Calicut (Kozhikode) who in turn vested the right of control to various princely families. It is widely referred to that the area was under control of Moopil Nayar's family and Elarpad Raja.

During the British rule, Attappady area was a village, listed in Malabar district under Valluvanad *Taluk*. During the formation of the state of Kerala in 1956, Attappady was listed under Perinthalmanna *taluk* in Palakkad District. After formation of Malappuram district and Mannarkad *taluk* (in Palakkad district), Attappady was listed under Mannarkad *taluk*. During the formation of panchayats in 1962, Attappady was represented as a single panchayat. In 1968 Attappady, panchayat was divided into three panchayats, namely, Agali, Pudur and Sholayoor.

Sl No	Grama Panchayat	*Irula* Hamlets	*Muduga* Hamlets	*Kurumba* Hamlets	Total
1	Agali	53	18	0	71
2	Pudur	43	5	19	67
3	Sholayoor	44	1	0	45
4	Total	140	24	19	183

Table 2 *Adivasi* Hamlets Grama Panchayat wise

The *Kurumbas, Mudugas* and *Irulas* were the early inhabitants of the area. Since they are early (*Adi*) inhabitants (*Vasi*), they are called *Adivasis*. It is believed that, among them the

Kurumbas are the earliest inhabitants followed by The *Mudugas and Irulas*. (Muraleedharan et al, .1991). The *Irulas* are believed to be the latest among the *Adivasis* of Attappady   moved into the area in the 17th century. The *Irulas* are mostly present in the eastern part and *mudugas* in the western parts and the *Kurumbas* in the deep forest. *Tamilians* and *Malayalis* are later settlers from the beginning of twentieth century. The *Tamilians* and *Malayalis* are settled in the eastern and the western parts of Attappady respectively. The *Adivasis* were dependent on forest resources for their livelihood. As a result of the inflow of the settler population and the establishment of government institutions they have become less self reliant as they depend upon the settlers for their livelihood. As a part of the government's forest conservation measures their freedom in depending on forest for their life has greatly come to a stall. Today they are part of the most downtrodden "poorest of the poor" to use the terminology of the developmentalists. Among the *adivasis* of Attappady the social relations, economic conditions, and health status are better off among the still forest dwelling *Kurumba*s. [Muraleedharan et al 1991; Mathur 1977]

Linguistic differences notwithstanding, the different *Adivasi* tribes of *Irulas*, *Mudugas* and *Kurumbas* had many commonalities. They engaged in activities like collecting forest resources like honey, food and other minor forest resources. Slowly they also started to engage in agricultural activities and animal breeding. The *Adivasis* used to get sufficient resources from the forests. They had an economic system that was deeply related to the 'ecology' and nature around them. Land and other items were never seen as a commodity. The hamlets were concentrated around the areas where water sources originated to form rivulets or streams, and such hamlets were called the *'oorus'*. The dwellings of *Adivasis* consisted of small thatched huts, with walls covered with mud and cow dung. The roofs consisted of grass and bamboos. These dwellings also had special granaries for holding their food-stock and every *ooru* had a place for ancestral worship.

Ragi, Cholam, Thina, Mustard, *Kambu, Varagu, Pandi, Thuvara* etc were the food products that the *Adivasis* were fond of cultivating. These cultivation patterns also were changed with the 'settlers' arrival. Cotton, Ground nut, Rice, Plantain, Tapioca, Coconut, Arecanut, Tea, Coffee, Pepper, Ginger etc got into the agriculture system of *Adivasis*.

	Area	SC	ST	Others	Total
a.	Below 1 Ha.	447	3006	3604	7057
b.	1 to 2 Ha.	188	3043	4169	7400
c.	2 to 4 Ha.	90	344	751	1185
d.	4 to 10 Ha.	--	11	215	226
e.	Above 10 Ha.	--	--	7	7

Source: http://www.ahads.org/Atta_basicinformation.htm

Table 3: Details of cultivated lands

Every *ooru* had a council of *moopans* (elders) who were vested with the responsibility of guiding the members of the hamlets with reference to their livelihood activities such as cultivation, hunting, food gathering and fishing, inter and intra community amity, family relationships, and also liaisoning between the *Jenmi* (land lord) and the community. The *Ooru Moopan* is the chief of the *Ooru* and he is assisted by the other members of the council of *moopans* designated as *Vandari, Kuruthala,* and *Mannookkaran*.

Significant among the cultural activities of *Adivasis*, the folk songs and dances were considered to be part of their expressions. *Adivasis* also had their own forms of *'natakams'* and *'koothus'*. They also had mastery over many ethnic wind and percussion instruments like *'para', 'thavil', 'peeki', 'mangai', 'therali'*, etc.

The migration of the 'mainstream' *Tamilians* and *Malayalis* into the area in search of agricultural land begun in the early 20th century and increased in the mid 20th century. The settlers emerged a major economic and the only political power within two decades of their settlement and presently outnumbered the *Adivasis*. They could manage to take land on lease from the Jenmi and later they could claim ownership of the land. This has resulted in the *Adivasis* losing control of the land before they ever become aware that land could be owned or sold as a commodity. The table given below shows the *Adivasis* becoming minorities at Attappady since 1960's[58].

Year	Total	*Adivasis*	%	Non *Adivasis*	%
1951	11300	10200	90.26	1100	09.74
1961	21461	12972	60.45	8459	39.55
1971	39183	16536	42.21	22647	57.79

[58] Of the total *adivasi* populations of Attappady, 77.7 % are *Irulas*, 14.4 % *Mudugas* and 7.9% are Kurumars.

1981	62246	20659	33.19	41857	66.81
1991	62033	24228	39.06	37805	60.94
2001	67672	28711	42.00	34171	51.00

Source(s) : Census Reports upto 1991, 2001 ICDS Survey Report, 2002

Table-4. Table showing minoritisation of *Adivasi* population at Attappady

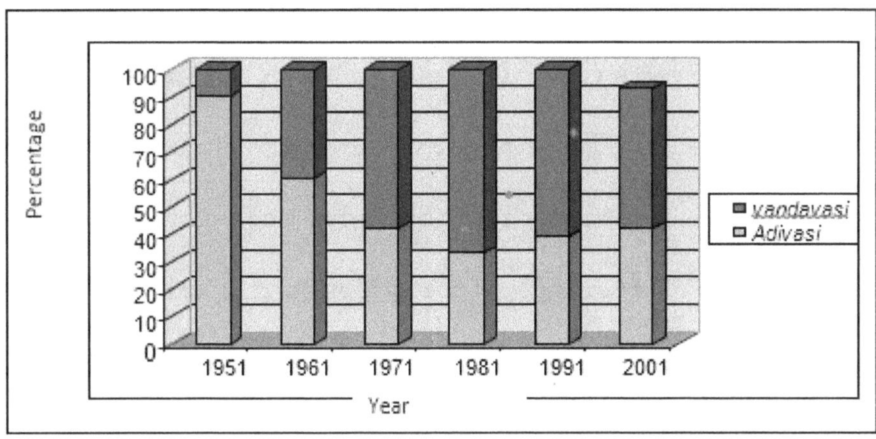

Fig. 8 Minoritisation of *Adivasi* population at Attappady

For their livelihood, the *adivasis* were depending on the forest in the past and they depend on the settlers in the present. The forest was providing them food, shelter and water. Theirs was not money economy even five decades before. The use of money among *Adivasis* of Attappady became widespread only since 1970's. Land had never been a commodity. The *Adivasis* on request from the settlers always let the settlers to occupy the lands nearby their lively hood. Claiming ownership, building fences, keeping a cleared land as an owned property were unknown to *Adivasis*. *Adivasis* of Attappady of course were practicing agriculture before the arrival of the settlers. They were following the practice of shift and burn form of agriculture practices. Agriculture for them was always rain fed. Irrigation was not part of their practice. Monoculture is not a preferred agriculture practice among them. They were sowing about thirteen varieties of seeds on slashed and burnt lands and they were using a land only till it yields. Harvesting of the yield is done as and when different crops mature throughout the year. They leave a piece of land approximately after continuous cultivation for three years.

Adivasis were practicing community agriculture. The community agriculture was called *Kambalam*. Men and women prepare the land as a collective and they share the yields. As all other walks of their life, the practice of agriculture too accompanied with dances, songs and playing of musical instruments. They even had jesters to entertain them during the labour hours. Participation in the *Kambalam* was voluntary. Alongside community agriculture there were also family agriculture practices. In family agriculture families or groups of families participate. Allocation of land for agriculture purpose is done by the council of *moopans* headed by *Ooru moopan*. The *Ooru moopan* collects tax in return to be paid to the *Jenmi*.

Among *moopan*s the most revered is the *mannookkaran*. *Mannookkaran* is the ritual head of agricultural practices of hamlets. *Mannookkaran* is also revered as an expert in soil and agricultural practices. It was believed with the loss of sacredness of *mannookkaran* the land would stop yielding. *Mannookkaran* decides the cultivability of a land, sows the first seeds, and initiates the first harvest. *Mannookkaran*'s wife is responsible for the food preparation from the first yield. The *mannookkaran* loses his sacredness when he gives up ethical way of life (*neethi* and *neri*) as it is conventionally followed. The *mannookkaran* never attends death rituals, as it was believed that participating in death rituals pollutes him.

With the government takeover of the forestlands, government's wild life protection initiatives, settler inflow, establishment of governmental bureaucracy, familiarity with the settler practice of commercial agriculture, deforestation, soil erosion, displacement demanded by the 'development' and so on the traditional practices gradually became irrelevant and the *adivasis* were reduced to daily wage labourers depending on settler entrepreneurs.

Documented property rights, their new labour status, establishment of money economy, decline of the traditional community governance by the elders, loss of traditional agriculture, the introduction of arrack into their culture, the settlement of the outsider and the ecological degradation has its role in defining the present status of familial relations too. The net effect of the changes is that, women lost grip on property rights, neither men nor women have to be dependent on each other as they work as labourers for the outside settlers rather than working together for the food requirement of the family or the community. This has diluted the necessity for 'ena[59] relationship as well as that of the strong community relationships. The parent children relationship had become very different from the past. In the past the family as a unit were collectively working towards food production and gathering. In the present life pattern, it is a rare occasion that all the family members sitting and conversing together. In most of the families by the mid teen age children become labourers whereas in some other families children stay at residential tribal schools. In either of the case, the bondage between children and parents is fast declining. Children earn money independent of their parents and hence for them there is no necessity to be guided by their parents. Everything happened so sudden to the *adivasis*, before they take stock of things in their life, life simply escaped their purview and took its own turn making drastic changes in their familial relationship with the changes brought with the settlement of outsiders and other events they had hardly any control over. As a result, the familial and community relationships as well are devastated and their life has become something very unfamiliar and uncertain to themselves. The collected life experiences show the general trend in the *adivasi* community that, as children they are neglected, at their teen age they enter into a weak conjugal relation, with childbirth they grow their children with meagre support from their husbands and other relatives and at the late age deserted. The story of the men is also not very different.

In the past as well as in these days the formal marriages are rare. Boys and girls, start live together when they find suitable partners. To start living with a girl, in earlier days the boy had to work for the parent of the girl for about a year. This is called '*Penvela*.[60]' The boy has to pay '*Penvela*.' The boy had to pay the 'bride price' to her parents. Today, the custom is fast fading. Some boys started demanding dowry. *Penvela* is not practiced these days. In the past, during *Penvela*, it was common that the pair eloped and stayed at the forest for days together. This was called '*kalavu.*' Usually the elopement is legitimated and they were allowed to live together. If parents of the girls are impressed by the boy who performs *Penvela*, the girls are given to boys in a ceremony arranged for this or asked to live with him. The consents of the girls mattered less.

In the past as well as these days, the boy sets a house after he had found a girl. Earlier, there was no scarcity of land and neither there were land documents. The children settle near the house of either of the parents, mostly near the parents of the boy's house. As land has become a documented property, the freedom to set a house at the place of preference could no longer be exercised on these days. These days it is usual that the girl goes and stays with her spouse at a place owned by the boy's family. As law prevents the tribal lands from being sold from tribal to non-tribal, and also because tribal people are not usually that wealthy enough to buy land, girls do not enjoy their parental property, even though it can be given to her as per documents. Her brothers will usually enjoy her land.

The *adivasi* society is gradually inventing patriarchical norms. For example, dowry that had never been heard among the *adivasis* is gradually emerging as a custom. The *adivasi* youth, especially the educated among them similar to the settlers calculate

---

60   The term *Penvela* literally means, "girl-work." It is the labour performed to get a girl as spouse. With the performance of *Penvela*, the boy convinced the parents of the girl and the girl herself that he is capable of providing her a secured life.

the financial status of the bride's family. The *adivasi* women say that present men unlike the men of older generation less involved in household works. Child rearing, bread winning, family maintenance and household jobs are becoming women's sole responsibility. As most of the men are alcoholic, they even abuse their wives. Today, it is common that both men and women suspect their spouse of illicit extramarital relations and this has become a major reason for household feuds. This was not the case with the older generations. In contrast to the marital relationships of the younger generations, even today the elderly people of the *adivasi*s can be seen always with each other's company either at home or at outside. They were always together even in their young age. There will be nothing that one knows hidden to the other. Today, this can be rarely seen. Women and men go to work at different places and come back to home only in the evening. Generally, by the time the men come home they are drunk. They do not share all the information with each other. Men and women have many things to hide from each other. For example, women hide the amount of money with her because, if it were told, the man would take it from her. Similarly, men have many common things they do with their workmates and others they meet at their workplace. This has distanced the spouses apart each other. They know less of each other and they fight.

Decades of encounter with the settlers and the interference of government mechanism in Attappady resulted in ecologically denuded situation and the social, cultural and economic impoverishment of *adivasis*. The combined effect of ecological denudation and impoverishment is hunger, ill health, malnutrition and the loss of community life.

The so-called 'tribes' of Kerala, especially those belonging to Attappady[61] are classified as 'poor' or 'persistently poor' in the documents of government and Non-Governmental Agencies' welfare and development programmes. They are called poor because of their poor income, vulnerability to hunger and starvation, lack of easy accessibility to minimum needs such as fuel, water, and other basic amenities. Their difficult life situation could also be linked to infertility of the lands belonging to them, their dependence on food stamp and food rationing, nutritional deprivation, declined employability, impoverished kinship and familial relations and their political and social alienation. The personal acquaintance with the people reveals that because of the severity of life situation the *adivasi*s of Attappady these days die young. 'Unnatural' deaths are very common, [Appendix 9] women are abused and to cope with severity of the adverse life conditions they resort to alcoholism. Whatever may be the indicators used, their life appears hard and difficult. During the intimate conversations of the fieldwork, both men and women burst into tears thinking of their actual hardships.

---

61   Attappady region is classified as an administrative unit called 'Block.' Attappady block consists three 'grama panchayats' namely Agali, Pudur and Sholayoor. The *Irula*s, *Muduga*s and *Kurumba*s are three groups of 'tribal' population settled at Attappady of which *Irula*s live at the relatively low lands, *Muduga*s at mid lands and *Kurumba*s at the high lands. The high lands are mostly protected the forest area. Of three, *Irula*s are closer to the mainstream and the *Kurumba*s are distant from the mainstream. All the three groups are integrated into the money economy and settled into hamlets. Of three, the forest dwelling *Kurumba*s appear to be healthier and happiest. *Moopans* of *Kurumba* hamlets command more respect than those of *Irula*s and *Muduga*s. All these groups live in nuclear families where it appears for the outsiders the *Kurumba* families better enjoy the resources of inter and intra familial relations than the other two groups. Of the three, the *Irula*s have a few people in government jobs, *Muduga*s have fewer and *Kurumba*s usually do not prefer government jobs. Of the three, mostly democratically elected leaders come mostly from the *Irula*s. As the scope of the thesis is limited to give an account of Praxis Intervention Practice, we do not elaborate the details of the 'tribal' population of Attappady. (See appendix for more details)

Health

The commonly prevailing ailments are fever, diarrhoea, anaemia, worm infestation, dental diseases rheumatoid arthritis, tuberculosis, leprosy, and diseases related to thyroid glands. Most of the diseases prevailing here are direct consequence of malnutrition, alcoholism, excessive use of tobacco, usage of un-potable water for drinking purpose. The block panchayat project report of 1997-2002 states, that among the 'illiterates' of Attapaddy the Infant Mortality rate is 132/1000. Among *Kurumba*s the infant mortality rate is as high as 280/1000. The infant mortality rate among *adivasis* of Attappady is very high. The average infant mortality rate for Kerala is 16/1000.

Health Facilities available at Attappady are:

COMMUNITY HEALTH CENTRE	1
Primary Health centres	3
IPP sub centres	28
Homeo Dispensary	4
Ayurveda dispensary	1

Table 5: Health facilities

Literacy and Education

The literacy rate among *adivasis* is low. *Adivasi* children perform poorly in education as education does not appear interesting to the children. With the new syllabus, the children are expected to make projects based on audio visual and newspaper reports. As the children have no easy access to the audio visual as well as visual media, and also due to the marginalised socio economic background they find it difficult to continue with their education. However, children in the residential schools are better performers, as they are not severely limited by the marginalised socio economic background of their parents.

Community	Sex ratio (per 100 males)	Literacy %	Female Literacy %
Irula	988	29.3	25.7
Kurumba	906	22.6	15.2
Muduga	983	24.3	17.1

Table 6: Literacy rates of tribal communities in Attappady

The educational infrastructure locally available for the *adivasi* children are:

MODEL RESIDENTIAL SCHOOLS	1
High Schools	7
UP schools	4
LP schools	18
ST Hostels	12

Table 7: Education facilities at Attappady

Occupation

The *Adivasis* of Attappady are generally agricultural labourers. *Adivasi* children and the elderly people involve in the occupation of cattle rearing labour. They rarely cultivate in their own lands, as mostly their lands are sloppy and infertile. Only less than 2% of the *adivasis* have found their occupation in Government or private sector and in the collection of minor forest products , all put together [KFRI 1980; Block Panchayat Report 1997-2002]. As the *adivasis* of Attappady are comparatively more marginalised than *Malayarayas* of Idukki and Pathanamthitta, *Kurichiyars* and *Kurumars* of Wyanad, they loose out the benefits from the positive discrimination strategies of the governments to the better off among the *adivasis*.

Ecology

Attappady is a continuing hot spot of ecological destruction. Despite it had been blessed with fertile soil, three perennial rivers, well spread adequate rainfall, equitable climate, a forest cover ranging from sub-temperate montane shola-grasslands to evergreen forests and semi-deciduous vegetation and also with people capable of maintaining the ecological balance its degradation is dramatic within the past few decades. The ecological degradation of the area had begun since the colonial government's intervention through its forest policies and it became acute since it had been integrated with the Kerala state in 1957 [Nair 1988]. The major activity that destroyed the eco-system of a deep forest into a desert like landscape is the conversion of forest into arable land by settlers. Deforestation and the introduction of non-eco friendly agriculture practices have degraded the vegetation cover almost beyond regeneration. With the loss of vegetation, subsequent massive soil erosion changed the local climate and made rainfall erratic. This has resulted in the loss of perennial nature of the rivers of Attappady as their catchments area has become relatively drier due to eco-destructive human involvement [Nair 2002].

Development

Attappady is notorious for failed high-expenditure development projects and subsequent studies enquiring into the possible reasons for the failures[62]. There had been several tribal development, irrigation, eco-restoration, agriculture development, animal husbandry, fisheries development, diary development, sericulture, forestry, soil conservations, watershed management projects sponsored by the government and non-governmental agencies. Invariably all of them met with failures in achieving the results set by themselves [appendix 7]. The sagas of failures still continue. Corruption, insincerity, lack of relevance, poor planning, poor understanding of the ecology and the conditions of people and the very internal biases of developmentalism, formal party politics and bureaucratic mechanism could be pointed out as the reasons for these continuing failures [IRTC 1998]. The decentralization initiatives after 73rd and 74th constitutional amendments presently being carried out are propagated to bring changes in the lives of the *adivasis* by the government machineries.

Most of the developmentalist projects claim that they exist there for the restoration of ecology, management of watershed, improvement of drinking water availability, improvement of health and nutrition among the *adivasi*s, facilitate the hamlet based community organization, strengthen grassroots democracy, bring about participatory spirit etc. Looking back into their history, one would not find they were ever poor in these respects and rather poverty in these respects was introduced into their life and into the region through the development projects and the government schemes. The experts

---

[62]　GOK 2003: 3-4; IRTC 1988; Menon 1982; Vijayanand 1997; KFRI 1980; BES 1977

invariably being 'outsiders' trying to 'develop' the *adivasi*s seem to be invariably trapped into their own biases. For example, a study [Vijayanand 1997] presumes that there is poverty among the *adivasi*s because they are 'excluded' from 'development.' The 'exclusion' can be corrected with 'genuinely' participatory methods of project administration. The genuine participation is imagined as flowing from the initiatives of 'motivated government functionaries' and 'social animators.' The premise of the study is that the poverty exists because of non-participatory methods of project management[63]. Madhava Menon Commission's Evaluation Report on Integrated Tribal Development Project [ITDP], Attappady is another example of outsider bias on the *adivasi* 'development.' The committee report blames the 'ignorance, negligence and malafides of the project staff about tribal realities and tribal interests,' for the poor performance of government sponsored development initiatives. To make development possible among the *adivasi*s, the

committee 'strongly urges' that it should be obligatory on the part of every district head of the offices from collector downward to spend at least three continuous days on duty in remote hamlets preferably on foot.

To make the tribal development a reality, the report also recommends

[The] involvement of forest authorities in many of the development activities including irrigation structures in the Attappady Valley. This is vital in the case of primitive groups (*Kurumba*s living in the forest area.)

Further, the report suggests:

A senior direct recruit I.A.S[64] officer with four to six years of seniority should be

---

63   Vijayanand's study is an uncritical application with minor modifications action of Jules Pretty's typology of participation on the *adivasi* context. Jules Pretty categorises participation into seven ordinal categories from 'passive participation' to self mobilisation.' [Pretty 1995 :173].

posted for the tenure of at least three years in the job [of Integrated Tribal development Project officer].

The report also observes, "The provision of pump sets and irrigation construction are very vital for the development of tribal cultivation."

The Madhava Menon committee report seems to have been written with the premise that:

- 'Tribals' are primitive anthropological segments.

- 'Tribals' are objects of development projects.

- For anybody involved in the 'tribal' development a specialised knowledge of 'tribals' is required.

- Senior direct IAS recruits, Senior forest officials, district collectors and institutions like Kerala Agriculture University etc., could make the 'development' of the 'tribals' possible.

- The 'expertise' of senior bureaucrats, tribal development experts, agricultural scientist etc, should be passed on to the 'tribals' by strict management of 'extension officers.'

The "Evaluation Study of Schemes implemented in the Tribal development block" conducted by the Bureau of Economics and Statistics in 1977 asserts that the reason for failure of development activities is:

Topography of the region – mostly hilly with barriers in communication …traditional outlook and fatalism of the tribals, and inadequate extension service.

The report recommends exploring scope for 'changing the cropping pattern of tribals to

64   Indian Administrative Service.

achieve a better rate of economic growth.' The report identifies introduction of tapioca[65] through extension work as a success story of bringing changes in their cultivation practice. The study grossly misunderstands the community organisation pattern of the *adivasi*s and suggests things like,

for each hamlet a cottage industrial unit should be started. The initiative should be taken by concerned village extension officer and the *Ooru moopan, Mamookaran, Bandari* and *Kuruthalai* should manage this Unit (*sic*)[66].

The appointments of personals, institutions, supervision and other such aspects are seen as the most important for 'tribal development' in Madhavan Menon I.A.S' Committee Report; for Vijayanand I.A.S, it is the application of tools and techniques of what he calls 'participatory development' assumes the paramount importance. The common thread in these studies is that development is an external agenda requiring external expertise. Common to all these is the 'visionary' project of shaping social life according to categorical schemata [Green 1983:3]. There had also been criticisms from the government itself that its initiative to decentralise local governments also could not yield expected results as the powerful among the non *adivasi* sections tactfully made use of the projects meant for *adivasis* for their own benefits [GOK, 2001; GOK 2003:3] The 'Government Order' issued in May

---

65 Cultivation of tapioca actually worsens soil erosion. The major reason for topsoil removal in the slopes of Attappady has been tapioca cultivation.

66 The community organisation pattern among the *adivasi*s has greatly changed. The traditional *Moopans* do not have so much of command over people as they were having a few decades before. Secondly, they had never been governing or managing communities as the modern governments or bureaucracies do. It seems that it is arrogant and demeaning to assume a village extension officer to be made a decision making partner with the *moopans* even if we go along with the logic with which *moopans* are taken to be the leaders of the *adivasi*s. It is obvious that the studies of this sort could not even understand the surface realities that could be understood with a minimum of sincerity.

2003 points out:

In spite of the high human development in Kerala and its features of equity, most of the tribal communities have continued to be outliers always subject to the danger of being pushed further away from the development process. A quick analysis of the tribal situation in the State reveals the following features.

(i)   Extreme levels of poverty, deprivation and vulnerability.

(ii)   High levels of exclusion both developmental and social.

(iii)   Extremely low levels of empowerment – political, social and economic.

(iv)   Rapid marginalization due to unfair, unequal and exploitative relations of production and exchange between tribal communities and others.

(v)   Low level of access to entitlements

(vi) Practically zero participation in development matters with no autonomy in any form of decision-making.

(vii)   Abnormally huge siphoning off of developmental resources and benefits meant for tribal people by middlemen.

(viii) Poor human development with low levels of literacy and access to health care.

(ix)   Rapid alienation of assets like land.

(x)   Alarming depletion of social capital especially traditional forms of organization and leadership.

(xi) Quick deterioration of traditional knowledge systems and cultural attainments.

(xii)   Fast increasing tendency to use tribal people as cat's-paws in criminal activities like illicit distillation, cultivation of narcotic plants, stealing of forest wealth etc.

(xiii)   High levels of exploitation of women by outsiders.

(xiv)   Weak delivery system of public services.

(xv)   Dependency - inducing developmental programmes relying on distribution of benefits rather than building up of capabilities.

(xvi)   Implementation of ad hoc and stereo-typed developmental progammes in the absence of proper planning.

(xvii) Very weak monitoring systems.

Pre-Praxis Field Work and Household Survey

To prepare for the *praxis* intervention the research team undertook our field survey with *Kurumbas, Mudugas,* and *Irulas* at Attappady and with *Kuruchiar, Thean Kurumars, Urali Kurumars, Adiyars* and *Paniyars* of Wyanad in randomly selected hamlets. In interacting with the *adivasis*, the researchers were reminded almost every moment that they asked wrong questions in trying to understand the *adivasis*. For example, at *Nakkupathi Ooru*, an 'Irula' hamlet at Agali, Attappady, when a question such as 'what is that they think the reason for their poverty' was asked, after talking to them for an hour, an old man among them calmly answered in his language, without any passion that "We are not poor. We are the original inhabitants of this place (*Adivasi*). You made us poor." ("R§Ä BZnhmknIfmWv \n§fmWv R§sf Zcn{ZhmknIfm¡nbXv"). There were inhibitions among the members of the group of their voices being recorded. They also expressed their displeasure of being addressed 'poor.'

At Thirunelly (in Wyanad District of Kerala), the reearch team was walking aside an '*Urali Kurumar*' household. There they saw a very old man sitting on his buttocks folding his legs and his face on his knees. He was unable to lift his head, as his neck was not strong enough to support his head. His face was full of wrinkles and surrounded with yellowish white beard. He may be around 90 years old. He was sitting on the veranda of his house. While passing, they just enquired his well-being and asked him to compare the life these days with that of his younger days. He did not answer for a moment. He looked at their face for a few minutes and looked at their feet. Pointing at their footwear, he recollected, and said,

In my younger days, I remember, even the British officials if they wanted pass by our households, keep their footwear there (showing a place about ten meters from the location where the researchers were standing).

Then he paused for a few minutes and continued with his feeble voice folding his hands as a sign of respect (probably he mistook them to be the welfare bureaucrats) showing the partly tiled and partly thatched construction of his house, "Can you help me if there is government support in repairing the roof?" He was silent once again. He was coughing looking down the soil. The moment to moment of the fieldwork experience with the people located in the economically impoverished, culturally de-capitalised, socially marginalised '*tribal* field' could teach that the effort to understand their 'de-capitalised field' with questionnaires posed to individual members of the fields are too inadequate and the answers the researchers have marked in the sheets hardly represented their on-the-spot understanding despite their understanding itself was inadequate.

They have also undertook a household survey in randomly selected 16 *Irula*, 7 *Muduga* and 8 *Kurumba* households. The details of the survey are represented in the following tables.

Average family size of an *Irula*, *Muduga* and *Kurumba* families are 4.69, 5.14 and 5.75 from the data collected.

However, more households have to be studied to arrive at an error free figure of the statistics.

Community	Average Family Size
Irular	4.69
Muduga	5.14
kurumba	5.75
Overall	5.19

Table 8: Family size

Of 31 households 15 families have an income below Rs.1000, 12 households have an income between Rs. 1000 and 2000 and only three households have an income above Rs.3000. The data collected shows that generally all segments of *adivasis* of Attappady are subjects of economic poverty.

	Below 1000	1000-2000	2000-3000	3000-4000	Above 4000
Irulas	8	7	0	0	1
Muduga	4	3	0	0	0
Kurumba	3	2	1	1	1
Overall	15	12	1	1	2

Table 9: Family Income

On the average the *adivasi* household is of 200-300 squire feet size with minimum amenities. The houses are of more or less of similar size with some basic amenities. The size of the house, its floor or availability of hand pump near their living place is no longer an indicator of their poverty condition as the indicators are managed through poverty eradication projects. However, the life of the *adivasis* continues to be characterised by many kinds of poverty such as economic, social and cultural kinds.

	100-200 sq ft	200-300 sq ft	Above 300
Irulas	2	14	0
Muduga	2	5	0
Kurumba	1	4	3
Overall	5	23	3

Table 10. Size of the houses

The houses have only minimum furniture in them. The households usually do not have modern electrical or electronic kitchen equipments.

	Dining table		Cots		Beds With Sheets		Electric electronic Kitchen equipment	
	Yes	No	Yes	No	Yes	No	Yes	No
Irulas	0	16	0	16	0	16	0	16

Muduga	1	6	1	6	1	6	0	7
Kurumba	0	8	1	7	1	7	0	8
Overall	1	30	2	29	2	29	0	31

Table 11: Household furniture

Of 31 houses surveyed only three houses have separate bedrooms.

	Households having special sleeping rooms	Households not having special sleeping rooms.
Irulas	1	15
Muduga	1	6
Kurumba	1	7
Overall	3	28

Table 12: Availability of sleeping rooms

Accessibility to water has been managed by the government programmes by providing each *Ooru* with a hand pump drawing ground water. It is not the availability, but portability of the water is the source of concern at Attappady.

The marital relation and its stability seems to have been affected with the degree of integration with the mainstream. *Irulas* are more 'mainstreamised' than the other two groups. Of 16 households surveyed, four have strained marital relationship. Where as, of the eight *Kurumba* families surveyed none of them has a strained marital relationship. *Kurumba*s live in the reserve forest with comparatively least contact with the mainstream.

However, it has to be admitted that the size of the survey sample is too small to make any conclusive statement.

	Stable	Unstable
Irulas	12	4
Muduga	6	1
Kurumba	8	0
Overall	26	5

Table 13: Stability of marital relationship

Most of the *adivasi* households surveyed at attappady have legal rights to the land they possess. *Kurumba*s live in reserve forest.

	Not having documented property rights	Having documented property rights	Forest land
Irulas	6	10	0
Muduga	2	5	0
Kurumba	-	0	8
Overall	8	23	8

Table 14: Nature of Land Rights

The *adivasi* households prefer to remain nuclear. In case of non-availability of land or resources to build a separate house, they maintain joint families, that is, families of sons staying with their parents till they get an opportunity to build a new house. As per the development report of Attappady Block Panchayat, 130 *Irula* families, 24 *Muduga* families and 17 *Kurumba* families are landless. The report also states that 'of 5262 *adivasis* families, 3400 are homeless".

The *adivasis* of Attappady are economically, socially and culturally impoverished people. Their economic poverty is indicated by their poor income[67] [GOK, 2003] disproportionate to their requirement, social poverty is indicated by not having a socially honoured community[68] status of influential leaders, highly placed entrepreneurs or senior bureaucrats among them and their cultural impoverishment is indicated by their self-assessment as 'unclean, ill educated, superstitious, non- scientific, in capable of producing for the Market, having 'inferior' marriage or death rituals, 'poor' familial/ community relations, lazy, lacking entrepreneurial attitude etc [Table 15].'[69]

---

[67] The survey conducted among *adivasi*s of Attappady shows that the average family income of *adivasi*s of Attappady is ranging from Rs. 1000 to 2000, where as the average family size is 5.19.

[68] The *adivasi* families at Attappady usually do not have persons holding jobs of regular income. The *adivasi* community of Attappady do not have political or community leaders of high social stature. The local politicians from the *adivasi* community at Attappady expressed their concern of being treated as the bonded labourers of the mainstream political parties. A Bureaucrat, writing on the formal politics at Attappady comments,

The Attappady experience shows that it is difficult for the elected tribals who constitute 45% of the panchayat membership to resist the pulls of cooperation and seek grass-roots level mobilisation. In spite of their numerical strength, they serve the dominant interests by *allowing themselves to be manipulated*. [Vijayanand 1997; IRTC 1998: 204]

[69] The [*adivasi*] participants were asked to compare themselves with the '*vandavasis*' in the first phase of "Praxis intervention". The participants came out with the observations cited above.

4 PRAXIS INTERVENTION EXPERIMENT

An Outline of the Project

The *Praxis* Intervention project when carried out had seven phases of which three Phases were in the field and four in the classroom covering a duration of six and a half months. There were three kinds of participants in the project: the researcher-*adivasi*-participants [hereafter RAP], non-*adivasi* participants [hereafter NAP] and the hamlet resident participants [hereafter HRP]. The RAPs were the elected *adivasi* representatives of the local administrative bodies of the *grama*[70] and block[71] panchayats[72] of Attappady and some hamlet residents. There were 35 registered RAPs, of whom 30 were regular. Among the regular RAPs, 15 were elected representatives [hereafter ERAP]. There were 13 women and 17 men took part in the project regularly for the entire course. The RAPs other than elected representatives (hereafter Non-Elected-Researcher-*Adivasi*-Participants [NERAP]) were manual labourers except one. One participant was a plus one (11th standard) student. All the participants were advised to select

---

70   *Grama* panchayat is the village level local body of governance.

71   The "Block" is the second tier of three tiered local bodies of governance namely the *grama*, block and district panchayats.

72   Panchayat is the name of local bodies of governance.

a hamlet for their field location. Each RAP selected a field location (mostly his/her own hamlet). Among the NAPs, there were two kinds of participants: the project undertakers (hereafter Project Undertaking Participants [PUP]) and the external experts [hereafter EE] associated with the project. There were seven PUPs of whom one was an *adivasi* activist from an *adivasi* community, two were *dalit* activists, one was a scholar in woman's studies, one was a research student of history and anthropology and one was an activist of the Kerala science - literature movement [KSSP][73], and the present researcher.

The project period was from 28th May 2002 to 10th November 2002. The planning for the project had begun in January 2002 and it was consolidated in a workshop called for the purpose on 28th and 29th of January 2002. In the workshop, it was decided that:

1. *Adivasis* of Kerala from the districts of Idukki, Wayanad and the Attappady block of Palakkad district would be the participants of the project for the first three years in three batches.

2. Each batch would be from any one area thickly populated with *adivasis*.

3. Each batch would be undertaking a research for about 4-6 months with intermittent classroom and fieldwork phases.

---

[73]   Kerala Sastra Sahithya Parishad.

4. There would be combined annual workshops with the batches completed their research for consequent three years in which all the batches completed would be joining in. The annual workshops could be used to promote state-wide *praxis* intervention strategies with the *adivasis*.

5. The RAPs would constitute of Elected Representatives of the panchayats and the 'tribal promoters'[74] working as animators under the Tribal Development Department.

6. The RAPs would be independent researchers who would be undertaking research and speaking their mind rather than just remaining participants of 'our' project in which 'our' minds are put through participatory tools or techniques [see appendix 3].

Contrary to the plans the PUPs had, the project could not have the participants from the 'tribal promoters' as there was unwillingness from the tribal development department. As the tribal promoters were not permitted to take part in the project, it was later decided to invite participation from the hamlets. The participants from the hamlets were recommended by the ERAPs. Owing to some unforeseen technical reasons the researcher could complete only one batch of the project.

The project of *praxis* intervention had phases arranged in tune with the spontaneity of the participant's learning. The learning had elements of discussions, debates, arguments, games, songs, dances, role-plays, writing charts, viewing movies, listening to lectures, fieldwork assignments, self-evaluations, tours etc. The practice of *praxis* intervention could produce, 127 chart sheets

---

[74] Tribal promoters are the persons appointed by the Tribal Development Department of the GOK to function as a link between the community and the department.

consisting bullet points of classroom discussions or presentations, 27 fieldwork journals, six songs compiled, 21 days of classroom sessions, eight workshops with PUPs and EEs, four workshops with RAPs at field location and six months of fieldwork [See appendix 1-5]. The steps followed in the *praxis* intervention project are represented in the figure 9.

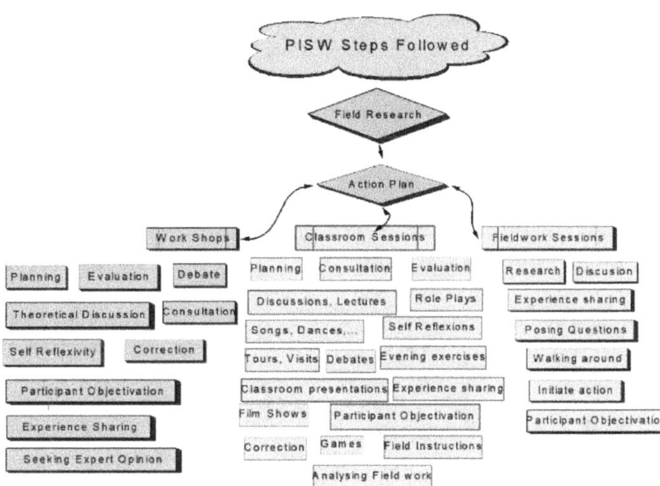

Fig. 9 *Praxis* Intervention- Steps Followed

Phase-I: Introducing the *praxis* Intervention

To begin with, the participants[75] arrived for an exercise in which the RAPs would reflect in groups on what they think about their '*adivasi*ness[76].' After hours of debates, the participants brought out the following chart, in which what the RAPs felt to be the *adivasiness* is contrasted with the *vandavasiness*[77] [table 15].

Adivasi (Tribal)	*Vandavasi* (Settler, non tribe)
1. Lacks education	Has high educational qualification.
2. Mutual support is less	More mutual support.
3. Does not look after children after the age of 5.	Looks after children until they are fully grown up.
4. Eats conventional food like *Ragi Puttu*, Cholam, mustard leaves etc.	Eats 'sophisticated' food like rice, *idli, dosa, appam* and various varieties of food.
5. Lackadaisical.	Alert and prompt.
6. Does not save money for future.	Saves money for future.
7. Rituals related to marriage, death, first menstruation are different from that of the *vandavasi*s. Dead are buried only after three days, Marriages are uncommon.	Rituals are different. Marriages are more important than the celebration of first menstruation. Some do not celebrate first menstruation at all. Dead are burnt or buried according to religious norms.
8. Does not practice intensive agricultural cultivation in their land.	Planned cultivators.
9. Does not approach Banks for support.	Takes bank loans. And enjoys other services.
10. Does not cultivate for Market. Agriculture is chiefly for self-consumption. These days *adivasis* rarely cultivate.	Cultivate for Market.
11. Has less money.	Has more money and wealth.

---

[75] The word 'participants' here means all the participants present during the event of making decisions. This includes RAPs, PUPs and EEs.

[76] The word '*adivasi*' is the local expression for the formal term 'tribal'. The term tribal or tribe is used in government literature.

[77] The word '*vandavasi*' is the local expression of the formal term 'settler'. The literal meaning of the term is the people who later settled.

12. Travel less	Travel more.
13. Belongs to Attappady and nowhere else.	Belongs to some other placed and settled at Attappady.
14. Cultivates food crops for consumption.	Cultivates cash crops for market.
10. Unclean	Clean
11. No Caste/ religious divisions.	Have caste/ religious divisions.
12. Does not practice family planning, or birth control	Practices family planning and birth control.
13. Stays at the fringes or in the of forest	Stays at cities and towns and some settle at tribal area converting that area into a small town.
14. To marry pay bride price	To marry pay dowry.

Table-15 *Adivasi Vandavasi* Comparison

The production of chart is a work done by the RAPs after two hours of discussion in small groups. What they reflect on the content of the chart is only secondary to the production of the chart in which they have articulated the differences. It can be observed that in production of this chart the RAPs could cross the limits of conventional thinking about themselves. The RAPs here could draw the contours of their social space in contrast to that of the *vandavasis*. Moreover, by doing so they were also engaging in an act of 'identification' i.e., they were drawing out their differences from the *vandavasis*. They undertake the act of 'identification' by 'differentiating' themselves from their 'other.' The work has set the opportunity to negotiate further with the identification and differentiation based on conceptual, political, historical, temporal and contextual assumptions. The criteria with which the identification is made are based on their emerging positions in the social space and the signs with which the process is carried out. There is a realisation that the positions they occupy are weakening; the 'signs' that decide their position are market compatibility, urge to colonise the future, consumption of 'elite' food stuffs, practice of 'elite' rituals, becoming 'employable' in the 'elite' social order and so on. This opens the possibility to think further whether to let their *habitus* modified by the signs that assumed symbolic superiority or to evaluate the signs themselves. Evaluating the signs themselves that determine their position in the social space is an option to be political.

We can observe that the chart as it is presented has little to express their political will. The chart just describes them: illiterate, divided, not caring for their children as the *vandavasis* do, eat crude food, lackadaisical, without a future, ritually backward, not well linked with the institutions of the state, poor agriculturists, have no market sense, economically deprived, locked within a small area of Attappady, unclean, have no sense of family planning and have no social practices of grand marriage functions and so on. While presenting, an RAP was expressing the 'shameful' practice of keeping the dead bodies for three days before the burial for ritual performances and dances. He also pointed out that invariably the rituals are accompanied with arrack. This expresses a sense of 'shame' rather than a will to be political.

Social thinkers have pointed out that shame is a sociological phenomenon occurs only among the socialised and domesticated [Heller 2003: 1016-17]. Shame for Heller is a 'social affect' that has no natural trigger. Shame when internalised becomes guilt, an individualist emotion characterising one's *habitus* and thus its reproductive schemata [Lynd 1961: 66; Bourdieu 1990: 57]. Guilt is about what one did; shame is about the self, what one *is* [Lynd 1961: 66]. Some Marxist scholars identified shame as the "hidden injury of the working class" related to the respectability of the class and the occupational position the working class enjoying in the larger society. [Sennett and Cobb 1973: 80-85]. For Goffman it amounts to 'embarrassment' and 'loss of face' [Goffman 1967].

Shame is understood in the sociological literature as an outcome of threat to social bond one is enjoying [Scheff 2000]. From another perspective, this would be an instance of the 'civilising process' [Elias 1994].

What should be the professional response from the "Social Work" that is recently called "Social Care Work"[78] in addressing the question of socially ingrained shame? No doubt, for a profession of social care it is an important question to be addressed. Can 'shame' be properly attended with the conventional social work categories such as casework, group work or community organisation alone? Is it sufficient to address the sociological and political phenomenon of 'en-shame-ment' with tools and techniques of counselling and other psychological approach alone? What kind of social action could be addressing the issue of shame? These were the questions haunting the PUPs hearing the presentations.

The RAPs could also point out that there are some differences between *adivasis'* and *vandavasis* in their understanding of family, community relationships, social stratification, ritual practices, religious beliefs, life motives, and the way in which agriculture, environment, landed properties and education is looked at.

The RAPs also undertook an exercise that takes stock of their present perception of gender relations. The details of group discussion are presented using the chart [table. 16]

---

[78] Meagher and Parton: An *idea(l)* of care been at the core of social work values, theory, and practice since social work's inception, and we argue that rehabilitating the ideal of care can counterbalance pervasive and corrosive managerialisation. Unless care is relocated at the centre of debates, policies, and practices, what makes social work (and social care more generally) distinctive will be lost [Meagher and Parton 2004: 11]

The University of Wales introduces its social work course as 'social care work'. In England the codes of conduct drafted for social workers is titled as "the *Code of Practice for social care workers."* [Jordan 2001: 533]

It can be noted that man-woman relationship is conceptualised as a relationship of authority, in terms of man's authority over woman. The relationship is also understood from the perspective of the degree of freedom enjoyed. Men are seen freer than women. Viewing from the responsibility angle the participants point out that men are less responsible compared to women. The comparison also brought out the weakening of trust between genders. The decline is seen as an outcome of doubting 'chastity' of their partners and over the sharing of responsibility in maintaining family life.

The chart points out that the women in the *adivasi* community hardly enjoy their gender identity. It also throws light on the presence of discursive as well as performative production and regulatory practices of gender coherence [Butler 1990:24]. Elspeth Probyn's remark that the self is a doubled entity is pertinent here. She says:

> it is involved in the ways we go about our everyday lives, and it puts into motion a mode of theory that problematises the material conditions of those practices. Unlike the chickens which are presumably sexed one way or the other, once and for all, a gendered self is constantly reproduced within the changing mutations of difference. While sex is known, the ways in which it is constantly re-gendered are never fixed or stable. One way of imagining the self is to think of it as a combination of acetate transparencies: layers and layers of lines and directions that are figured together and in depth, only then to be rearranged[79].

---

[79]   Probyn 1993:1

Man	Woman
1. Has authority over the family.	Is a member of the family.
2. Enjoys more freedom of movement.	Freedom to move is restricted especially in the night hours.
3. Gets a higher wage compared to women.	Gets lower wage compared to men
4. Only a portion earned of money is spent on family	Every penny earned is spent for the family
5. Less number of boys continue after upper primary education.	More girls study after upper primary education.
6. Less involved in household works	More involved in household works.
7. Does not wear *thali*	Wears *thali*.
8. Come forward in [formal] politics	Less interested in public affairs.
9. Does not respect women	Does not respect men
10. Does not conceive and give birth	Conceives and gives birth
11. After marriage need not go away from own family.	After Marriage has to go with husband.
12. Doubts the sexual morality of wife.	Doubts the sexual morality of husband.
13. Enjoys property rights	Practically no property rights.
14. Has to pay bride price.	Paying Dowry is only very rare.

Table 16. Man woman comparison

The presentation of the charts however provided a ground for the PUPs for provoking questions of social construction of gender identities. There was a nine-month-old child with one participant. In an interactive session, the participants were asked whether the child knows that it was *he* and *he* was an *adivasi*. The participants thought for a moment and one by one came with responses. One response was that the boy is hardly grown up to know that *he* is a boy and he is an *adivasi*: but, in due course of his life, he would *learn* that he was an *adivasi boy*. It was further probed, whether the boy would become like other *adivasi* boys had he been given a chance to be grown among other communities. They were also asked what would be the result if a non-*adivasi* child were grown among *adivasis*. Their answer was unambiguous: the children will grow up into persons according to the way they were brought up. The discussion went on to the extent of stating as a conclusion, that the *adivasiness* or *vandavasiness* has no inherent *adivasi* or *vandavasi* nature, rather these identities are constructed by the social, cultural and economic conditions in which one is placed. Through a dialogue, it was brought out how history and arbitrariness of historical trajectory along with the biographical trajectories, the process of socialisation, habituation, legitimisation and reification construct the content of our consciousness, personhood and identities [Berger and Luckmann 1991].

It had been highlighted that to understand the current social relations it is important to inquire into the historical processes that had led to the developments and changes we witness. Therefore, it was collectively decided to probe into the importance of the 'history' of the present-day practices, beliefs, and other things [Burkitt 1991: 164] [80].

Following the discussion, an eminent historian[81] introduced the idea of history and the means to explore it. He demonstrated the method of probing 'local history' with the participants. He was dialogically inquiring with them into the possible events that led them occupy their present hamlets, the *Kurumbas* occupied the top hills, the *Mudugas* the mid-hills, the *Irula*s the foot hills and the settlers on the riverbeds. The questions raised only had hypothetical answers and the participants were encouraged to raise similar questions with the elders in the hamlets to verify their hypothesis. The EE was not actually probing into their history but merely demonstrating how data could be gathered from the field through methods of dialogue. It was emphasised that the dialogue should not be a mechanical survey rather it should be provoking the HRPs and the RAPs themselves to think and imagine the past from the present with critical perspectives. The dialogue should be a tool for inviting people for further participation in the *praxis* intervention. The participants were also introduced that if anything exists in their social practice that should have some historical precedent be it a tumbler, a glass, a table, the gender relations, the settler occupation, their food habits, or their cultivation practices.

The participants enacted role-plays as a rehearsal of their intended fieldwork activity. The role-play was a demonstration, with many subtle comical interludes included. There were three role-plays presented by three sub groups   involving everybody in the classroom. They were evaluating each other's performance critically. They were correcting the possible mistakes they could commit in the

---

[80] For Elias the process with which the present is constituted historically by the chains of reaction of habitués is figuration. By figuration we mean the changing pattern created by the players as a whole – not only by their intellects but by their whole social selves, the totality of their dealings in their relationships with each other. It can be seen that this figuration forms a flexible lattice-work of tensions. The interdependence of the players, which is a prerequisite of their forming a figuration, may be an interdependence of allies or of opponents. [Burkitt 1991: 164]

[81] Dr. K.N. Ganesh, Reader in History, University of Calicut, Calicut.

field, like acting like a bureaucrat, being mechanical and formal, etc. The subjects to be explored were indicated: the history of hamlet settlements, the traditional pattern of community organisation and the present status of the community, the patterns of agriculture of the past and the present, gender relations of the past to present, and the changes occurred as the settlers and the government machineries arrived. It was also decided that the RAPs would probe into the personal histories of men and women in their hamlet in order to look at the historical changes from the biographical perspectives of individuals by invoking people's memories of their childhood, ranging over experiences such as teen age, getting into marital relations, work and labour, household activities, child rearing and old age[82].

To equip the participants for probing the local history the workshop provided them with information on the pattern of land settlements at Attappady; history of *adivasi* struggles all over the world with special reference to India and Kerala; developmental history of Attappady as it is documented in various studies; the present demography of Attappady; on the ecological conditions of Attappady; the health status of *adivasi* according to the secondary data available; laws prevailing in the country with special reference to the rights and privileges of *adivasis*; the opportunities available within the decentralisation drive of the Kerala government etc.

There were group discussions and presentations on the observations made in the lecture sessions. For example, after the lecture on the history of development at Attappady, there were heated debates on the issue of development failing to restore their well-being. The

---

[82]   While gathering the information of personal history, the PUPs told RAPs the need to be confidential about the names of the information providers.

classroom sessions ended every evening evaluating that day's learning and its contribution to their research. The morning sessions of the day after always had group presentations evaluating the previous day sessions. This gave the organisers an opportunity to correct their mistakes and fill in the gaps. The practice helped the *adivasi* participants gradually to exercise their control over the project and developed a critical consciousness and self-reflexivity.

The first phase of the project could introduce the idea of *praxis* with games, discussions, debates, theoretical analysis, and information and generate a curiosity to undertake a field research. By the end of the first phase, they could fix their field research agenda to explore: the history of land ownership patterns of the past, and its present status; land use practices from the past to the present history of *ooru* (hamlet) and that of whatever is present in and around the *ooru*, the personal history of at least three persons among whom at least one being a woman. There were detailed discussions on the methodology to be adopted in probing the details. It was stressed the probing should not be limited to asking questions rather it should be an invitation to the collective action to be started in the forthcoming phases.

Phase-II: Exploring the *adivasi* life-world

In the second phase of the project, the RAPs undertook fieldwork at their selected hamlets. The RAPs went to the households and told them about the objective of their visit; they sat with the family members discussed every evening on the issues of history, personal life, on myths, shared their family problems, discussed local politics, walked with them to their landed properties, and talked about the community issues. In general, they accompanied the people at the hamlet in exploring the life-situations and   its historical trajectory. The HRPs did not hide their puzzlement and suspicion over the RAPs interest in knowing their life. They had to face the questions such as, whether they were probing these questions on behalf of the Government to initiate any new welfare measures; has the inquirer, or one among them, got new job? any external agencies want details about them through the participants in order to meet any of their needs and so on. One participant recorded an event, typical of the initial contact:

> On 5-6-02 I went to Kuravanvankandy *ooru*, met the *Moopan* and told him that I got classes on history of *adivasis* of Attapaddy from KILA, Thrissur. When we were about to start conversation, Masanan and Chelli the neighbours of the *Moopan* came next to me and asked, "what is the matter?" I told them I wanted to know the history of our *ooru*. My reply made them very happy… They became happy because they said nobody had come so far asking their history. I said, "Whatever you know of the history of our people should not be allowed to die; rather it should be imparted to the future generations." Chelli agreed to this. Then I asked, "how did our Kuravankandi originate?" "Why are you asking this question" asked Masannan *Moopan*. I replied to him, "this is for knowing *ooru* and to discuss with our people about the history of our *ooru*…compare its past with present and to think about a better future for all…"

The participants also had their own share of puzzlement. When they asked the elders to narrate the history of their hamlet and of their initial settlement, instead of narrating history, some of them narrated the myths about the human origin and mythologies explaining division of people into *kulam*s etc. The RAPs too reproduced these mythical narrations as history. The myths narrated were about formation of different *kulams*[83] (subgroups) among the *adivasis*, about how different *oorus*

83   The classification of *Kulam* appears to be similar to the caste groupings.

got their name, justification of community ethics prevalent or wished, the origin of human life in the world and of their deity *Malleswaran (Shivan)* and His wife *Malleswari (Parvathi)* etc. The *Kulam* Myths they have collected appeared to be the justification for ritual status of *kulam*s during special occasions, namely who among the *adivasis* should light the torch at the *Malleswara* peak, the justifications of the names of the *kulam*s etc. The myths surrounding *kulam*s portray the biases of one *Kulam* over the other. There were even myths explaining ill health, early death among *adivasis*, taboos of menstruation, taboos of certain burial practices and so on.

According to a belief shared among them, the dead become their guardians. The dead are buried with merriment and dances. They are expected to become the *Pesadh* (spirit) that guards their community. *Pesadh*, of elders, is the most revered divinity among them. A ritual urn that is maintained in the households of lineages is believed to be representing all the spirits of their elders who had passed away. A master ritual urn, the *Pesadh* of entire hamlet is kept in a hut called '*Pesadh koora.*' Lord *Malleswaran* represents the *Pesadh* of all the three *adivasi* groups live at Attappady. The ancestors are believed to be living in the present as Lord *Malleswaran.* Lord *Malleswaran* is a living deity for them. According to their belief, as the people die, they also join *Malleswaran* and continue to live. Lord *Malleswaran* is represented by a peak[84] [*Malleswaran Mudi- Malleswaran* Peak] of Western ghats located at Attappady that has a semblance of the hair-tie [*Mudi-Kettu*] of the Lord *Malleswara.*

---

[84]   The *M[...]*n be better understood
with *L[...]*stralian *adivasis* identify
thems[...]r origins mythically to
these [...]sisted, "can therefore be
nothir[...]nder the visible form…"
[Durk[...]

Fig. 10 *Malleswaran* Peak

Malleswaran is usually the central character of their myths about the origin of humanity on the earth and of their ethical concerns. In their Myths, *Malleswaran*, equivalent to lord *Shivan* of the Hindu faith is seen as the well-wisher of the *adivasis*[85]. He is presented as kind, compassionate, understanding, listening, teaching, guiding, helping and always visiting them with His pair *Malleswari* (*Parvathi*). They are portrayed as '*ena*' (pair) always walking together, similar to the *adivasi* view of couples. *Malleswaran* and *Malleswari* are presented as the most trustworthy and intimate friends and leaders of the *adivasis*.

One myth narrated an event after a great flood that had destroyed most of the people. After the flood was over, *Malleswaran* and *Malleswari* were wandering in the forest searching for the surviving lives. While walking together they noticed smoke from the forest. *Malleswaran* and *Malleswari* suspected that there should be some humans there. They walked near the source of the

---

[85] From Durkheimian perspective god is nothing more than society apotheosized. [Durkheim 1995: 236-245]. Durkheim observes that the pre historic societies do not regard their gods as hostile, malevolent, or fearful in any way whatsoever; on the contrary, their gods are friends and relatives, who inspire a sense of confidence and well-being. Durkheim considers the social construction of God is not an out come of hallucination rather it is based on 'reality'; for however misunderstood, there actually is a real moral power -- society -- to which these beliefs correspond, and from which the worshippers derive their strength. Durkheim observes: The most barbarous and the most fantastic rites and the strangest myths translate some human need, some aspect of life, either individual or social. The reasons with which the faithful justify them may be, and generally are, erroneous; but the true reasons." [Durkheim 1995: 1912: 14-15, 255-262; Jones 1986: 115-155]

smoke and found a small hut. Standing outside the hut, *Malleswaran* asked who are all the people living in the hut. The man replied that he and his daughter are inside the hut. *Malleswaran* requested them to come out, as He wanted to see them. The man replied, "My Lord, I cannot come out because I am naked." Hearing this the Lord *Malleswaran* torn a part of his attire and asked the man to use the cloth to cover his body. The man came out. He was a very old man. *Malleswari* told him that she wanted to meet his daughter. To this the old man said, "She cannot come out because she too has no cloth to cover her body." Hearing this *Malleswari* too torn a part of her attire and gave it for the woman to come out. *Malleswari* found that the woman was in fact a young girl. When both of them came out, *Malleswaran* and *Malleswari* turned them into young pairs with their magical spell and advised them to live as couple and have children. They also advised the young couple that they should not stay alone and they should always stay in company of other people in a community at least surrounded by ten *enas* [pairs].

In another myth collected, *Malleswaran* was once again portrayed as a compassionate person: long ago, there was an acute famine and the *adivasis* were starving. *Malleswaran* did not want them to starve. He identified fruit of a tall and slippery tree as edible, and recommended the fruit for eating. The fruit was juicy and tasty. *Malleswaran* told them to eat the fruit only when it falls. He asked them not to climb the tree because the tree was very tall and its trunk was slippery. Unfortunately, tempted by the taste of the fruit, people wanted to climb and pluck the fruit from the tree. Some of them died in their effort to climb on it. When *Malleswaran* came to know the incident, He felt sorry for that. He came to the tree, plucked one fruit, and squeezed it with his fingers; from then onwards the fruit was not juicy and it has become inedible. The *mathi* fruit's cylindrical star like shape as if it were squeezed out with fingers, is given as an 'evidence' for the event.

There were several myths collected having the theme that 'greed is dangerous'[86]. A myth of "*Asaka* Rock" is an example of such a myth: Long ago, people were honest and bound by *neethi* (justice), *neri* (righteousness, honesty), *nela* (stand point, position, state of affairs) and *nyayam* (reasonableness, fairness). They always honoured their commitment. As people were righteous, they could communicate with gods. Gods were concerned about the people, about their food, dress and shelter requirements. They had nothing to worry as the gods were with them. Then it was a custom that the *adivasis* should wear new cloth during the *Malleswaran*[87] festival. For the participants of the festival at the foothills of the *Malleswaran mudi*[88] (*Malleswaran* peak), gods supply garments from a cave, namely the *Asaka* cave. The garments would be kept there and the devotees could use them for a night on the eve of the festival. After using it for one eve, they should return it to the cave. The people were using this facility for years. As the *neethi, neri, nela and nyayam* [hereafter 4Ns] declined in the community, once a woman did not return her garments to the cave. As a consequence, it is believed, that the cave was closed by a huge rock namely the "*Asaka* Rock." Though *Asaka* cave was closed, it was not closed forever. With the recovery of *neethi, neri, nela and nyayam* accompanied by a penance and repentance it could be opened again. For the cave to be opened again a person from the *Devena Kulam* should perform a ritual for all the *adivasis*. The ritual

[86] Durkheim in his lectures presented in "pragmatism and sociology" observes that the "myths are groupings of representations aimed at explaining the world, systems of ideas whose function is essentially speculative." He further states "What lies at the root of myths is not a practical need: it is the intellectual need to understand." For Durkheim, in myths "a rationalist mind is present there, perhaps in an unsophisticated form, but nevertheless enough to prove that the need "To understand is universal and essentially human." Myths, for him, "were bodies of truths which were considered to express reality (the universe), and which imposed themselves on men with an obligatory character which was just as marked and as powerful as moral truths." [Durkheim 1983]

[87] *Malleswaran Pandikai* (*Shivarathri*) is the most auspicious of all festivals among the *adivasis* of Attappady.

[88] *Malleswaran mudi* is a holy spot for the *adivasis*. *Malleswaran mudi* is a peak at the Western Ghats. The *adivasis* believe that the peak represents *Malleswaran*'s presence at Attappady. The *Mudi* is an object of worship among the *adivasis*.

should be performed between twilights in the night. According to the myth the *Devenan*, should sow one bag of grain on the roof of a hut with devotion and reap them within that night and should eat all the grain cooked with meat of a Buffalo[89] before sunrise. The belief is that with the recovery of the 4Ns the performance of the ritual would not be impossible. The myth indicates the irrecoverable loss the *adivasis* suffered with the loss of the 4Ns- *neethi, neri, nela* and *nyayam*.

Erich Neumann observes that 'the world and the unconscious predominate and form the object of myth' [Neumann 1954: 5]. Myths are rather symbols gathered around the things to be ordered, explained understood and interpreted. Hegel too in his lectures on aesthetics observes:

> All mythology is…essentially symbolical. This would be to say that myths, as creations of the human spirit, however bizarre and grotesque they may appear, contain in themselves a meaning for the reason; general thoughts upon the divine nature — in a word, philosophemes.[90]

Myths for Neumann are representations of 'collective unconscious' that amazingly rises up from the depths of the human psyche in answer to their unconscious questions. The unconscious in Jung's perspective is 'transpersonal - or the archetypes and instincts of the collective unconscious - as the *deposit of ancestral experience*[91]. Distinguishing the unconscious from the conscious, Neumann observes, "It neither attempts nor is able to seize hold of and define its objects in a series of discursive explanations, and reduce them to clarity by logical analysis" [Neumann 1954: 6]. To Neumann, the act of becoming conscious consists in the concentric grouping of symbols around the object, all circumscribing and describing the unknown from many sides. Myths are grasped as, "the symbolic story of the beginning, which speaks to us from the mythology of all ages, is the attempt

---

89   Traditionally, buffalo meat was not a part of their diet.

90   Hegel in Lectures on Aesthetics, Part I, Of the Symbolic Form of Art, WWW.Marxist.org

91   Quoted from Jung in Neumann, 1954: 23.

made by man's childlike, pre-scientific consciousness to master problems and enigmas which are mostly beyond the grasp of even our developed modern consciousness" [Neumann 1954: 6-7]. For Neumann the unconscious is the foundation for consciousness that unfolds historically:

> The ascent toward consciousness is the "unnatural" thing in nature; it is specific of the species Man, who on that account has justly styled himself Homo sapiens. The struggle between the specifically human and the universally natural constitutes the history of man's conscious development. [92]

It is interesting to observe that the RAPs and HRPs take the myths to be history. In the mythologies presented by the RAPs, the difference between ordinary and extra ordinary is blurred. The time reference given to the myths is always 'long ago.' All these things said and happened 'long ago' is expected to be the guiding principle for the present day life-world. It appears the traditional *adivasi* worldview places myth where the historical societies place their history. Durkheim while classifying historical consciousness from the mythological unconscious observes that unlike history mythologies are not directed towards the future[93]. For the HRPs, as they are yet to be full-fledged participants of the norms of historical societies we can presume, they blur history with mythology.

Historical societies construct their present on the derived historical consciousness and 'progressively' proceed towards colonising the future. The historical communities thus objectify time and plan towards conquering the future. Similarly, the historical societies find means to spread

---

[92]   Neumann 1954: 14.

[93]   Durkheim: According to pragmatism, knowledge is essentially a plan of action, and proposes practical ends to be attained. Yet the mythological beliefs encountered in primitive societies are cosmologies, and are directed not towards the future but towards the past and the present. What lies at the root of myths is not a practical need: it is the intellectual need to understand. Basically, therefore, a rationalist mind is present there, perhaps in an unsophisticated form, but nevertheless enough to prove that the need to understand is universal and essentially human. [Durkheim 1983]

spatially. Thus we find colonisers expand their territory and as settlers or rulers. The tendency to expand is found in the present social world is explained in terms of *globalisation* or *futurisation*. The globalisation is the spatial spread of ideologies and discourses and the futurisation is the project of making investments in the future and constructing the ideology of the future from the present. In this regard, Barthes identifies the ideology that operates from the unconscious of the historical society to conquer time and space expressed 'innocently' or 'naturally' in their everyday life styles itself as mythology[94].

For *Adivasis*, at least till they were exposed to the historical society of the 'mainstream' (which seems to have inherited a sense of history from their colonisers), it seems time meant something different. It is not a 'time' that progresses into future; rather whatever exists exists for the present, as there is nothing to be done towards changing its course into an imagined future. However, the time as something left to itself has already become what Ulrich Beck calls a 'zombie category': a category that is dead and still alive. [Beck and Beck 2002:203-4]. The time in the spatially globalised and temporally futurised world has already become a *new zombie* category, *to be born yet alive*. That is, despite their institutional participation in the historical time that is already *futurised* the people remain in the ahistorical past of the mythical time. This event put the NAPs into puzzlement; if they conceive 'time' so differently then the question remains as to whether it would be possible for the NAPs to grasp what the *adivasis* say and do. That the myths narrated by them have no element of violence or cruelty does not escape the notice of the NAPs. The myths are non-totalising and devoid of self-heroic narrations. It is about food, shelter, dress, community life and a mutual life of non-violence. The myths are about the *adivasis* themselves. There is no pretension, in *adivasi* myths, of explaining the ultimate reality, primal being, the perfect originary state of being,

---

[94]   Barthes, 1972: 242; Barthes 1975: 14, 40, 131; Cook 2001:154; Kroker 2001:84

primal deity sufficient to itself, authoritarian god, as that can be found in the religious mythologies of the settlers. The human beings are seen in *adivasi* myths as engaging in life as it exists. The *adivasi* myths the RAPs presented do not project a future in the forms of hell or heaven. This should be seen in contrast to the myths orienting its holders' unconscious towards a future to be consciously built; towards attaining 'heaven' or avoiding 'hell' or towards totalising everything. The myths of *adivasis* do not project them towards the virtual future. Instead, the *adivasi* myths express care, concern, and compassion. The myths also warn its believers of greediness, individuality and un-concern. *Malleswaran* and *Malleswari* were portrayed in the myths, as a couple with full of care and concern; they were presented as non-judgemental, righteous, sensible, co-present and compassionate; they are not characterised as omnipotent or omnipresent as it was customary among the settlers.

If it is true that the myths show the unconscious of the people, then the settler myths of authoritarian gods, myths regarding the primal being inclusive of all, the myth of life proceeding towards heaven or hell show settler unconscious, that is immersed into the tendency to futurise, totalise and colonise within which ecological conservation, *ena* relationships, and a caring companionship could hardly be found.

Probably, guided by the deep-seated 'unconscious' inscribed with unconcern, un-care, and the profound motives to totalise, expand and conquer, the settler civilisation that invaded the *adivasis* brought disillusionment and despair to the *adivasis* and their physical and social environment. Thus, we find the *ena* relations are broken and in its place we hear sexual abuse, murder and unnatural deaths among *adivasis*[95]. The cases registered on the atrocities against *Adivasis* throw some light on

---

[95]   Bijoy 2002; Bijoy, and Raman 2003; Surendranath 2003; Prabhakaran 2000, 2000a

the issue [see appendix 9]. The leadership emerging from formal democratic exercise seemed less self-righteous as the parties that operate from a distant social space from which compassion, care, or sensibility could hardly be expected, program them. What the *adivasi* myths warn of has emerged as the virtue in the world outside the *adivasi* mentality. The world outside the *adivasi* mentality in fact promotes competition, individuality, smartness and a business spirit that looks at every resource to be converted into one or another variety of capital. In order to become 'developed' they have to give up the ethos so strongly represented in their myths. The contradiction is so sharp that what is recommended as 'development,' seemed such as leading to ill being [see appendix 7].

The *praxis* intervention exercise in the beginning itself put the PUPs in a dilemma, whether to explore further into the deep-seated *adivasi* ethos or to get them trained in the modern habit of placing time as a progressive phenomenon. Despite their poverty of understanding, the NAPs proceeded to expose the difference between history and myth and highlight the importance of exploring history. For NAP's, people locating themselves in history is a political project. This academic bias and the bias NAPs have inherited from their middle class habit could not open their eyes towards understanding the worldview conveyed by the *adivasi* myths. Nevertheless, there were sound reasons for PUPs to accompany the *adivasi* participants towards exploring their history. In spite of themselves *adivasis* already been subjected to the historical developments. They are located in the historical time that informs who they are and what they are expected to do. The history as it had imploded into their life-world and not their native myth is the reference point that is instrumental in shaping their rationality. Before the settler invasion, it was the myths that handed over values from their tradition: then, it was the myths that defined who they are and what they should do. History had now already virtually replaced myths, demanding from them a competence to handle the historically emerged life situations. History had already begun its mission of locating their subjecthood. Alternately, there is no way left other than gaining historical competence. Gaining historical competence involves mapping their subjecthood within the historical space: that is, it involves knowing where one is historically located at present. Hence, the PUPs thought that gaining historical competence is inevitable, if one has to overcome the *historically* imposed poverty. However, the historical competence comes as the whole baggage of instrumental rationality, individuation and rational objectification.

The Oral recollection of history provides particular opportunities to examine the role of memory in reconstituting the past, as a process, which occurs in and through language [Murphy 1986: 157]. The exercise according to the NAPs would provide the opportunity for those who never spoke speak, those who never heard hear, those who had never been heard heard, those never interpreted history interpret and uncover the lived texture and intimate experience of everyday life. [Thompson 1978: 2,18,158,226] In this regard, Paul Thompson observes:

> the practice [of recollecting memories] brings history into, and out of, the community. It helps the less privileged, and especially the old, towards dignity and self-confidence...Equally, oral history offers a challenge to the accepted myths of history, to the authoritarian judgement inherent in its tradition. It provides a means for a radical transformation of the social meaning of history [Thompson 1978:2]

Oral historians also point out, "For working people to speak for themselves, about their own history, is somehow a political act in itself" [Yeo 1981: 46]. John Murphy, extending the argument points out to make the oral history political it is not sufficient to let them speak rather there should be opportunity for the people to interpret their history. [Murphy 1986: 160]. In narrating history, what becomes pertinent is not keeping a record of the past, but interpreting the present. The practice as John Tosh observes, "has had more to do with the re-creational than the explanatory side of historical enquiry" [Tosh 1991:226]. In this respect Zygmunt Bauman in his critique of oral history points out that the 'remembered history' as the collective historical memory if not used as 'pool of metaphors and analogies necessary to make sense of the present' by the people who face the history it fails to act upon the social world as an interpretive framework. [Bauman 1982: 2, 27, 28]

> Underlining the *praxis* perspective of history Peter Friedlander notes:
>
> And if there seems to be structure and coherence in history, then there must be structure to *praxis*. The formal, abstract task of history as a dialectical science *sui generis* is therefore to formulate a conception of this structure of a specific historical *praxis*, a *praxis* which originates within a social personality and in relation to which the "individual" becomes an object of study rather than a presupposition.[96]

In this regard, Nancy S. Struever points out that perceiving history from *praxis* perspective is pertinent, as the structuralist understanding of history though maps totalities and coherences showing how a particular system of reciprocal relationship maintains its identity fails to explain the radical discontinuity that characterises the transition between coherences [Struever 1974:411]. As the life histories constitute themselves not only in the vertical dimension as a temporal connection of the cumulative experiences of an individual but also formed at every moment horizontally at the level of the intersubjectivity of communication common to different subjects it becomes necessary to probe into history that occurred interactionally [Habermas: 1972 155-6].

---

[96]   Friedlander 1975: 18.

As the fieldwork was going on as part of follow-up measure, the PUPs also participated in some fieldwork sessions. The RAPs then shared about the initial inhibitions of the hamlet people in responding to the query. This is attributed to their embarrassment when they found something unusual about their fellow members asking questions and probing them as never before. After initial embarrassment, the people started involving in the process. In a workshop arranged at the field location, the RAPs presented the myths they have collected thinking that they had really collected historical information. In the workshop, the difference between myth, and history was discussed and, the RAPs were encouraged to explore historical details of settlement into hamlets, land use patterns, personal history and so on. It was in fact a revealing experience for them to know that history is something different from myth. As the difference was made between myths and history, they have collected information from their real life. Then onwards they probed into stories of initial settlement of *adivasis* and the beginning of the settler arrival.

It followed from their narration that the plot of their history thickened with the arrival of *vandavasis*. The process of history reveals the manner in which the 4Ns (neethi, neri, nela and nyayam) they had drawn from their tradition through myths had gradually been dismantled.

It was about 50 years before the settlers started coming to Attappady. The *adivasis* could identify the *vandavasis* just by their white shirts and dhoti. An *adivasi* woman narrates the incidents of settlers at the beginning of *vandavasi* arrival:

Then I was a small girl. Whenever we see a man with white dhoti, we make no noise and hide behind trees. This was because our parents taught us the men in white Dhoti are child catchers. We were terribly afraid of them.

Regarding the initial settlements of the outsiders an RAP noted in his field diary:

The settlers who first came here approached the *Moopan*s and begged them to offer some place to sleep. Those days the place was thick with forests and leaches were everywhere…(It is because of leaches (*Atta*) the outsiders named the place - Attappady). They were not just offered a place to stay, but also *raghiputtu* (a food item made of *ragi*). Later they started occupying lands and claimed ownership of the land.

Some RAPs also recounted the memories shared to them:

Long before, we were not staying in one place. We were looking for places to graze, and cultivate *sama, ragi, cholam*, mustard, and green leaves. We were sowing all the seeds together. Then, we go around the forest searching for honey, tubers, bamboo shoot, and catching animals using traps. Staying at one place was not important. To store food for *panja masam* (draught season) we dig a pit in the centre of the house and keep them there. The pit will be like a mud pot. On the top of it, we would cover. It will be opened only in the Panja Masam….Kandiyoor is a place where we keep our traps. (*Kandi* means trap) because animals go this way. We keep traps and hide here. That is why we call this place Kandiyoor even today…

The RAPs could gather information that displaces the assumption that the *ooru moopan*s were indigenous leaders of *adivasis*, existing as the authority from time immemorial. The information gathered also showed that all those who are presently called *adivasis* were in fact settlers of an earlier period. The narration of an *adivasi moopan* illustrates the recent origin of *adivasi* settlement:

My grand father came here from Tamilnadu for grazing purpose. Then I was 5-year-old child. We came to Ilachivazhi. Then there were only two houses at Ilachivazhi and there were only four houses at Thazhe Mulli. At Mele Mulli then there were four houses. Then this place was a thick forest. We cleared some land and started cultivation with the seeds we brought from Tamilnadu.

In another field note, there is a narration of '*adivasi*' settlement at Kandiyoor:

Long before my great grand parents came from Tamilnadu to the place now called *Nadukkal*. They stayed for some time at *Nadukkal*. Later they settled at the place now called *Kottathara*. From *Kottathara*, we came here to *Kuravan Kandi*. Moopil Nair made my grand father a *moopan* and through him, the *jenmi* was collecting taxes… *ooru moopan*s were given golden bangles by the Moopil Nair as a sign of his position

A *moopan* from the melechundappatti during the fieldwork told a participant:

My grandfathers were living at Mysore forests. Fearing British, they come to Attappady via Tamilnadu (*Nilgiris*) When they came the land was already under the control of the *Jenmi. Jenmi's* representatives told that they had to pay two *anas* as *Karam* [tax] per acre for cultivating there…As the family expanded, the *ooru* came into existence. Their daughters brought their husbands from neighbouring *oorus*. Based on the *Kulam* norms then existing, among our family members, some assumed the positions of *mannookkarans*, *kuruthalas*, and *vandari's*. The *ooru moopan* was appointed according to the wishes of the Moopil Nair and his men. Later these positions became hereditary.

An RAP records Mari *Moopan's* statement of how his family (belonging to *anu moopan kulam*) became a *moopan*:

"…the *kariasthan* (agent or manager) of Moopil Nair made my grand parent a *moopan* and my grand parents were collecting *karam* (tax) for him…we still continue to enjoy the position…"

The observation based on the field data collected shows that the position of *ooru moopan* is a creation for tax collection by the Moopil Nair. The observation came as a surprise to the participants. Some of the RAPs questioned the veracity of the observations. As the purpose here was not to explore history as it had happened, the facts behind the statements were not verified in this project. However, the observations made here are worthy of serious historical research.

There were also interesting stories about *Kulam*s. Some of the informants claimed that *kulam*s were actually representations of the origins of the place they came from. Raman, a 75-year-old *moopan* told a participant that his great grandfathers were from 'Devena puram' in Tamilnadu and later they became devana *kulam* among the *adivasis*. Another participant remarks in her field journal that *Kulam*s were actually later invented by an *adivasi* ruler called *Kolambi Raja* in a meeting convened at Kollan Kadavu for that purpose. In the meeting convened the various *kulam*s such as *Sambava, Anumoopu, Vellakal, Devanan, Kurunakal, Uppuward…* and *Kuppali* were formed among the *Irula*s based on the original place from where they came or based on the rituals they perform. There were also divisions made within the same *Kulam*s. For example, among the *moopu kulam* one group performed annual rituals for their dead and the other group performed their rituals for dead once in three years. Based on their ritual practices they were divided as sub *kulam*s.

There were also some narrations of the life in the past. An RAP recoded the mode of collecting the food. It is represented in the words of a *Kurumba* woman:

> …Mine was a small thatched hut …we were not doing any agriculture those days. We used to collect food from the forest. Later we started the practice of cultivation. On the sunny days, we used to take our little ones to

the forest. We dig pits on the earth and put the kids inside the pit with some toys.... go for food collecting....

Another field record, in which a participant writes about the memoir of a sad incident told by the grand daughter of nachhi *moopathi* revealed how precarious the life of *adivasis* have become:

> ...Nanchi *Moopathi* eloped with her lover. After marriage, they started agriculture. During those days, they used to take their kids to the forest, with them. They keep the kids inside the holes of the trees and sing songs while working, to soothe the kid to sleep.

> ...One day she put big lumps of firewood in the '*choola*' to prepare rice. The "*choola*" was burning. She went out to the paddy field to work. She had put her third child in the cradle before she went. The fire caught on the cradle, and the kid was dead when Nanchi *Moopathi* returned.

An RAP recorded the beginning of agriculture practice as told by an old *kurumba* woman:

> I met an old *Kurumba* couple during my fieldwork. The husband's name is Chathan, and his wife is Maruthi. Maruthi's father is Kakki. Maruthi recollecting their experience of growing food crops for the first time, years before, told me that after her marriage as they were finding it difficult to gather food they started cultivating food crops. She said that prior to their experiments with the cultivation of food crops they were depending on the *Noore* tuber, bamboo shoot, bamboo rice, honey and other wild fruits for meeting their food requirement. Mango, Jackfruit and jamoon fruits were available. Finding food crops were difficult in the rainy seasons.

Rain was heavier those days. They thought it would be better if they too cultivate food crops following some other among themselves. In the beginning, they did not know the methods and techniques of agriculture. They cleared a piece of land and sow *Cholam*, *Ragi*, *Chama*, *Thena*, Mustard, *Thatta Payar* (a variety of pea), Ashgaurd and other crops. During heavy rain, the seeds just flood away. Later they tried preparation of land for cultivation using the '*kotthu*[97].'

An RAP recounts the story told by Ponni *Moopathi* remembering the hardships in her past:

Today you have food at home. In my young days, we were never certain that we would get food. We were wandering and collecting tubers and roots. When we come back home collecting roots and tubers and fuel wood, it would be already past the afternoon. We boil the collected food material after coming back home. This is the daily routine. It was a difficult life.

An RAP, tracing the history of the settler arrival notes:

The first settler in Attappady is Mathechen who lived at Kukkum Pallayam. At first, he came for trade. It is said that *Nair* came after that for trade. Then a *Chetty*[98] came ... The nature of the trade was this. They brought head loads of rice, oil, soap etc and exchanged them for the locally available things.

---

97   *Kotthu* is a hand tool used to prepare land for sowing on slopes.

98 *Chetty* and *Nair* are caste names

The RAPs also traced the coming of money into their economic life. An RAP viewed that the *adivasis* living in the forest started using salt very late. Once they started using salt as the people who settled later introduced it, they required money to get salt. The *adivasis* take honey and other materials and go to *Thadakam* near Coimbatore to get salt. Later, the *adivasis* were given money in exchange of the forest products they take to the Tamil traders. Among *adivasis*, they were not using money in those days. The persons who went to purchase salt for the *oorus* were later called *Uppili Kulam*. (*Uppu* means salt).

In the words of Nanchan, a hamlet resident, money appeared among them along with the wage labour. He says, "I did not require money until I was 25. It was only after that I started using money." What Mani, a 70-year old man, says too must be read along with.

> In those days, it was difficult to even think of having money. There were enough food grains. Things grown at home were exchanged for articles (like salt, chilly, onion etc.) ….afterwards all necessities were managed through money earned by selling grains or labour. It was not easy to get wages everyday. On those days wood, timber and bamboo from the forest would be cut and taken to the shops in exchange of money.

Their fieldwork gave them a fair account of history of the *adivasis*. One cannot be sure on the authenticity of the historical data they have collected. However, It is certainly important that they could objectify their history and gain their historical competence. The notes from the field show that they were not only collecting data but also were interpreting and using their hermeneutic skills, throwing away their ingrained biases about their *adivasiness* and their *kulam* identities.

Phase III: Collective exploration of the data collected

Field visits always followed faculty workshops wherein the fieldwork details were shared and the planning for the next classroom sessions were made. In the faculty workshops, it was decided that the next classroom phase should accommodate the participants' sharing of their fieldwork experiences. To make their experience sharing more effective it was decided to break up the classroom sessions into workshops concentrating on specific topics such as workshops on local history, personal history, land use pattern and on deciding the next fieldwork phase. It was decided to allocate the first day for general discussion and the fourth day for providing information for the next fieldwork along with introduction of new themes and the fifth day for the fieldwork planning.

The third phase began with a participant's metaphorical note:

> I can explain my fieldwork experience by an anecdote. There was a box with glass cover placed in the corner of a house that never attracted any body's notice. Nothing inside the box was visible because dust gathered over year had made it opaque and unattractive. One day, somebody, who knew what was there in the box visited the house and asked the house owner to remove the dust and look what was there in the box. The house owner accordingly cleaned the surface and looked into the box. What he found in the box was amazing. There were priceless treasures of precious stones and metals. The household could not believe his eyes. He just wondered his status of living in poverty despite having such rare treasures in his house. *Praxis* intervention is such an experience. We never tried to look into the treasures we own. This exercise helped us to look at ourselves and understand our worth.

The RAP was referring to the *adivasi* past, before their historicisation, that was rich with natural resources, plenty of food resources, human warmth and congeniality of which he heard from the participants from the hamlet.

The discussion was later guided to be specific. To begin with, the participants required to form sub groups and present their observations on primary socialization of the *adivasi* children. The point of reference for their presentation on primary socialization was the statement, "our children grow (spontaneously) whereas the *vandavasi*s bring up their children" which figures in the chart they earlier presented [table 15]. The observation made was an example of the participants' exploration of their own potential for critical hermeneutics. The *adivasi* children could grow spontaneously as there were no social threats and social expectations from them. *Adivasis* seem to treat children more as biological entities than social entities. The importance menstruation assumes in their collective life may be attributed to this. Girl children's first menstruations were celebrated in the past with the traditional art forms of *koothu* and a community gathering. (These days 16 MM films replaced the traditional performance of art forms.) The expenses are usually borne by the entire community rather than by the girl's parents. RAPs notice the importance given to the first menstruation of the girl children in the following words:

> "Girls get menstruated by 15 years of age. They have to sit in the corner of a room in their house for seven days. No males should see them during those days. The girl will not come out... will not take bath. On the seventh day, she takes bath... in the early morning... Then nobody should see her other than the women who go with her for bath... Sister-in-law puts oil..."

> "....Sister-in-law will spill the oil three times; afterwards she will be allowed to smear oil on her head... From the first day, up to the eighth day, normally, she is not supposed to smear oil on her head...Later after a bath, she will be allowed to have food prepared by *Guruvan*[99], along with Sisters-in-law. After the feast is over

> everybody will give "*Mooy*" - an amount to the girl's parents for the *cheeru*[100] expenses."

> "As and when they 'attain their age,' the girls will not disclose the matter to mother and father. They will hide themselves somewhere in the house. Later she will tell the issue to some of her relatives. Parents will inform the *morapayyan*. He will come and construct a hut near their home and the girl will be there inside the hut... After seven days, the hut will be destroyed and torched; then also she won't be let to enter the interiors of the house. Till the 45th day she will be staying outside the house, on the *thinna* (the raised portion of the floor before the entry door) ... those who are well off economically, will conduct a feast one day, between 15th to 30th day after the menstruation...Parents will decide a day for "*cheeru*," inform it to the *moopan* and *thai maman* (maternal uncle). Uncle will bring dress materials, ornaments, bangles, *bindi*, groundnut, sweets etc., as gifts to the girl. Parents also will buy all these items."

> "On the first menstruation, girls are instructed not to be seen anywhere near the sight of her uncle. Maternal uncle is usually the first choice ritually prescribed to be the spouse of a girl." [The symbolic mechanism of masculine domination can be observed here.]

It can be observed that the biological events like childbirth, menstruation, and death assumes priority over the social events such as marriage, naming, or initiation ceremonies. Similarly, the basic needs such as food, water, shelter and clothing and others assume priority over the institutions of education, formal religion, 'growing' children etc. The observations made by a participant in their field journals illustrate this:

> "Children up to 4-5 years old remain with their mother. The family looks after them. After that age, they grow among everybody in the *ooru*. Children may not return home even for sleeping to their home. They would stay wherever they please in the neighbourhood. When they are about 10 years

---

[99]   A ritual position

[100]   Community gathering for celebrations or mourning.

old, they go out to the forest and hills, sometimes taking animals for gracing. Throughout the day, the boys and girls remain outside. They do not come back home till it becomes twilight in the evening. They spend all their daytime grazing animals, searching for fruits and tubers, trapping small animals and eating their flesh burnt….After menstruation girls are expected to remain at home. Even after that, the girls go out to the forest to fetch fuel wood and other needs. However, they return home every evening. In the case of boys sometimes they will not return home for a couple of days and nobody will enquire about their whereabouts."

"There were no marriages. The girls were taken to live with their husbands. Parents decide the partner. Girls are just supposed to just obey them"

"when the boy becomes 15 to 16 years old, he goes to uncle's house for working ("*Pennvela*") indulges in agriculture, cattle fielding etc. and try to earn good name with the girl's father (i.e., uncle). The girl would be then allowed to live with the boy. There were no formal marriages. The girl's consent did not matter much."

"Even if the girl disliked the boy who came to her father for "*Pennvela*", she would be forced to live with him, if her father decides to "give her to the boy". In turn if she likes to marry the boy and her father had no interest in him then she would not be allowed to go with him."

"I understood that Marriage was not happening as it happens today. There was no practice of the boy and girl selecting each other. The boy's parents visit the girl's house and decide whether she is suitable to his son. Both the girl's parents and the boy's parents inform their respective *ooru moopan* on the boy's parent's visit to the girl's house. Then the girl would be sent to live with the boy. There were no special functions or feast celebrating the occasion"

"Immediately after childbirth, during the period of a woman's labour bed [ninety days] it is the responsibility of the husband to look after his wife. Others do not touch her...after seven days of child birth all the cloth used by her would be burnt...It is a difficult time after child birth… it becomes the husband's sole responsibility to earn for the family's living and … the husbands have to cook, wash cloth and do everything. Until seven days over after childbirth, she has to remain outside the house in a *pandal*. Only after seventh day, she would be coming into the house... only after three months the other relatives come home… until then nobody will drink even a drop of water from there...If they want to see the child they look at the child from a distance..."

According to the participants' account marriage seems to have emerged later as some among the *adivasis* found themselves capable of affording it. Obviously elaborate socialising process was absent. *Adivasis* were less bothered to bring up their children as the *vandavasis* do. As the socialising process is heavier among the *vandavasis*, the performance of the children in a variety of aspects such as being well dressed, having better food etiquette, being better schooled, married to socially well placed persons and other things affect their 'honour'; honour, like shame is a social phenomenon. For *adivasis* it is not honour, but 4Ns (*neethi, neri, nela and nyayam*) that are of paramount values. *Neethi, neri, nela and nyayam* though essential 'resources' to lead a community life, are hardly 'social capitals' as the 'honour' is. Looking from the *adivasi* point of view the heavy social content and the capitals that frill the *vandavasi* sociality gives the impression that the *vandavasis* are more socially bonded than the *adivasis*. The heavy social content among the *vandavasis* also indicates acute individuation, which itself is another 'social capital'. Traditionally among *adivasis*, being individuated had been considered as a liability to the community life.

The participants also noted that in course of time significant changes occurred in marital relationships. In the past, it was generally the boys who had to equip themselves to get a girl as a partner; the boys were expected to please the girls' parents for letting them to live together. On the contrary, these days, it is observed that generally the boys choose their respective partners and live together. It is also observed that these days there are rare incidents of boys demanding dowry from the girl's parents. However, only the educated boys hailing from the families that had acquired 'honour,' demand dowry.

In the 'ahistorical' past, when there were apparently no documented title deeds, both the couple work on the piece of land allocated by the *ooru moopan* (hamlet chieftain); there was no sense of ownership over the land. An RAP notes:

> "Primarily no one has private land... they lived in the forest since they didn't like to live by possessing it.... Land was then no one's private property, they moved without restrictions of any kind... in those days the *adivasis* just had to seek the permission of the *moopan* to cultivate at the place of one's preference..."

> "There was no practice of giving land to any body. They just go and settle somewhere. The land and house in which parents are living usually goes to those who take care of them till their death"

> "They had no knowledge of registering land or owning it. Outsiders introduced the system and using the nitigrities of the system they have taken away community lands and made them as their individual properties"

> "Land was used only for the purpose of agriculture. The ownership was not an issue in the past. Only with the coming of Outsiders and the government, land has been treated as a possession"

With the introduction of title deed documents, the girls practically lost control over their lands especially after marriage. This happens because after marriage she stays with her husband. This prevents her to be in charge of the land legally belongs to her. As law prevents the lands belonging to the *adivasis* from being sold to the *vandavasi*s, she cannot even sell her land that easily. As one RAP notes as she was informed by a HRP:

> Nowadays land goes to men only. If at all there are no men in a family then the land property will be that of women.

Another significant practice emerged in due course of their historicisation is that of *thali*[101] tying at the time of marriage (Tying *thali* constitute part of the event). This practice some observed is an imitation of *vandavasi* practice. However, some participants observed *thali*-tying practice was present though it is from a different sense than that of the *vandavasis*. *Thali* tying appears to be symbolically representing the *ena* bond between the couples rather than the social obligation of the women to men. The practice of tying *thali* even after the death of the woman on her corpse among the *adivasis* may be signifying this. *Thali* tying does not simply appear as the woman being tied to their men, rather the woman's inclusion into the man's family or *ooru*. In sum, *thali* tying among *adivasis* represents the woman being included into the man's family and community rather than an abstract social institution demanding woman's social obligation to the man she lives together with. Regarding this, some participants remarked:

> "Tying *thali* was not a practice in those days. Only those who formally marry were tied *thali* by the elders of the boy's *ooru*. Others who go to live with

---

[101]   *Thali* is a 'holy' twine tied to the woman's neck during marriage indicating the woman is tied to the man in marriage.

their husbands do not wear *thali*. *Thali* was tied in these cases only after death.”

“In the olden days, when girls and boys attain their age, they choose their partners and they settle together. There was no practice of tying *thali*. There was no gathering of relatives. Neither there were any feasts. They were just starting to live together. It was not elopement. The parents of both sides were giving their consent. About 50 years before, there was a little change in the practice. There were elopements. Girls were eloping with boys. Girls were attracted to the boys who were good singers, dancers, drumbeaters, and players of other instruments. About 40 years back, the custom of marrying ‘*Morapayyan*[102]’ was the practice. Sons and daughters of the uncles were ‘*Morapayyans*’ and ‘*Morapennus*.’ The marriage between them was fixed even when they were children and rituals of marriage were introduced. When the girl attained her age[103] she was married to her uncle’s son in the presence of *moopan*s from seven *Kulams*. Earlier we were tying only ‘*keera pasi*’ later it was replaced by *thali*. *Thali* is a twine dipped in turmeric paste with a piece of turmeric tied on it. The *moopan*s of seven *kulam*s[104] were tying the *thali* across the girl’s neck. It was not the boy who was tying the *thali*. About 30 years before, the boys had to do *Penvela*. During *Penvela*, the girl’s parent judges whether the boys were capable of taking care of their daughters. If they were convinced, they would give their daughter to the boy in marriage. Boys with the ploughing, hunting, and food gathering skills were preferred. The parents were deciding the matrimonial choice of their daughters. Sometimes the girls elope with the boys before formally given to

---

102   *Morapayyan* means the default boy. If nobody else is preferred, the *Morapayyan* will be marrying the *morapennu*. *Morapennu* is the default girl.

103   The beginning of menstruation is called age attainment.

104   *Kulam* is the subsection of the tribal community.

the boys. It was called '*Kalavu.*' It was since the last 20 years, we find girls frequently elope with boys. Parents allow this to happen. This happens when parents do not take effort to get their sons and daughters married in time. It is only from the past ten years, we see, that they elope, but do not always sustain their married life. They develop problems of doubt, disbelief, suspicion and quarrel with each other and find it difficult to run a happy married life."

Some participants observed that *thali* tying was there, but it was not necessary to tie *thali* at the time of marriage:

"*Thali* has come to symbolise marriage only recently, the *adivasis* were not used to the concept of tying *thali* at the time of marriage. Instead, they were tying *thali* at the time of giving birth to a child, or at menopause, if this does not happen… after death, on the way to graveyard. They tie *thali* on the dead body of the woman… This is part of old tradition… it is being practised in some *oorus* even now."

An incident reported by an RAP gives an account of a man tying *kola kola* (*thali*) to his wife in order to qualify her to participate in the death ritual of his father:

To perform a death ritual, it requires at least two volunteers closely related to the dead. The dead man whose ritual I was attending had a son and a daughter in law. The son and the daughter in law were living together as it is the common practice here. Since, the son and the daughter in law are the most related to the dead they were supposed to perform the ritual. As the couple was not formally married, the daughter in law was not wearing *Kola Kola* (*thali*)…to facilitate her participation in the ritual the *moopans* present there asked the son to tie *kola kola* to his wife…. Only after the performance of the *kola kola* tying ritual, the girl was allowed to participate in the death ritual. The body was buried following the death ritual.

It was observed that, with the advancement of time, the traditional patterns of settlement of marital disputes also waned. One of the participants writes in this regard in his field diary:

When a marriage had gone bad, if it were informed to the *ooru moopan*[105], he would guide the *kuruthala* to manage the issue in secrecy; if *kuruthala* could not solve the problem, the matter comes to *vandari*; if the *vandari* fails, *moopan* would tell *mannookkaran* to solve the problem. *Mannookkarans* were respected in the *ooru*s; even these days they are respected. Their words are usually observed with reverence. If that could not be solved at that level, *ooru moopan* sends his wife to solve the problem. *ooru moopan*'s wife would talk to the women in the family to explore the issue and solve it. If the problem was not solved even then, the *ooru moopan* interferes. If the problem was not solved still, it was publicised; everybody in the *ooru* would be called for a meeting and the matter would be discussed in public. If the issue was not being settled still, the *ooru* would even assume the authority to punish; and in the extreme cases, they would decide to excommunicate the erred person. There existed a similar method of solving the problem when problems arise between husbands and wives belonging to the different *ooru*s.

105   The Division of labour among *moopan*s: *Kuruthala* is responsible for information of death, *cheeru* and decisions of the *ooru moopan* (hamlet head); *Vandari* is responsible for measurements, collecting tax and distribution of the yield from the community agriculture; *Mannookkaran* is responsible for *Bhoomi Pooja* (earth worship), identification of cultivable land, sowing, harvesting the *first* crop; *ooru Moopan* is responsible for the overall governance, allocation of lands for cultivation, decides on land tax and its collection; informing *Kuruthala* his decisions; participates in *cheeru*s .

The *ooru moopan*s of the respective *ooru*s will meet only if it is not solved at the levels of the *vandari* and *mannookkarans* of the respective *ooru*s. As *moopan*s have no control over the residents of a hamlet, these days, there is no mechanism to settle disputes between couples.

The family life of the past, and the present was brought under the critical gaze. Some participants pointed out that in the past the family life was much more sincere and peaceful as there were stronger affinity among the family members as they were living and working together.

A participant quoting Kuppan *Moopan's* observation notices:

"There were no conflicts with their women in those days. They were listening to each other. Today, men expect women to obey them, and women do not obey them. They suspect each other and fight with each other. There is no mutual respect"

Another participant points out:

In those days, we do not see men and women walking separate after deciding to live together. Even today, our old couples always walk together. They always consult with each other. They get up early in the morning, cook food together, and go to work together and come back together. The young couples are not such *enas*

In contrast, the present day gender relationship is depicted as a life full of suspicion and mistrust. Stories narrated by the participants explain the extent to which the marital relationships have worsened. An unmarried participant girl writes:

The last death that occurred in our *ooru* is that of Karumi. Her husband, Palani, killed Karumi. Karumi was alleged of having an illicit relationship with other men…. I do not know that whether this allegation had any truth in it. It was usual that he was beating his wife… the incident had shocked me. It is risky to trust even one's husband…

Another participant reports a murder and a suicide recently happened in his hamlet:

Ponnan and Ponni were husband and wife staying at Padavayal. Ponni was pregnant. They had a daughter of four years old. Thursdays are *chantha* (weekly Market)* days for the people at Padavayal. On that day, everybody goes to *chantha*. On *chantha* days, nobody remains at home. Usually on *chantha* day, people visit their relatives. Ponnan did not go to *chantha* on the pretext of headache. His mother took his daughter to her relative's home … that night, Ponni and Ponnan were alone at their home. Ponnan thrust a towel in her mouth cutting her throat to death… and he killed himself hanging.

One participant reporting his brother's suicide observes in his field diary:

My brother is just 25 years old. He mixed poison with arrack and consumed it to kill himself. He was living with his wife in a separate house here at Chindakki. They were not living happily. They were always fighting. The reason for the fight was that his wife was alleging that he had developed an illicit relationship with another woman… he was taken to hospital. He died there at the hospital. My sister-in-law then married to another man recently.

There were stories of husbands deserting their pregnant wives and wives deserting husbands, grownup children abusing their helpless parents; *adivasis* joining with the settlers harassing their brothers and sisters and settlers harassing *adivasis* and so on. Some of the participants pointed out that all these things happen because these days family members hardly work together. Each one goes searching for one's own job, but returns home fully drunk. Usually the men come home drunk and quarrel with their wives. The wives earn and look after their children.

In a critically oriented discussion, it was remarked that the common space among the family members is shrinking. The major factor that was maintaining the family affinity in the past was the collective labour of the family members; the family members were working together to make a living. Presently, as the collective or family agriculture practices had almost ended, family members rarely work together. They work for the settlers individually. The changes brought in their social life made the members of the family economically independent as every adult could earn an income, however meagre, to meet their minimal needs. The economic independence, especially when their income is meagre, let the individuals remain aloof from one another, holding on to their individual income. Neither in the past, nor in the present, the social pressures such as being responsible to one's family, maintaining 'family honour' keeping one's family 'renowned' were operating on the *adivasi* individuals. The economic independence of the individuals in the absence of social pressures and without rigid familial norms, had contributed to the reduction of the shared space among the family members. Rather, sometimes it has created shared spaces in the work places. The family members staying under one roof having private spaces in the absence of institutionalised family norms had in fact aggravated dissimilarities, suspicions and disputes among the individuals. As, the mothers are expected to take care of their children, the women were the worst hit as they have to struggle for their own and their children's survival. Husband deserting wife and coming back is not a rare experience among the *adivasi* women. The following narration given in the classroom as it was told to an RAP by an HRP woman, pictures the plight of the *adivasi* women:

> I was a housemaid at a *vandavasi* house even as a child of 10. We had no food at home; therefore, I had to work as a housemaid. Later I started going for work outside. I used to get Rs. 35 a day. Of that, I would get nothing as my share. My parents would take all that I earn. I got married when I was 18. Today I am 28 years old. ... My husband deserted me when I was pregnant. My days of pregnancy were the days of hunger... I delivered at my parents' house. It was a stillbirth. After months, my husband returned. By that time, he was ill. I conceived again and gave birth to my son ...later two children were born. My husband's illness became severe by that time. We took him to hospital and the doctor said he was affected by Tuberculosis. As he was ill, he could not go out to work. I had to manage everything from earning to cooking. As we feel hungry, sometimes we live by eating mustard leaves.

The participants could think over the fractured marital relationships prevalent among them. A story narrated by a participant as he heard from his fieldwork captures the fragile marital bond, as it exists today:

I am given in marriage to my husband's family when I was barely 16 years old. There was no marriage ceremony. I was taken to my husband's house. I saw him for the first time at his house. It was like that. Then there was no marriage. Girls were just taken to the boy's house. Parents decide the partner. We just had to obey them. … Then, my husband was 23 years old. We were happy. I became pregnant after eight months of living together with him. I gave birth to a boy at home. …later I gave birth to three other children. When I was eight months pregnant of my fourth child my husband just absconded from our *ooru,* without informing me about his whereabouts. Nobody knew where he went. Usually it should be the husband who should look after his wife during pregnancy and after Childbirth…. My husband's mother was too old to maintain the family and me, especially when I could not earn. She also had to take the burden of my three children. Amidst these difficulties, I gave birth to my fourth child. My mother-in-law could not toil further to meet our both ends needs. She felt sorry for her un-viability in looking after my children and me. She asked whether I could go back to my house until my husband reappeared. My parents were informed. They came and took me with them. Six months later, my husband came back. Knowing that he had come back, I went to his house the next day. My mother-in-law was angry with him. She felt sorry for her son's behaviour. She told that he does not deserve my love. She also said that it is foolish to come to him, as he had been too cruel to me. To her and to me, he promised that he would never leave me. As it is the custom that we should live as a separate family after childbirth, he said that he would settle a house at Chindakki. This is because, at Chindakki, finding a job was comparatively easier. We came here, and he became a regular worker in the farm. … Later we settled at Chindakki with children…. Years passed. The children grew up. … My second child studied up to the 10th standard. My children got married….

Now my husband has left me once again. He got his retirement benefit Rs. 45,000/- with that money, he went to his home and now living with his brother... He accuses me that I used black magic against him. I know that now he has another woman. I am now alone, and I have just five goats.

The unfair family relationships as it exists are further illustrated by one participant's life experience:

My father died when my mother was having me in her womb. As my father demised, she had to go to her parents, to give birth to me leaving behind our home. For nine months, my house was left unoccupied. Using this occasion, my paternal uncle, who was settled nearby, taken away everything he found useful from there. When my widowed mother returned to our house, she found it was empty. Everything including grain, utensils, etc., were taken away. When we returned, none of my relatives from my father's side were kind enough to inquire our well-being. When asked why they did they emptied the house my uncle told that he had taken away everything because they belonged to his demised brother. He justified his action saying that my mother could have no claim over the things he left during his death, as it was not her earnings. Despite hostility from my father's relatives, my mother stayed there, as she thought that was only proper. My mother stayed there and struggled for our survival. It was not easy for her to survive. When everybody had men at their home to prepare land for shift-and-burn[106] cultivation, we had none on our side. In fact, according to the practice existing in the community, men help women in distress and widows in clearing the forest for cultivation. Whoever came to help us were stopped

---

106   Prior to 1950 it is a common practice that the forestland was cleared by slashing burning plants over a small area, and cultivating food crops. The land will be used for three years and the cultivation would be shifted to another location. This practice is called " shift-burn-agriculture."

from helping us. Without somebody supporting, it was impossible to make a living. As my mother could not live there, leaving everything behind, she left my father's place and settled near her parent's house.

The story of Masani, an *adivasi* woman worked as a house cleaner, as her son told it to one participant, sketches the torn life of *adivasis*:

My father's name is Maniyan, and my mother is Masani. I have a younger brother and a younger sister. We were living at *Nakkupathy* Pirivu…. A *Malayali* family lured my parents to work for them. Driven by hunger, my mother agreed to work as a house cleaner at the *Malayali* household.

She was doing every work from looking after their cattle to washing and cleaning at the *Malayali* household. For her work she was just paid two rupees a day, and stale food. My father was working as a firewood cutter. They could manage to bring home stale food from the *Malayali* household and about ½ kilo of rice every day.

At times, she had even to 'steal' stale food from the cattle bowl meant to be given to the cattle to feed us. … My father died when he was 25. Then I was seven years old, my sister was five years old and my brother was just three years old. …After his death, we had no means to live. My mother somehow managed to bring us food. She was with us for about a year….

Living in an unbearable poverty, she obliged to run away with a *Malayali* man leaving us at abeyance. As she left, we had nobody to look after us and we grew by ourselves begging, wandering and sometimes working for the settlers. My brother was taken by my uncle as his servant; my sister was taken as a housemaid at Calicut and I became a hotel boy at Coimbatore…

After working many years, we came back one by one to our *ooru*. My sister came back first and we brothers followed. As the *Malayali* deserted my mother, she too came back to us, but as she had left us at abeyance we did not allow her to stay with us…She was wandering here in the streets for a few days and went back to the *Malayali*. One day, we got the information that the *Malayali* had beaten up our mother to death. When we went to the *Malayali*'s house, we saw that our mother was tied and strangled to death…we brought her body and buried at our *ooru*…

The story of Masani depicts multiple dimensions of *adivasi* life in its relation to the settler sociality. The new social reality that imposed servitude on the entire family within an unsafe socialisation in the making had taken its hard turn on the family.

Not everybody agreed that the life of women is deteriorating only today. Some participants observed that even in the past the women were sufferers:

"Women were slaves during early periods…. those days women used to work hard both in houses and forests. Nowadays there is change in attitudes. Women have positions in government bodies. These days *adivasi* women can become panchayat members representing even the *vandavasi*s. This could not be even imagined in the past."

"Earlier men were getting property… No property to women… but nowadays both men and women gets land property…"

Some had pointed out with the arrival of *vandavasi*s there were more restriction on women:

> During our childhood, we were not allowed to go to schools. If girls get out of the house they were told, the *vandavasis* will take them away. So, they were confined in the houses looking after the younger ones.

The narrations suggest that the social life of *adivasis* is undergoing a change of which the individuals or the community has no control. Individualisation process that has currently spread its effects the world over has made deep impact on the *adivasi* life-world. It has withered away the community and family bonds among them. There was no historical necessity for the *adivasis* to go under the rigorous socialisation as the settler communities and other religious/historical communities had. While the rigorous socialisation could mitigate the effect of individualisation among the settlers, its absence made *adivasis* vulnerable and unrepairable with the later 'development' efforts that could hardly look beyond economic criteria. The settler society in this context took the role of both as an actual and effective agent of change in the life of the *adivasis*. Despite the fact that the change has only brought the *adivasi* suffering and dismantlement, the exposure (to the settler ethos) has destined them to look at the settler society as the model to be emulated.

The discussion on the changes occurred in their family life is followed by the discussion on the emergence of labour relations among the *adivasis*. The participants after discussing in groups came out with an observation: The idea of money was unknown to the traditional community. Money when it was introduced had only ritual significance. Money emerged as the medium for bride price. Working for others to earn money was unknown to them. They were working for themselves under the guide ship of *'mannookkaran'*, the ritual head of agricultural practices in the traditional social system. *Mannookkaran* identified the lands suitable for shift and burn cultivation. The *ooru moopan* accordingly allocated the lands to be cultivated to the families in the *ooru*. The *ooru moopan* in return collected tax in kind to be handed over to the *Jenmi*, the landlord. *Adivasis* were practicing rain fed cultivation. They cultivated varieties of maize, pulses and leafy vegetables. There was a practice of sowing 13 varieties of crops together and harvesting them throughout the year. Under the British rule, they worked as labourers in cutting trees in 1940s. Moopil Nair, the *Jenmi*, used their labour extensively to cut trees in the 1960's before he had to hand over the land under his control to the government. In the late 50's the settlers occupied lands, mostly in the riverbeds. As the *adivasis* preferred to stay in the slopes, there was no clash with the settlers. Settlers from Tamilnadu and Kerala brought new crops such as onion, new vegetables, coconut, new varieties of paddy, plantain, banana, sugarcane, groundnut, cotton and other crops. The Tamil settlers introduced irrigated agriculture. The *Malayali* settlers brought with them new crops like arecanut, coconut, new varieties of paddy, pepper, cardamom and other horticultural crops. Initially settlers brought their labourers with them and later *adivasis* became their labourers. Among *adivasis*, *Irulas* first became labourers followed by the *Mudugas*, but *Kurumbas* restrained themselves from becoming other's labourers till date. The traditional system of *adivasis* working collectively under the leadership of *mannookkaran* gradually collapsed as the shift and burn cultivation was banned by the government. Since, the settlers already occupied the riverbeds, the *adivasis*, were given title deeds by the government to 'own' lands on the slopes. As slopes are hardly re-usable under frequent cultivation, the lands belonging to *adivasis* became unusable and infertile because of soil erosion. This had led them depending on the *vandavasi*s for labour and livelihood. The *adivasis* becoming labourers had altered their daily life cycle and food habits. Hotels emerged at Attappady to accommodate the food requirement of the labourers. Hotels introduced, new food items like *parotta*, tea and beef. Rice was known to them earlier. They were traditionally cultivating rain fed varieties of rice. Rice was not a major food item. Rather they were more familiar with varieties of millets, maize and *ragi* as their staple food. Millets, maize and *ragi* required pounding. Compared to millets, cooking rice was easier and rice gradually emerged as their major staple food. In the process, men and women were introduced to arrack, consumption of which was unknown to them. Later they also learnt to distil arrack at their hamlets. There were practices of bonded labour, under which the entire family was expected to work for a settler family for a sum of Rs. 1000- 3000 a year. Later, the system of bonded labour was abolished by law. Presently, the *adivasis* hardly practise any agriculture in their land, as the land does not yield. Further, the increased number of wild bores and frequent crop destruction by elephants prevented them from undertaking agriculture. As the cumulative effect of all, that had historically happened to them the *adivasis* became impoverished. The recognition of their impoverishment followed by government sponsored development activities and the presence of non-governmental organisations working towards 'development'.

Later, they undertook a critical over view of their history of agriculture practices and came out with observations: Traditionally, *neethi, neri, nela* and *nyayam* were considered to be integral to the practice of agriculture. It was believed that the *4Ns* of the *adivasi* community had direct link to the agricultural yield. It was believed that *Mannookkaran's* ritual purity and personal conduct are decisive factors in a better agricultural yield. Hence, the *mannookkaran* to preserve his ritual purity avoided attending death rituals. With the *vandavasis* practicing agriculture with no reverence to the 4Ns, and yet having better yields gradually broke *adivasi* faith in the relation between the 4Ns and the agricultural yield. Practicing agriculture for commercial purpose was unknown to the *adivasis*. Cultivation was always for consumption and for saving the grains for the lean seasons. As the granaries were full, there was no fear of hunger. Further, unlike today, the rivers at Attappady were full of fishes in the past. The *adivasis* were free to trap wild bores and deer for their meat requirement. Deer meet was part of their rituals. There were specific places where traps to catch animals were kept. Kuravan kandi was one such place. *Kandi* means trap. These days the forest laws prevent them from trapping wild animals. The results of these developments were non-availability of food, starvation, malnutrition and loss of health.

The participants brought to discussion the traditional practice of collective agriculture among the *adivasis*. The collective agriculture practice was called *kambalam* or *rarukambalam*. *Rarukambalam* refers to the whole festivity of cultivating *ragi* and millets where the young and older womenfolk together sing and dance to make the labour less burdensome. For this work (*rarukambalam*) nobody is given wages.

A participant reporting on the practice of *kambalam* among the *Irulas* as he learnt from an 85 years old man recounted:

> In those days, the forest was so dense that the earth had never felt the heat or light of the Sun. Even in those days, not everyone was equal. Some had more grains than the others. Some were managing hundreds of people in clearing forest and undertaking cultivation and some others were not. Some were not part of the collective agriculture practice. Those who were not part of the collective practice of *kambalam*[107] would usually suffer in the rainy season and would go to those who have grain to help them. In those days, there was no system of credit. If one has grain, they share with the other, but with a condition, that they would have to join in the next *kambalam*. If they do not oblige, then they will not be supported when they face shortage of grain. The person, who coordinates *kambalam*, would be taking the lion's share of the yield.

The narration continued:

> When *kambalam* was the general practice, a person called Kunju-muhammad came here. He could manage engaging about 2000 people in his agriculture activities. Unlike the people who organise *kambalam*, he gave wages. People were happy, as they need not wait until harvest to get their share. He employed the *adivasis as* his labourers. He was cultivating tapioca in acres of land. ...he was generous enough to share the yield with the *adivasis*. He was even giving wage to the people who trapped rats to prevent his crop from the rat attack. ... . One had to produce the tail of the rat for proof. Since, rats were cooked and eaten by the *adivasis*, they enjoyed this proposal and caught them enthusiastically. Then there were *Kokko*

---

107   *Kambalam* is a collective agricultural practice found among *Irulas* and probably among *Mudugas* too. According to the field notes submitted, becoming part of *kambalam* is voluntary and the participants would share among themselves the yield. The unique thing about *kambalam* is that it is accompanied with songs and dances. The *kambalam* team consists of singers, dancers, and jesters to cheer those who prepare land for sowing or those who harvest crops. The singers, jesters and dancers were also given a share of the harvest.

Paattan and *Minukki Paatti*[108]. Kunji Mohammad was attracted towards Minukki Patti and he was living with her. Minukki Patti was kind to the *adivasis*. For one-day labour, he was giving one *padi* (an unit of measurement) of *ragi*. Later, with the influence of Minukki Patti, the labour was paid in two *padis* of *ragi*…Kunjumuhammad also fell trees from the forest. To transport them to Mannarkad in those days, there were no proper roads. With the help of the *adivasis* and others, he cut a road to Mannarkad and transported them to Mannarkad. It is during this time the first teashop came. The first teashop was set up at *Kakku Padi*. That shop later became a provisional store. People started buying things in exchange of money from then onwards.

The anecdote presented here traces the gradual shift of *adivasis* from collective farmers to agricultural labourers. They also critically looked at the changes the new agricultural practices brought to their cultural practices. A participant brought an interesting observation on the consequence of cotton cultivation, as it was narrated to him by a person called Lacchi *Moopan* at his hamlet:

To cultivate, our traditional crops we never needed money. All that needed was willingness to work. With the introduction of the Cotton cultivation, money becomes important in agriculture. Traders introduced the cotton cultivation here. The *adivasis* were given credit by the cotton dealers. Earlier we never used to give credit or get credit. They gave seeds, fertilizers and pesticide as credit to be repaid after the harvest. They take the cotton and give us the balance money. Sometimes instead of money, they gave us cloths…. They have also given us the reason for wearing new cloths. They introduced the *Ayyappan Vilakku* festival, which coincided with the harvest of cotton… Then it became a routine to buy new clothes for *Ayyappan Vilakku* festival…

108   *Paattan* is Grand Father, *Paatti* is Grand Mother. The words is used for referring ancestors too.

Later the cotton cultivation was not profitable and the traders stopped giving credit. However, the Ayyappan *Vilakku* festival continues…

The narration while elaborating the emergence of new practices in agriculture among *adivasis*, also illustrates how new gods emerge out of new economic realities. Another narration as told by a *Muduga*[109] *Moopan* to an RAP illustrates, the historical origin of the faith in *Malleswaran* as a deity and the ritual status accorded to *Mudugas* in the performance of rituals at the *Malleswaran mudi*:

> Earlier there were only the *Muduga* and the *Kurumba* people in Attapaddy. They were dwelling in the forests. The *Irula*s came later from Tamilnadu. They were believers in various gods. The *Mudugas* and the *Kurumbas* didn't have much faith in personal gods. They were worshiping their ancestors. The *Irula*s started worshiping their gods at Attapaddy (keeping stones under big trees)… In the beginning, they didn't know the way to the *Malleswara Mudi*. They sought the *Muduga's* help to light the holy lamp there on *Shivarathris*. So they hired the *Mudugas* for lighting the holy lamp on the *Malleswaran Mudi* [*Malleswaran* peak]. For that, they were giving the *Mudugas* 1¼ *panam* wrapped in a yellow cloth. Later it became a ritual that the *Mudugas* should light the Holy Lamp on the top of the *Malleswaran mudi*. Then Attappady was under the control of the King Zamurin. The King Zamurin was a believer of the lord *Malleswaran* (Shiva).

When the narration was presented in the classroom, the classroom was divided on the issue as many of the RAPs disagreed and claimed that the faith in *Malleswaran* is a time immemorial practice.

In another narration reflecting on how a deity *'Ganapathy'* became the *ooru* deity a participant narrated the following story from her life experience:

---

[109] The participants also learnt that the *Mudugas* were so called by the later settlers as they were carrying their children on their back (*Mudhuku*) in a bag-like device bag-like device around the forest

In our *ooru*, there is a *Ganapathy* temple. Earlier it was not there. A few years before roughly when I was 12, the children of my age made a mischief. We were more interested in playing… than going to school. We played make crude models of temples. Thus, one day all the children of the *ooru* made a model temple on the roadside. Then we brought pebbles from a nearly stream and fixed them as the idol. Then we placed an old photograph of Lord *Ganapathy*. We used to perform the *poojas* there… However, our playfulness sow the seeds of serious thought in our elders who never thought of making a temple. They began thinking of making a temple there. Now there is a *Ganapathy* temple. I think the most of the things that become part of our habit or beliefs have some trivial start like this. Nevertheless, once we start believing it however illogical or trivial it is we cling on to them[110].

Through their research and their group discussion on their research findings, the *adivasi* participants located themselves in the history. They have done the exercise collectively for the first time in their life. It helped them to find their present life situation within a historical trajectory of which they had little control. They organised their findings and presented them neatly in the classroom. There were historians and other social scientists present in the classroom. Their presentation evoked awe inspiration and surprise among the learned audience. The social scientists also actively participated in the discussion asking for

---

[110] The present researcher was informed that in a *Kurumba ooru* it is a usual practice to worship the odd-looking stones collected by children and playfully kept at the bottom of trees. In most of the cases the *ooru* is not ignorant that it was the children who begun the worship playfully. In this case Neumann's observation that some tribes consider the state of childhood proximate to the state of divinity should be seriously considered. Neumann observes: The original knowledge of one who is still enfolded in the perfect state is very evident in the psychology of the child. For this reason many primitive peoples treat children with particular marks of respect. In the child the great images and archetypes of the collective unconscious are living reality, and very close to him; indeed, many of his sayings and reactions, questions and answers, dreams and images, express this knowledge which still derives from his prenatal existence. It is transpersonal experience not personally acquired, a possession acquired from "over there." Such knowledge is rightly regarded as ancestral knowledge, and the child as a reborn forebear [Neumann 1954:23].

more clarity in their presentation. One eminent historian[111] present there remarked, "I have come here expecting ignorant *adivasis* listening history from me, rather they taught me history well researched."

As the part of the project the specialists in health and environment had delivered their lectures to them in preparation for their next phase of fieldwork. The lectures concentrated on providing basic facts regarding the health status of the *adivasis* and the environmental status of Attappady. There were some lectures delivered on making use of the decentralisation initiatives of the Kerala government. They were also motivated to undertake action projects alongside their research as they have already established a good relation with the people in the hamlet.

It was the fifth day of the third phase. A participant, M, took leave from the classroom session on the second day of the phase because his wife is about to deliver a baby. On the fifth day, the classroom debates continued without any drop in enthusiasm. Everywhere in the hall there were chart papers hanging. As the four walls of the classroom were not sufficient, charts with their group discussion inscribed were hung on twines knotted across the classroom. One of the participants in an emotionally charged moment said:

> this classroom is divine as we have with us the representation of the world
> in which our ancestors lived. If we are sensible, we can feel their spirit being
> present here. We have invoked their spiritual power as we were discussing

---

[111] The statement was made by Prof. Raghava Varrior, en eminent historian from Kerala.

the times they lived. For us they are our God. We will also soon become the spirit. As we revere them, our future generation would revere us. However, now we should reflect whether we are really worthy of our future generations' reverence. Are we not corrupt? Have we not given up our *Neethi*...?

The discussion was ethically charged. Everybody was involved in the discussion. After a while, they were discussing the futility of development and the damage it has done to their self-respect. They were discussing their inability to demand quality when anything is given to them free by the government officials. They were referring to the weak structures of the houses the government built for them. While this discussion was going on the participant, M who took leave entered the classroom, and commented reacting to the discussion then going on, that nobody is sincere about them, and if the roofs of their houses collapse because of the weak structures they just die and nobody bothers. Hearing this, the entire classroom in a chorus spontaneously said "WE *ADIVASIS* NEVER DIE." Not just the NAPs but M too was stunned by this response. One still feels the sound of the chorus in one's ears.

At the end of the phase of the classroom session, there was an appeal from the participants that what they have learnt from their fieldwork and from the classroom sessions should be given to their people. There was a suggestion that at the end of every classroom phase, they should write a song consolidating their learning, and they should design dance steps too for their song. On the fourth day itself, they came with the song.

They composed two songs collectively and they were much eager to present them before the classroom with dance. The songs were written on chart papers. The first group consisted of the elected representatives and the second one the persons nominated by the elected representatives. The content of the songs was on the history of the *adivasis* since the coming of the settlers. The songs were capturing the aspects of pre-settler occupation of Attappady: the rule of *Jenmi*, the beginning of agriculture, the beginning of settler agriculture, their being turned into the labourers of the settlers, the coming of money economy, deforestation, deprivation and drying up of their water resources, decline in their nutritional consumption, illness affecting them, the demise of *neethi*, the onset of party politics, presence of dishonesty and corruption everywhere, and the need to restore food security, and resistance to corruption, their dream of the future etc., The elected representatives had written in their chart "Elected Representatives" appearing to claim the authorship of the song. (See appendix 8) The claim of authorship by the elected representatives did not go well with the others. They resisted the claim on the authorship of the song, whose ideas had come from all the participants' fieldwork. They decided to boycott the song. There was a debate on the ethics of claiming ownership of ideas that had been collectively generated by all. Later, the elected representatives removed their name from the chart pleading an apology for their mistake. Only after a settlement reached, both the groups combined presented their songs with dances.

The final session of the third phase was set-aside for making decision on the research activities to be carried out in the next fieldwork phase. The participants decided that the next phase of fieldwork should concentrate on the issues of health. The research agenda for the next phase was fixed upon as follows:

1. Understanding health issues, tracing the interconnectedness of food nutrition, water quality and other such issues.

2. Intensifying the studies already taken up.

3. Improving the dialogue possibilities with the people in the selected hamlets for *praxis* intervention and gradually taking in them as partners in the reflexive process and social action.

4. Study of the ecological degradation/improvement in the past four decades.

Phase IV: The Beginning of Collective Action

The fourth phase is marked with the beginning of field level activity. There was a project at Attappady namely Attappady Hill Area Development Society [AHADS]. It is a multi million project, aimed at restoring the ecological fertility of Attappady. The project for some reason distanced itself from the institutions of the local governance. There were no healthy communication existed between the local governments and the project management. The project had its field level micro units. People associated with it gained as the project gave daily wage employment through its micro units. While the researchers of the *praxis* undertaking their field research, they observed that the persons from the AHADS project were removing shrubs, herbs, creepers and climbers including small bushes on the hilly landscapes of Pudur. When the researchers asked the micro units of AHADS the logic behind clearing off the hills of the plants, they could not give a proper answer. For them, it was only an employment opportunity. Later the researchers learnt that the plants were removed to plant new trees in order to raise forests. The answer was not appealing to the RAPs, since the knowledge they gained from their research and their lived experience was that those hilly areas were suitable only for the shorter plants already existing there. They felt removing them would only increase soil erosion. As summers are hot here, trees planted there would have only little survival possibility. Besides, their research had revealed to them that most of the shrubs, herbs, creepers, climbers, bushes and thorny plants grew over there were believed to be plants having medicinal values. These plants were also giving abode to the birds, reptiles, insects and small animals. Some of the plants were ideal for honeybees to have their hives. Pointing these things, they wanted to stop the plant clearing activity. The local officials of AHADS were not willing to stop the activity. The people involved in the clearing activity did not want the activity stopped, as it gives employment to them. Some of the researchers involved in the protest against clearing the plants were elected representatives. They had a problem in intervening as it would result in antagonizing a few who were seeking employment through this activity. However, they decided to resist the activity as it appeared to them an activity detrimental to the ecology, soil health and other living beings living over there. The ERAPs from Pudur panchayat subsequently passed a resolution in their panchayat against clearing the plants and stopped the activity for a temporary period. Later, when verified with ecologists, one was told that the insightful activity of the participants was in fact justifiable in terms of the knowledge available about the conservation of the eco-system.

The *praxis* intervention project had brought obvious changes in the participants' behaviour. In some cases, extreme changes were observed. There was a participant called J[112]. He was an elected representative too. People observed obvious changes in his behaviour. He had stopped drinking and started attending his official works. Earlier, he never used to comment on anything while attending public meetings whereas he had become sharp in his comments. A government doctor residing at Pudur expressed surprise over the changes happening to J. It appeared that he had taken things to an extreme; he was advocating to everyone that they should return to the traditional *adivasi* life style. He has rather himself started practicing the traditional *adivasi* life style as he learnt from his fieldwork. He stopped eating rice; instead, he consumed only the traditional *adivasi* food. He was not practicing agriculture for years as he was in active party politics and later became a panchayat member. He re-started agriculture practice, claiming that he would set an example for the others. His parents complained that some "evil spirit" possessed him bringing changes in his behaviour. His parents visited the doctor and enquired whether he had gone mad. For the local doctor there appeared nothing abnormal. Later his parents took him to people who claim to drive away evil spirits. J was reporting all the things happening around him with a smile.

During the follow-up field visit to Pudur, the PUPs stopped at a hotel for Lunch. The hotel owner came out of his cash counter and showed his respect folding his hands for minutes. The hotel owner came down to them and said, "You have done a great service to us." He further continued:

---

[112]   The real name of the participant is not given here.

We never expected the people to be transformed by training programmes. Our J has become entirely changed person. We never saw him in his senses before. He was always drunk. He has given up drinking. Whenever there is meeting, J never uttered a word even though he is our elected member. These days he could talk intelligent things… All our people are indebted to your service…"

As for the PUPs, they were quite unsure as to whether to take the changes happening in J as an extreme 'identity' position or an instance of meaningful transformation. However, J, along with other researchers had mobilised many young men and women to practice in rain fed agriculture to ensure their food security and health.

The researchers suspected that arrack consumption and poor food intake among the *adivasis* are the reasons for their poor health. At many field locations the participants advocated rain fed agricultural practice and spoke against arrack distillation, consumption and selling. A participant from the *nakkupathy ooru* called a general meeting of the hamlet resident and explained that the hamlet should be made arrack free. In the meeting, it was decided to ban arrack selling in the hamlet. They collectively filed a complaint against the sellers at the local police station with 51 signatories. Based on the complaint, the police conducted a raid. Arrack selling was thus successfully stopped at *Nakkupathy*. Unfortunately, the person who was making a livelihood selling arrack attempted self-immolation. However, his life was saved as he was taken to the Palakkad Hospital and given medical treatment.

In another incident, a participant from Chindakki, called a general meeting of the hamlet people and discussed all that he learnt from the classroom. He initiated three-fold action for recovering health status of the people. First, he gave a call for action against the arrack menace, second, he initiated action towards food production and agriculture and third he mobilised people to clean the water source of the hamlet and fixed an announcement board requesting the vehicle owners not to clean their vehicle in their water source. His threefold action met with a good success as a collective force was formed against alcohol selling, everybody in the hamlet came forward for cultivation and the vehicles drivers listened to the community's request and stopped cleaning their vehicles there at their drinking water source.

At *Oothukuzhi*, another participant intervened to solve the water issue. Water problem was acute in *OothuKuzhy*. There is a public water supply system at *OothuKuzhy*, but that was not properly functioning. The participant met the water supply line repairers and told them of the difficulties. They immediately came and corrected the problem.

There are two wells in the *OothuKuzhy Ooru*, of which one was out of use as the colour of water has turned black. Later, they found the water in the other well also had some problem. The *ooru* people noticed that there were frogs earlier, but later all of them died for some unknown reason. Instead, there were worms in the water. The water by its colour appeared dirty. Later the water was tested in a laboratory and found to be not potable. The researcher sat with the hamlet people and enquired what might be the possible cause of the water being spoilt. They suspected that it was because of the excess of pesticides used for the cotton cultivation in the land just above the well. The pesticides and fertilizers used there might have spoilt their water.

The fourth phase could witness participants bringing out their learning into visible action. They were also seen sharing their learning with the other people at their hamlet and probing with the people in the hamlet and thus multiplying their learning.

Phase V: Deepening the Learning

The participants returned to the classroom phase after their fieldwork. The participants were proud that they were researchers. They thought that they have conducted a meaningful research on themselves. They acknowledged during the presentation hours that they could discover that Attappady was greener and more fertile in the past than it is, at present. From their research they could state that the rainfall had been better in the past and their *uravus* and rivers were with full of waters; and it had dried up only with the arrival of the 'settlers' and the 'development.' They have associated the 'development' with the deforestation, land alienation, party politics, drying up of their water resources, depletion of traditional food resources, and the introduction of labour-hood commencing with the settlement of the outsiders at Attappady. They were confident that their findings were correct and authentic as their elders who lived through the changes informed it to them. They were confident of their findings also because the responses they got from one corner of Attappady matched with that of the other. In one of the Classroom sessions, N, a resource person, was listening to the presentations carefully and said that what they were stating need not be accepted as the undisputed truth as they do not produce sufficient evidence substantiating their findings. They were obviously dissatisfied with N's comment and tried to defend that, what they stated were facts they have collected from the field. N told them that despite their reporting what was said to them by their informants it may be in danger of being misrepresented, therefore need further investigations. To prove his point, he asked them about sunrise, i.e, where they think the sun rises. They answered it rises in the east. N challenged them saying, it is only apparent that the sun rises in the east, as a matter of fact the sun does not rise at all. The sun appearing as rising in the east is an illusion caused by the earth's going around the sun; similarly, it is important to realise that what they were finding out may be the seeming truths and it requires scientific inquiry to prove the actuality of their findings. They were quite shattered as they were challenged at the things they believed to be unquestionable truths. Then N discussed with them how to look for evidences for what they were claiming.

The participants had a group discussion on their fieldwork experience and opined that the major issue they confront among *adivasis* is their health. They observed the health of the people fast deteriorate because of poor food intake; poor quality of drinking water available; high consumption of alcohol and women not well cared for during pregnancy and after the childbirth. An RAP field-working at Kujur emphatically pointed referring to the worsening health condition of the people and their increased dependence on hospitals, "If you want to see anybody at Kunjur, just go to the Agali Government Hospital. You can find them there. Such is the health condition of the people here." The statement sums up the health situation of the *adivasis*.

The participant narrating what was told to him at a meeting with the people at Kunjur:

None of us is healthier than our parents or grandparents. The main reason for this is that we do not eat as they were eating and second we do not work, so much as, they were working. Our parents were having food grain storage at their homes. Moreover, they could also get the meat of deer, wild bore, fish and they could find plenty of wild fruits, leafy vegetables, tubers and honey. Arrack was unknown to them. The hamlet itself was inside the forest. There were huge trees in the hamlet itself. Water availability was not a problem. There was plenty of water in the *uravus* (sub surface water flow that springs out*).* Plenty of land was available and *kotthukadu*[113] cultivation was possible. If a piece of land did not yield, they were shifting to another piece of land. Today, there is not even a trace of forest existing here. We do not have water, we do not have food grains at home, nor do we get a regular wage. Everything has changed fast just before our eyes.

There are plenty of references in their field records expressing people's concern on deterioration of their health condition such as early deaths, child mortality, tuberculosis, poor vision, rheumatoid and other diseases incapacitating their mobility, high prevalence of psoriasis and 'smoke disease' [a disease caused by excessive smoking resulting in their fingers decaying and dropping], fatigue, anaemic complaints, skin diseases, frequent headaches, stomach ailments and so on. The participants narrated the stories of ill-health they gathered from the field and expressed their concern.

The women, they pointed out, in the *adivasi* communities suffer lack of care during their pregnancy and childbirth. The pregnant women, generally, are not fed with nutritious food. Their food intake becomes poorer during their pregnancy days, as their income comes down with the woman's earning is reduced. During pregnancy, according to the *adivasi* custom the women remain

---

113   Shifting cultivation on the slope of the hills. The forestland newly cleared for cultivation was called *pudukadu*. The forest burnt for cultivation was called *Karikkadu*. The land that is processed with *kotthu* instrument in the second year of cultivation in it is called *Kotthu kadu*. Plain land prepared for agriculture is called '*Airkadu*' or *Vadikadu*. *Airkadu* means the ploughable land.

with their husband. It is the convention that the parents do not visit the couple's house until the 90 days after childbirth. In the crucial period that requires care, protection, and better nutritional food the women remain starving as they could only depend on their spouses' income.

It is also observed that the traditional food is now considered to be representing backwardness. The *adivasi* traditional food is considered less prestigious in the households that have children educated at the residential tribal schools. The children get accustomed to the *vandavasi* food habits in their hostel life and expect similar food at home. They refuse to eat the *adivasi* food and parents are supposed to buy rice and vegetable available at the market to feed their family. This puts pressure on them to earn money by selling their labour. It also discouraged them in cultivating traditional agriculture crops. As they go out to work for others, the parents too get accustomed to the *vandavasi* food items like '*parotta*' and tea. As the husband and the wife go out in search of work, often no food is prepared at home. Everybody in the household ends up eating outside. Once used to the *vandavasi* food women also find it difficult to cook the *adivasi* food because, to make food out of traditional grains like *ragi*, required pounding the grains; whereas cooking the rice is easier. For all these reasons, the quality of the food intake has come down which in turn affected their health. The observations made remind us of Bourdieu's analysis of taste in *Distinction*. Bourdieu remarks that the desire to have the food that is symbolically given a prestigious status could be associated with particular *habitus* and position in the social field [Bourdieu 1984]. The whole purpose of *Distinction* is to counter the view that the judgements of taste are disinterested and free of the influence of the *habitus* and the struggles of the social field

[Sayer 2002]. The symbolic value associated with certain food in fact overrides the real worth of the food in terms of their nutrition or in terms of their cost of production.

One reason they point out for their starvation and poor food intake was deteriorating neighbourhood relations. People in the neighbourhood used to be more considerate than they are at present. Food grains were shared among them. A participant reports what had been informed to him by the hamlet people:

> "Deer, Wild bores were available in plenty. We were not using guns to catch them. We use traps made of bamboo and coir…Once we get these animals, we take them to *ooru moopan*. *Moopan* share them to every family. Today, if anybody catches them, they keep it secret; they just share with their neighbours. They even sell them to settlers. They get Rs. 50 for a Kilo…"

> "Hunger was not a problem during summer as there would be plenty of mango and jackfruit. Only a few had these trees. Those who have them share it with others."

The instances quoted here are instances in which modernisation has left a community half way into social crisis. The deterioration of neighbourhood and the disintegration of community life is only a symptom of a larger social mechanism in operation. Though the 'social resource' of the community got depleted, it was not replaced by any workable social system. The 'social resource' here means the resourcefulness of the social relations such as trustworthiness, mutual support, community care, mutual concern, a feeling of warmth in being social and having a dependable community relationship. Individualisation, the invention of the historical process alien to the *adivasis*, through their engagement with the settlers and the outside social world in general replaced their communitarian life style. Individualisation without the effective social system (with its public institutions or orientation towards such institutions) leads to general negligence. Mutual co-operation, though it was a practice prior to the invasion of modernity into their life, was not institutionalised among them and hence with the onset of modernity their social resources could be flooded away.

The system of credit was unknown to them. Those who have, share their grain with others who do not have them. It was not expected that those who had taken grain should treat it as a credit and return it. These days, it is not necessary the neighbours help one another even if it is known that there is hunger and starvation at the next door. Unlike in the past, if the neighbour is found starving, as there is the possibility of them approaching for credit, even normal social relations are suspended with them. The poorer they become the thinner becomes the community bond as it becomes economically unviable to maintain good relationships. With the gradual depletion of the social resource, their health condition has come at stake. Another argument put forward was, it was not food alone but the socially shattered status of the community as a whole that contributed to their ill health. The underlying theme of their discussion was that a community that has been psychologically pushed to depression, despite the provision of food material, would remain ill.

A participant stated in his presentation:

> One thing I have clearly understood is that the health issue is not just an issue of giving medicine for diseases. I understood from the *praxis* that, problem of health is problem of nutrition, problem of agriculture practices, problem of mental status, problem of arrack menace…It is often stated that if there are more hospitals, and more beds in the hospitals, it shows better health facility available. It is good to have the health facilities, but it signals the status of ill health if the beds in the hospitals are always full. We can say that we are healthy only if hospitals find it difficult to get patients. …

The participants could travel a long way from the taken for granted assumption that health has something to do with medical institutions to linking their health situation to the history of disempowerment, land alienation, decline of agriculture, drying up of *uravus*, consumption of ground water from the bore well, pollution of their water sources, growing alcoholism and so on. A better living for most of them is to live healthily with adequate food and to have trustworthy people around. They understand that Attappady has sufficient resources to keep people healthy with adequate food. With the inflow of settlers trustworthiness had gone resulted in the deprivation of food, nutrition and consequently the loss of health.

---

114   Attappady Block Panchayat, Development Report (2002-2007) 2002 : 94-9.

115   See the Government 'Order' issuing 'guidelines' for implementation of "Tribal Sub Plan" under its 'decentralised planning.' Government of Kerala, Planning and Economic Affairs Department, G.O. (MS) No 54/2003, Dated 31 may 2003: 3; Government of Kerala, Status of Panchayat raj in Kerala, Feb. 2000. Annexure-II. Section XII.

116   World bank too equates health to medical infrastructure and recommends cut in the government expenditure on health and promote corporatization (or 'public private partnership') of health infrastructure.[Alternative committee of International Forum on Globalisation, 2002: 7-9; World Development Report, 2003; Centre for Democracy and Governance, 2000: 13]

117   There exists a ban of liquor on any sort from local toddy to imported liquor at Attappady. A few kilometres away except arrack, all other forms of liquor are available. The claimed objective of ban on arrack was to save the tribal families from liquor menace. According to the participants of the programme, contrary to the objective, local arrack production and smuggling of arrack into Attappady became more profitable and hence the consumption of arrack has increased many a fold.

On the contrary, the scholars, bureaucrats, the local bodies of governance, and the 'world organisations' link their health situation to "health insurance" 'cleanliness'[114] "poor access to health care," "management of dispensaries and primary health centres," "sanitation," [115] practice of indigenous medicine, commercial health infrastructure and the 'public-private partnership' of medical infrastructure.[116]

There was also a discussion of why people consume so much of arrack than the previous generations. One reason they found was its availability. Ironically, its availability has been increased after the government ban on arrack[117], toddy, and other forms of liquor at *Attappady*. As it is more profitable than many other forms of labour, many are involved in the production of arrack. As it is over produced, the sellers keep their business live by supplying them at the households. This has increased the consumption. Even children are addicted to alcohol. It is not an unusual sight at Attappady that children about ten years old swacked by arrack. About this, the participants note:

"Arrack was never a menace as it is today. Today arrack reaches every household and hence even women and children drink. One need not go to the shop to buy them. This is the consequence of arrack ban at Attappady by the government. Earlier the *moopans* were not seen in drunken status. Now arrack reaches the *moopan's* house. *Moopans* too drink and fight in the streets; hence, they have lost respect and thereby control. After drinking, men and women fight at every home. Today, arrack has been so much habituated so that without it people do not even dance at death rituals. This has made the rituals less genuine. More over, because of arrack, people die young and hence they are struggling to live alone. As everybody has become indifferent to everybody else everybody suffers. They decided to handle the arrack menace collectively."

"In my *ooru,* I have called a meeting to discuss on the arrack menace, there was a discussion on why at all we drink, for that the people said they drink for various reasons such as 1. to get rid of fatigue, 2. to get rid of ill feelings and depression of their family issues 3. to get courage and talk at the face of the others 4. to get rid of body pains and also because 5. it had become a habit."

"It is a place of *ganja[118]*, arrack and sexual exploitation. About eight children are regular *ganja* users here. Even children drink arrack. We can always see men and women fighting with each other. There is no peace in families."

"Arrack came only during late 1970's. In 1970s we learnt to make arrack out of *Velam Patta.*"

"Today, throughout the day people drink arrack. Above half of the *ooru* is addicted to arrack; arrack is distilled here at the *ooru* itself. The *moopan,* who should question this, himself distils arrack. Since many make arrack, there is competition among the people in selling them at the lowest price, with the highest intoxication."

"Today, in almost half of the households people distil arrack. Even children of seven smoke *beedies* and drink arrack"

"If *Adivasis* learn to live without the arrack, and if they get proper environment to study and learn and live, *adivasis* would be definitely having a better life than the *vandavasi*s"

"Arrack was distilled and sold here in plenty. One day some members of a political party, with the help of *ooru* members destroyed all the tools utensils used for arrack distillation and stopped arrack menace. However, it is the same party men, who were instrumental in stopping arrack, produce arrack and sell them. Their party people know it. Nevertheless, when their party people do it they do not question it. This is how politics work in my *ooru.* ... there should be politics, but, people should

---

[118]   A narcotic plant.

not be made scapegoats of party politics"

"... women were not much introduced to liquor when there were arrack shops in the *oorus*. Arrack prohibition had been casual to the serving of arrack directly at the households, which introduces even the small children to drinking habit. Even little ones drink arrack"

The participants shared their experience of their struggle to make their hamlets alcohol free. An incident reported by a participant shows his perseverance and continued effort to bring an end to the arrack business at his hamlet:

I am the president of *Iswarya* Club. There is another youth club functioning here. Its name is *Thapasya*. Both the clubs joined to gather to call for action against arrack menace. The sellers of arrack were told not to sell arrack at the *ooru*. The sellers did not heed to our request. To catch hold of the liqueur seller red-handed, I gave ten rupees to a person instructing him to buy arrack. When he was buying, we went there and destroyed one litter of arrack. We searched for further arrack and found ½ litter. We poured the arrack on the road and warned them to stop the business at the *ooru*. We have given complaints at the police station and excise officials. Though the police came and taken the sample of arrack to the police station, no action was followed; the arrack business was going on as usual. We complained against the police inaction to the Superintendent of Police. After that, the police came and taken the woman responsible for that to the police station, she was warned and sent back to the *ooru*. Now the arrack menace is under control.

The participants have observed that other than arrack a major problem affecting their lives is poor food consumption. The poor food consumption is not an isolated issue. It is linked to the fact that the *adivasis* are not having food grains in their granaries. Their granaries were empty, for their lands were unused. Their lands were unused because their lands are usually in the slopes and it does not yield. Even if it yields, the animals like wild bore, or elephants destroy their crop. A participant during the discussion of the present day poor land utilisation pointed out:

> ...Maize was there right from the beginning. *Pandi, ragi* and millet came latter. Earlier, many *adivasis* lived inside the forest...we were not cultivating in the same land for years. We were cultivating in a land only for two to three consecutive years. Then we search for new land. We fell trees, cleared land and converted the land into a *kotthukadu*. Our agriculture was rain fed....later the forest department and the government became the owner of the forestland and restricted the shifting cultivation.... The lands in the slope are not suitable for permanent cultivation. As we were prevented from seeking new lands for cultivation, the traditional agriculture practice came to a halt. As the possibility of growing food crops dwindled, we were left with the only choice of working in the settler's land as the labourers. ... We had to go out in search of work.... Earlier, there were no hotels in Attappady...hotels came here only after we became labourers... With the coming of hotels, we were introduced tea, *parotta*[119] and beef. ....We did not know the value of land and its documentation procedures. Making use of this ignorance the settlers cheated and taken away our land.

One participant observed that people do not work on their land expecting it to yield rather they want immediate money they earn from their labour:

> *Adivasis* who once lived a simple and collective life now are suffering from starvation, poverty and suicidal tendencies. *Ragi* and millet have to be cultivated like earlier times for their survival. Each and everyone should be

---

119   A staple food item made of refined wheat.

prepared for this. The inhabitants of my *ooru* say that they are getting prepared for this.

Nowadays people are not willing to put in hard work. They do not think of working in the land and cultivating. Working in the field takes long time in yielding returns. People want money immediately at hand. Working as a wage labourer gives them money to be spent for the immediate purposes. Once they get their wages, it is just squandered away. They are not bothered about the coming generations. If this continues, our family and the inhabitants of Attappady will die soon. There is no water. Although educated they cannot find jobs. If this continues, they will die without any kind of existence.

A participant observed that it is not the presence of wild elephants that pose problem for their agriculture, as the elephants were always there. Elephants have their own fixed path to travel. When fences block their path, they take different routes and it results in destruction of crops. Individual property owners, especially the settlers fence their landed property; the AHADS project also fenced the land at various places without giving due consideration of the elephant paths. A participant expressed the issue:

> The Wild elephants were always there. In the past, they had enough food and water in the forest. Their path was not broken. These days, individual farmers, mainly the *vandavasi*s[120] fence their land. The AHADS[121] project people also build fences everywhere. The elephants have less food in the forest and their traditional

---

120   Outside settlers.

121   Attappady Hills Area Development Society, Attappady.

122   Raja means King.

paths are fenced. Therefore, they take different routes. They destroy our crops when they pass through our field. It is a tradition here that we do not curse elephants even though they destroy our crop. We call them Raja[122]....They trouble us only when we trouble them. To sum up, we are unable to cultivate as some others trouble the elephants.

Some participants countered the observation made by some others that the *adivasis* think only of the immediate present and they were unwilling to work hard. A participant pointed out:

The *adivasis* were hard workers; we were slashing and burning, hunting… Nowadays we are not willing to work hard…. Today, work means earn money for survival… what is that we can aspire? We cannot work in our land because it does not yield…. All that we can do is work for others. Per month, we get about ten works. … With this, nothing more can be earned or saved… When the present is just a hand-to-mouth survival, it is not easy for us to save for the future. When we are busily involved with hardships of survival, we can think only more about the present…. This is the reason why the wages we get from labour is squandered away …education is not a guarantee for jobs…our water sources are drying up…our land does not yield… This being our condition, I do not know how long we will be on the earth.

The agriculture of the past is contrasted with that of the present by most of the participants. Field notes also contain sufficient references about the condition of the present day practice of agriculture and the nature of difficulties they had to face while carrying out that practice. A participant observes:

Twenty years back whatever was cultivated on this land gave very good yield. Now it is time of chemical fertilizers. There is a reason for that. With the coming of the migrants, chemical fertilizers began to be used in plenty. When they spray fertilizers and pesticides in their land pest would move to land that has not applied the same. Then, we have no other choice but to use the same in our land also. Certainly, the intensive use of fertilizers became a common practice here only by the last 15 years.

To guide the participants to undertake their ventures of agriculture practices there was a session with an expert in agriculture science. In that session the agricultural practices that could be suitable for them was discussed. The difference between high input commercial agriculture and low input traditional subsistence agriculture was highlighted in the session and the suitability of low input sustainable practice of agriculture was discussed in detail. It was suggested in the discussion that Attappady is a draught prone area and hence it is better suited for low input agriculture. Further, it was insisted that the traditional crops grown with low irrigation input could be preferred for their higher nutritional value. It was pointed out that another important aspect to be considered in choosing an agriculture practice is the nature and texture of soil and the slope of the land. It was emphasised that any agriculture practice that would accelerate soil erosion has to be suspended at Attappady, as that would make the land infertile in the long run. The participants were also introduced to the practices of research that they could participatorily carry on.

Following the discussions, there were classroom sessions on legal aspects of women's rights over their property, and there was a session further deepening their research in tracking the *adivasi* history. After a dialogical session on history, the participants were introduced to the ecological history of Attappady.

An eminent ecologist delivered the lecture on the ecological history of Attapady[123]. In his presentation, aided by slide shows, about 350 of them, the EE traced the gradual ecological destruction of Attappady in the past 30 years. There were pictures of dense forests in the locations where today one finds barren land. There were pictures showing trees capturing moist from the air and passing it to soil; pictures depicting forests being set on fire to clear of the lands; pictures showing drying up of the catchments areas of rivers; pictures of a river (*varagar*) that was running live till recent times and has become dried up completely; pictures of extinct species of fishes in the river *BHAVANI*; pictures capturing the traditional agriculture practices of the *adivasis*; pictures showing sites destroyed by development projects and their construction activities and so on. The participants thoroughly engaged in the discussion followed. They could well engage in the discussion, because most of the places shown in the picture were familiar to them. More over they could see what the hamlet people were telling them regarding greenery that existed until the recent past. The session continued the whole day and the day after. The presentation brought out the futility and shallowness of 'development' thinking and practice.

There were also presentations made by resource persons who believed strongly in the efficacy and value of development projects. However the arguments from the 'developmentalist' perspectives did not appeal to the participants. It was felt that the

---

[123]   Dr. Sathish Chandran Nair.

development projects were mostly projects of raising concrete structures. The participants thought that the development projects just achieve their target of spending the allotted money rather than aim at the well-being of the *adivasis*.

The PUPs felt they were not successful in bringing the participant round to appreciating gender issues. A few examples would suffice to show the failure. Initially there was a lecture on gender relations in the classroom. In that lecture, it was mentioned that women should not think that any of the activities humans perform should be regarded as gendered. An example cited was, men climb trees so also can women; woman cook so also can men; women bring water for household purposes so also can men and so on. There were suggestions that discrimination against women should be resisted; women need not always be obliging and so on. These remarks apparently made no impact on *adivasi* women participants. Nevertheless, upon this their visit to Attappady for fieldworks the PUPs knew why. What they witnessed was the sight of a woman RAP fast climbing a tree in front of their eyes with no sense of hesitation to pluck some fruits for them. Expecting the woman to be docile is not as acute among *adivasis* as it is among the 'mainstream.' The PUPs have now come around to appreciate that there is a sense of non-difference between men and women of their present concern. The classroom lectures on gender relations seemed misfired because of its mainstream biases and poor understanding of the *adivasi* gender issues. Perhaps, different set of parameters needs to be considered. Problems certainly there were in gender relations among the *adivasis* but that did not come to light with the prevailing methodology. To accompany the woman participants in helping them to care themselves, the PUPs required a deeper understanding. The lectures delivered presumed that there would be heavy socialising content among the *adivasis* pertaining to their gender relations as it is the case with the 'mainstream'. The results of the fieldwork disagree with the premise. It appeared that the issue to be addressed is not dismantling the patriarchic socialisation content and its banes; rather it is the individualisation breeding indifference in the absence of strong institutions of socialisation. The appropriate approach the PUPs felt would be focusing on rebuilding *social resources* towards *trans-gendering* indicated in their mythical narrations of *ena*. The PUPs regretted that the realisation came late as the project had already passed half way through. The PUPs felt there should be an exclusive *praxis* intervention project on gender relations among *adivasis*. To handle the gender issue sensibly, two women resource[124] persons were invited to stay with them and learn their issues. The resource persons stayed with them during their classroom sessions and found that the trans-gendering phenomenon is more suitable than the narrow gender politics with a mainstream middle class bias. The politics of *trans-gendering*, the PUPs felt, is the politics of care characterised by attention, alertness, caution, judicious self reflexivity, self patrol, self defence, accompaniment and reinstatement of sensibilities [Ahmed 2005: 18,19]. Most of the discussion on gender held outside the classroom at a personal level. In the classroom only certain aspects of the obvious gender bias came up for discussion. In general, the message on gender relation delivered was that the historical trajectories and biographical trajectories one has gone through might have consolidated some perceptions on one's own

---

[124]   Ms. P.V. Shobha and Adv. Vijayamma

gender or that of the other. The NAPs as resource persons might have been subjected to the process of internalising the gender perceptions that were prevalent among the *vandavasi*s. All the thoughts sedimented on gender relations should be reflexively reconsidered. What is important is not one gender struggling against the other or any of one group consolidating their own gender bias rather one has to throw away the settled gender identities and look for humane relationships with one another. The message delivered amid towards diluting gender identities. This message obviously appealed to the minds of the participants. The reference to gender relations as it appeared in their field diary reveals the impact of the approach:

> "Earlier, I never used to do the household jobs. I was expecting the women in my family, should do these jobs. Now I do not expect women alone to do the entire household works. Now, I do several of the household works. This change happened because of my learning from the project."

> "The difference, between men and women, is only in their body. It is only a sexual difference. One can give birth to a child and the other cannot. Other than this difference, they are just human beings like men. Unfortunately, the misunderstanding of this difference creates problems between them. It culminates in a situation the women have no freedom for mobility and no decisive role in decision-making. At the same time, men have more freedom, better status in the society, more opportunities, and more power. With this, the men dominate women, and they think the women are their property."

"The training had helped me to understand my family members and my wife better. Now a days, I do not get angry with my wife. These days I help her in her family work, I look after my children."

A woman participant writes: I do not respect men more than I respect women. From the *praxis* intervention project, I learnt that many differences between men and women are just creations of our imagination…. We should understand that whether it is man or women, they are just 'fellow beings.'

The final day of the fifth phase had group discussions regarding their forthcoming fieldwork phase. They decided after the discussion to deepen the field actions they have already started. They also decided to explore ecological issues, undertaking experiments in agriculture, explore new opportunities in agriculture and food cultivation, deepen their understanding on the women's social life and labour life, and to explore what people think about 'development'.

The fieldwork conducted on the fourth phase and the classroom discussion of the fifth phase had helped the participants to come in terms with the issues affecting their health. They could relate that the unfriendly social set up, ecological degradation, poor quality of drinking water available, decline of their agricultural practices, excessive consumption of arrack, and their overall poverty condition, provides a fertile ground for ill health. This realisation is different from the attitude of treating ill health as bad luck or as something that can be handled by consumption of tablets or with the establishment of hospitals. This realisation did not merely make them more informed but went long way through their psyche by informing their action such as expanding their area of cultivation, preserving their water sources, and also starting their struggle against the arrack menace.

Phase VI: Deepening the Social Action

When they entered the sixth phase of the project, the participants had to face a difficult situation. Of the 15 elected representatives took part in the project 12 belonged tom the political party coalition that was ruling the state. The government of Kerala for some reason decided to divert the River *Bhavani* that runs through the *adivasi* concentrated eastern Attappady to Tamilnadu westward. The participants had the circular issued by the government to divert the river westward towards Mannarkad of Palakkad district in the pretext of supplying water for irrigation purpose. The circular issued by the irrigation department, instead of mentioning the name of the river to be diverted, made an indefinite remark about 'the diversion of a *stream* near Mukkali forest office'. As the only stream present there was the river *Bhavani*, the participants could make out that it was a plan to divert the river. There were suspicions in the minds of the people that contrary to what was stated as the intention of the diversification of the river i.e., for the irrigation purpose, it may turn out to be part of a plan to develop infrastructure at the public expense for a private hydel power company to be set up in the future. The Eastern Attappady was already facing severe draught and drying up of *uravus*, whereas the area towards which the water is planned to be diverted is already blessed with water sufficient for irrigating fields. The RAPs brought a copy of the circular to a meeting held at the fieldwork workshop at Attappady. They felt that it would make the eastern Attappady drier. They decided they should study more about it. As they demanded, another workshop was held at Attappady with the participation of ecologists and geographers analysing the implications of the circular. By that time, as the government unusually speeded up the project work of digging canals for the diversion, it became visible that it was the *BHAVANI* river that is going to be diverted. The participants resolved to register their protest. In order to show their protest, first they printed a notice collectively raising their voice against the project and distributed copies everywhere in Attapaddy. For the local people this came as a surprise for, the people belonging to the ruling party coalition were coming up against a government project. The panchayats of Agali and Pudur passed resolution against the diversion of the river. The eastern Attappady shares its border with Tamilnadu and the people speak Tamil. It also had settlers from Tamilnadu. The farmers of this place too joined the struggle initiated by the *praxis* participants. Unfortunately, the media and political parties interpreted this as a 'Tamil' struggle favouring Tamilnadu. The supporters of the project belonging to the ruling party coalition unleashed statements of hatred against the Tamilnadu government and the Tamil minority living at Attappady and spread *Malayali* chauvinism everywhere. With the messages of *Malayali* chauvinism spread, there were uneasy tensions at Attappady. The Participants had to give up their struggle as they were pressurised to do so by their respective parties. The participants (belonging to the ruling coalition party) however remained unhappy over the diversion. The incident showed them how powerless even the elected representatives could be in solving the real issues affecting their people. The incident hurt the non-politician participants of the project, as they felt internally disturbed about the behaviour and performance of the politician participants of the ruling coalition. It came as a relief to all when the Supreme Court intervened and stopped the state government from diverting the river westward.

As part of field visit, the PUPs went to various locations where the *praxis* intervention actions were initiated. Everywhere they went they could witness people busy with their newly begun agriculture activities. One could witness people engaging in traditional agriculture practice of cultivating 13 different varieties of millets, pulses, and leafy vegetables. Participants who kept usually silent during the sessions were now turned to be most successful in motivating people at their hamlet into cultivation. There was a woman participant who kept quiet in the classroom and was unassuming. The PUPs thought that she might be equally silent in her fieldwork too. For some reason she did not turn up for the fieldwork workshop held at Attappady. The PUPs decided to undertake their field visit to her location along with the RAPs present there. She was there at her home. She told them that she could not come because of some personal commitments. She accompanied them to her field location. The PUPs were surprised to see that she could motivate the entire hamlet to engage in the cultivation of rain-fed traditional crops such as *ragi*, *cholam* and some leguminous food crop. It was surprising because, in the classroom she never reported that she was successful in motivating her people in cultivating food crops. She also said that she never strained herself in motivating the people around her to cultivate them. Rather what she was doing was just talking to the people casually the importance of having food storage at home, as she has learnt from the classroom discussions. She also set a model by cultivating them. She was just having discussions and dialogues with them, what she was saying appealed to their reason. Somehow, the information spread from mouth-to-mouth that it would be good if they have the food grains stored at their households. The modest, mild, yet effective social care work of the participant is typical of the *praxis* intervention one witnesses in the field locations. It had an impact not only in the hamlets where the fieldwork was done but also in the neighbouring hamlets. Even the elected representatives who had given up cultivation due to their full-time political career had started cultivation.

For the PUPs, it was distressing to know that the political parties could dare to spread communal tensions for achieving their (party) political ends. However, for the RAPs the incident was a revelation in the sense that it exposed the weakness of the party based formal politics especially when it comes to address the real issues of the people. However, the incident was a moment of realising that their genuine concerns are of little value to the formal political systems. Nevertheless, the fieldwork proved to be hopeful as one could see that the concern for nutrition and health coming out of the participant's research had been given a serious listening and motivated collective action.

Phase VII: Reflexion and Evaluation

After the fieldwork, the participants returned once again to engage in the classroom sessions. It was already six months since the project started. The participants have come to share their experience in the fieldwork. Further fieldwork had reinforced their learning in the earlier phases. This time they have spent most of their time in explaining to the hamlet people what they have learnt from their research

In the earlier phase N's comment that they should be more careful in their studies and report because it is easily possible that their bias towards one or against other could lead them to arrive at wrong conclusions. N was pleading with them that they should not be compromising on collecting supporting evidences for their statements. This time when they came to the classroom after their fieldwork, the participant, who argued the most with N that their study was based on facts came to the classroom with photographs meant to substantiate his statements. He informed the classroom with the newly found evidence that the soil erosion has increased as the shrubs and bushy plants of the hill slopes were removed. He had taken the photograph of a slope cleared off by the AHADS before and after rainfall and the muddy water of the river beneath the slope after a rainfall to show the evidence for what he found. Similarly, to prove the point that the people of a family living in the forest cultivating for themselves traditional crops are better-off nutritionally, he presented the case study of a family of five members, where four work as labourers with no food crop cultivation for themselves are less secured and starving than a neighbouring family of six members all involved in their own agriculture practice and food grain at their home. He systematically presented the income, expenditure and asset in these two families and stated the *adivasis* who work for others as labourers go downtown daily in search of labour but often come home empty handed not finding any work. He was also producing the evidence, even in case of finding work, they end up spending more money on travel, food and arrack compared to the neighbouring family that concentrates on producing their own food. He was also citing the narrations of the family members as evidences that those who mostly work as family for their own food security are leading more peaceful familial life than the family that was reluctant to work on their own land. This incident demonstrated two things: one, with how much seriousness the research participants took the classroom lectures and discussions; two, responsible research is an attitude, which many people are capable of having without much formal training in academics.

During their fieldwork, they verified the working time and kind of works women and men do. It was obvious from their field study that the women were working more than the men as they have the burden of looking after the family including the younger ones and go out to work as labourers. The result of the study was on the expected line, but it could help them to drive away the taken for granted biases that, men work more and harder than women do. Besides, they also realised that most of the families survive with the money earned by women, even though, the women are paid only Rs. 40-60 a day whereas men's wage is about Rs. 80-120. They compared the work pattern of today's *adivasi* women with that of a few years before and found out that as time went on the workloads of women only increased. They have observed that earlier the division of labour between women and men was not as sharp as it is today. Both men and women were sharing household jobs as well as food gathering and cultivation. They also observed that even in the past women were more burdened with work than men were.

Their presentations were followed by a dialogical session reinforcing the *trans-gendering* argument. The participants were told that they should be careful not to be frozen into the ideas of identities such as gender identity or *adivasi* identity and struggle forward against all the life situations forced on them historically.

The participants were introduced to the idea of social space, the space within which they have to find their way forward with a proper awareness of the field within which they were operating and their position within the space. It was also explained how people symbolically construct their position within the social space.

The next day started with a presentation on informing about various central and state government agencies and projects with their objectives and about the means to make use of the opportunities offered by them. Following the lecture session there was a group discussion on how they could make use of the learning from the *Praxis* intervention in improving decentralised planning initiatives. The participants said that they had a wonderful opportunity to understand the decentralised planning and they have already started using the vision and confidence they have gained from the programme. They said that this time the development report produced by them would be of a better quality than that of the previous year. They requested that one of the faculty to visit them to perfect their planning process. They said that they would bring to the notice of the government that whenever any assistance is given to agriculture it is only for the mainstream crops and not the one they cultivate. Tools and implements supplied by the government are of the type usable only in the mainland and not useful on the hilly slopes. The participants made their voice heard at the appropriate centres, and they met with an initial success of gaining the government's attention. The Government order issued later in fact reflected their concerns. The government order regarding 'tribal development' issued on May 31st 2003 had thus observed:

> 4.1 The following development priorities are to be followed while preparing the plan:
>
> (i) Putting to optimum use the existing land in the possession of tribals preferably through organic agriculture giving priority to locally relevant crops as decided by the tribal farmers… [GOK, 2003:3]

The document also recognized the:

> Importance to understanding of the development situation by the tribal people themselves through a process of analysis, reflection and action to come out of the existing plight, realized in a framework for participatory planning from the grassroots. [GOK 2003: 4]

Their observation on the formal party politics was most revealing. Formal politics has been seen by the participants, including those who are part of political parties, as the major reason for the breaking up of the community life. They pointed out that with the advent of party politics, the *'neethi'* of community came to naught. Formal politics with the 'development' is seen as an outsider agenda thrust on them.

There was a debate in the classroom between the politician and the non-politician participants, in which the non-politician members challenged the morality of the politicians. For that, a representative from the politicians replied as follows:

> You people accuse us because you do not know what happens in the party politics. In politics, we have less freedom to do anything. We are

like the bonded labourers of the party we are representing. We do not have much freedom. Discriminating the *adivasis* is more in the politics than it is anywhere. The party never listens to us, but they always want us to listen to them. All that we are doing is according to the direction of the party persons senior to us. We are directed to speak certain things and not something else. We can speak only what we are told while approaching the voters. Only the hands that we hold and the body that walks are ours; the voice is somebody else's. After winning the elections, we have to carry out what is taught to us by the party. We are always reminded that it is with the party label we have won and expected to be loyal to it. With the *adivasis,* more loyalty is expected. It is in their service we divide *oorus* on party line. We have no voice.

A newly elected member said,

When I first stood for the election, during the campaign I could see "people." I thought I could do something good for the "people." I won, and even became the president of a Panchayat. After winning, I could never see "people"; I could see only individuals coming for their jobs done. "people" vanishing after the election is a new experience and a surprise for me.

The unhappiness of the politicians as well as the non-politicians over the formal politics irrespective of their party affiliation was obvious, in the classroom discussions. The party politics in fact operating as 'de-politicising machine' little relevant to the 'life politics' of the people has been resented in their discussion. It is well understood by the participating politicians and the other participants that the formal party politics is a vocational activity centrally managed.

The argument posed in fact holds us back to think whether the formal politics has any politics of the people it claims to represent. As Marx and, later Weber noticed, politics in its formal system of party politics could only produce a political bureaucracy and a self serving political class guarding itself by guarding the statues quo [Marx 1977; Weber 1994b; Heller 1991: 331]. The practical circumstance under which the formal politics is located, in other words the *habitat*[125] of formal politics, seems to have a compulsion to be "un-utopian" and playing its "life Politics" of immediacy with less scope for the people concerned to imagine and build their own world accordingly. It appears, in that strange world not everybody's *habitat* is equally uncertain, chaotic, ambivalent and non-determinable. While the formal politics seen from the context of the marginalized people and their formally elected representatives is uncertain, chaotic and ambivalent, the very formal politics is used as a structurating tool that conditions the lives of the people from a far away political space. From the remote controlling centres, whether they are persons or institutions, (institutions like economic and commercial systems, institutions of governance and administration, organised bodies like multinational corporations, persons or abstract ideologies - like the ideologies of neo-liberalism) the structuring institutions' habitat stands on a firmer ground than the structured institutions or persons.

---

125   The concept of habitat is explained by Bauman as a 'complex system', a term derived from mathematics which suggests firstly, that the system is unpredictable and secondly, that it is not controlled by forces outside of the control of the human agents that operate with it. There are no goal setting, managing or co-ordinating institutions within the complex system; this makes constraint fall to an absolute minimum. Therefore, the human agents or any other element cannot be discussed by reference to its functionality or dysfunctionality; and no one agency can determine the activity of any other agent. Although, Bauman explains that: " ..the postmodern eye (that is, the modern eye liberated from modern fears and inhibitions) views difference with zest and glee: difference is beautiful and no less good for that." [Bauman 2002 :354].

There were also discussions on 'development' at Attappady. The participants in fact had a good opportunity to witness the 'development' effort by the government in the instance of diverting the east flowing river westward. Some of the observations they got from their fieldwork on development were:

"I asked nanchi *moopathi* to tell me what is progress. Without hesitating she answered, 'Progress came through ration shops. It came through the free ration of wheat. We saw wheat for the first time through ration shops. Progress is using aluminium vassals, plastic items and so on. Progress was brought here by the *Kurumba Girijan* society"

"With settlers 'development' also came. It has come through the introduction of political parties."

"Our community cannot be developed by the government or any others. Only we can help ourselves"

"Development Projects are not for betterment of life situation; they are there to spend money allotted for certain purposes."

"Development is not just hospitals, schools and roads. It is something to do with the well-being of the people, health, practical knowledge, freedom of movement. The development projects at Attapady were doing something else which is not relevant to the well-being of the people."

"Development was first brought to Pudur by Muthu Gounder as he cut the *Moolakombu* road to take away timber from the forest....and also through the construction of the *Chavadiyoor* Bridge, which was also constructed for timber transportation."

"The 'development' had entered Jellippara with the widening of the *Kakku Palayam Jellippara* footpath into a road."

The quotations commenting development presented here is neither said nor written sarcastically. It is the casual representation of the 'development' by the people in the hamlets. The 'development' is sensed as something that comes from outside along with settlers, government institutions and with the market.

A participant critically analyses in his field journal:

> "The 'development' came through the introduction of money. It is not just the 'development,' but also our land alienation could be linked to the onset of money economy… It was only after the intervention of the government the need for money has come…now all the forms of cultivation have declined and only the wage labour remains…we had to lease out our land for money … Since money has become the medium of exchange all necessities were managed through money earned by selling grains… It was not easy to get wages everyday. In those days wood, timber, bamboo from the forest were cut and taken to the shops in exchange for money…To overcome contingencies we had to sell cattle we were growing…money thus got was spent for buying food and liquor…"

With the narration of the experience of a ginger cultivator, Kakki, a participant tries to explicate the ways in which the 'development projects' disturbed them:

> The government gave everyone a loan to cultivate ginger the next year. I had a quintal of ginger seeds with me. I got 2.5 quintals of Ginger seeds from the agriculture department. … I sow 3.5 quintal of ginger… Since, the ginger seeds I got from the department were of very poor quality, the yield was also very poor … It is not just yield, something happened to my land so that Ginger does not grow there any more even with better seeds…This is what happens if we depend on the government.

A participant reflecting her 'development' experience with an *anganwadi* (Pre-nursery childcare centre) writes:

I went to the *anganwadi* as part of my fieldwork. There were 15 children...the teacher said, "We were giving eggs to the children three months before. Now the scheme is stopped. Later there was a scheme to provide milk. However, that scheme is not useful for the children here. Milk is only for the children below three years old. Here there are no children below three years old...I thought it is better there are no children below three years. If there were children below three, they would be getting milk; whereas the older children would not be getting it. How can we do this?

She narrates another development experience in the following words:

Today some doctors and other staff came here to the *ooru*. There were two doctors and seven other staff. They examined the people free of cost. They gave free medicines. They had brought used cloth to be distributed. There were some good cloths. There were completely useless and torn cloths too. I felt sorry... our people just laugh at the cloth distributed. Why do these people come here with torn cloths? They should not insult us with these 'services'...

In their studies, they took care to be self-critical. They were critical of their past agricultural practices as these were not without the elements of exploitation. For example, they could notice the exploitative side of *kambalam*. They were not just self-critical, they were also critical of the lack of '*neethi*' and '*neri*' in the modern agriculture practices. When they were asked to study agriculture practices, they were careful enough to incorporate, the aspects of food, nutrition, ecological balance, health and their relatedness. The participants could look at things in its complexity. This was a surprise for the PUPs. The PUPs' surprise over the capability the RAPs evinced for perceiving things in its complexity was due to the former's prejudice about the latter's calibre. They could relate degradation of ecology, decline of traditional agriculture, impoverishment of their nutrition, their new status of labour, its impact on familial relationship, the decline of local community governance all in a single networked mutually reinforcing factors of impoverishment.

For the PUPs it was a new learning, as they could now see that the *adivasi* way of doing agriculture is not "less advanced" rather it is a practice that was followed with a deep-seated ethical character that constituted their *habitus*. The talks with the research participants, their presentations and fieldwork reports had the extra ordinary effect of a reversed *praxis* intervention for the PUPs; for this removed some of the latter's biases evidently. The *adivasi* conceptions of time, space, land, water, natural resources and work are far divergent from that of the mainstream. The important lesson for the PUPs was that the *adivasis* have their own understandings of things. PUPs seemed to overlook what the *adivasis* have. PUPs had no inkling about whether the *adivasis* were consciously /intentionally practising *neethi* or not. Before the *praxis* intervention, PUPs maintained that the *adivasis* are less advanced because the latter is ignorant. The *Praxis* intervention revealed to PUPs that they were on the contrary ignorant of the logics of the *adivasis'* thoughts and actions. Had their sense of *neethi* not been with understanding or discerning, there would not have been the mythologies referring to them. However, the logic of their practice, which they have culturally imbibed and preserved through mythologies, is ruthlessly destroyed by the mainstream that implodes into their life with no choices left.

On the final day of the project, the participants sit together to evaluate the project. In that meeting the participants made the following observations:

> "*Praxis* intervention is a process of developing our critical ability, trying to understand things in a new perspective, and we becoming aware of ourselves and our surroundings…"

> "In this training, everything was upside down. Usually the trainers teach us. Here, we were doing research and teaching our teachers."

"It is always the case somebody from outside teaches us on what we should do. They are so confident that we do not know anything. This is for the first time I have witnessed a training programme that was based on the information and knowledge collected by the *adivasis* from the *adivasis* is used to train the *adivasis*."

"The *praxis* intervention project helped me to learn our history, social formation, life of the *adivasi* individuals, issues concerning ownership and use of land, law, institutions, and the meaning of living socially… not only my self but also my family members are happy because I have become more considerate person than before… I have no formal education. Here I learnt a lot. Now I do not feel that I have no education… *Praxis* Intervention is not teaching, it is learning, action, and becoming oneself a thinker… I enjoyed my fieldwork. I did not do my fieldwork alone. Many people at my *ooru* were with me…"

"I did not know what the *praxis* is. I could understand only after the first phase that it is a training programme with research and action content. From this, I could understand the resourcefulness and competence of our people. It is already too late that only now we understand that our people too are resourceful and wise. We should start using these resources. It is better to use the wisdom and abilities we have rather than to lose everything we have at out hand by trying to catch up with the settlers… This experience is very much helpful in transforming my own life… I did not even know the simple thing, that we will not go hungry if we cultivate food crops… It is with the *praxis* intervention training, I could start thinking in this direction…I think that we should re-create the cordiality and togetherness of the *adivasi* life … We should love our people…these days when I meet people, words just flow from my mouth…"

"Even though I am an *adivasi*, as I am brought up among the settlers I never showed interest in knowing my community. I did not even know my native language. I did not know our songs, our dances or our history. I thought the *adivasis* are of an inferior kind of people. With this opportunity I could closely mix with my people… in the classroom there were many opportunities to dance, sing and talk on our people, their history…this has changed me a lot. Within the six months I have learnt that I should be proud of being an *adivasi*…I have learnt something about our history; heard many stories of our past. I could contrast our past with our present… I could influence the *ooru* people to cultivate food crops. Many of us cultivate our traditional crops once again. With this, we have a small hope for survival…"

"Before the start of the *praxis* intervention, three persons from Kila met me. I took them to *ooru*s to conduct surveys. I was invited for a training programme in which the elected representative from Idukki, Wyanad and Attappady took part… At every stage, we were consulted of the training programme. Finally, Attappady was selected by consensus during a workshop of all elected representatives of the three districts. Never before I attended any training was organised with such seriousness…. In this training programme, we are not instructed to do this or that… Rather we are exposed to a new philosophy… we are trained in thinking, understanding, and acting based on our understanding… for me this training is like a dream becoming reality… I had received other trainings too. In 1992, I took part in a training programme organised by The Socio Religious Centre, Calicut. It was a weeklong training programme. I could learn from that programme that we should claim our "benefits from the Government welfare Programmes," "rights" etc. They taught the procedures of claiming these rights and benefits. Now I understood that claiming these rights and benefits alone are not sufficient… The life of the *adivasi* has become as dry as the rivers here… The minds of the *adivasis* too are drying up. Not just the rivers and *uravus,* but also the minds of the *adivasis* have to be revitalised… I had felt and learnt this only through the fieldwork and classroom reflection of this training…I was longing for this kind of knowledge. I had many unanswered questions in my mind. This training has helped me to find answers for such long-standing questions… I do not think that working with the *adivasi* community with the learning we had here is easy. There are stakes in the society. They are very strong. They will oppose any action that comes against their stakes.

The politics is functioning based on the vote bank system. Politicians of all hues will oppose a genuine work. I also belong to a party. There is limit to my actions too. I cannot come out of my party. If I do so, it will be difficult for me to survive. This is my mental struggle...I am from a family that has undergone many a tragedies and difficulties. As I got an opportunity to do fieldwork among our people, I could understand they too have their personal tragedies and difficulties. This has made me aware that I should do something to end these miseries....From this project, I have understood that I should not just remain a people's representative alone, but I should work as a representative of the *adivasis* too. My responsibility lies in speaking for the *adivasi's,* whose interests are hardly represented anywhere... I learnt the importance of a life of freedom with no place for greed."

"With this experience, I have got the fire and commitment... I think it should be spread everywhere."

At the end of the *praxis* intervention project, an evaluation sheet was distributed, in that a woman participant had written the following with a subtitle: *"Please read."* Her reflexive account throws light on the unintended ways in which a *praxis* intervention practice helped in solving personal problems:

In my life, ... I had never been happy. I could know of my life through the *praxis* intervention project. I did not even know to which group of tribe I belong. As I am from another community, the people in my locality maintained a distance. They treated me as an ignorant person. To them, I am an ignorant woman; I did not know anything about the *Kurumba* community. Second, I am living with my husband for the last five years. I could not conceive for these many years. I wanted to consult a doctor so that I can get treatment for our infertility problem. My husband was not willing to come to a doctor. He was afraid to consult a doctor. Somehow, I managed in taking him to the Bethany hospital at Anakatti[126]. The people in the hospital said to treat us we have to pay Rs 5,000/- the amount, which we never had. As I was not bearing a child, my mother-in-law was disappointed with me. I was always scolded and insulted. My husband was kind. He never blamed me for my inability to conceive. I decided to commit suicide if it becomes impossible for me to conceive. Then, I got the letter from KILA inviting me to the training programme. As I thought that going out might help me to relive my tension, I decided to take part in the training.

God never helps directly; He helps us only through people. This is what I believe. The same has happened to my life. There was a session on health at KILA. You have invited the Local doctor, Dr. Prabhu Das, who is the medical officer, the government dispensary, Pudur, to lecture us. When you came to Pudur for field visit, I was also there. You have introduced all of us to the Doctor. In fact, he was also remembering us. He was a kind person. I told him my problem of childlessness. He advised me to come to the primary health centre at Pudur with my husband. I felt happy. I took my husband to him. He gave us medicines. Now I am pregnant. I am so happy, that I do not find means to express my happiness. Not only that you have asked all of us to study about men, women, children, land, history, culture, rituals, myths, environment, man woman relations and everything about ourselves. That was a great blessing. All the sudden the world has become different to me. Now it happened that I know more about my community than most of the people there. My husband was helping me in my fieldwork. My mother-in-law is happy about me these days for two reasons. One

---

126   Anakkatty is a place in the Attappady Block bordering Tamilnadu.

reason is that I am pregnant and second I know a lot about the community. In addition, the entire *ooru* is good to me as I am working for them, organising them, and talking to them on their own welfare. I never expected things would workout in such a way. Today, my life is completely changed. My life is changed upside down.

By the time the *praxis* intervention project ended, the participant researchers could realise that there is essentially nothing innate about their *adivasiness.* According to the data they have collected from their elders who could tell them what they have learnt from their ancestors they are migrants from Tamilnadu and Karnataka and called the *adivasis* only because they were the earlier settlers. According to them, their culture has become different from that of the mainstream Tamilnadu, Karnataka or Kerala only because of long years of seclusion from them. It was not difficult for them to understand that over a period their views about everything were changing. They learnt that their idea of marital relationship, community life, family life, celibacy, food, agriculture, religion, god, work, money, wealth, time, space, dress, education, politics etc., are going under drastic changes for the last few decades. This realisation has helped them to de-essentialise their identity. In the classroom, once they asked,

Who in the world are not the *adivasis?* We did not come to this world earlier than any other communities neither anybody among humans came earlier to us. In a sense, everybody is an *adivasi.* Nobody came to the world in the middle or in the end.

To ask such questions they should have gone deep under reflections.

It was the penultimate day of the *praxis* intervention programme. By eight o clock in the evening, the project ended. They were learning together for six months. They all were attached to one another and they were very much fond of the faculty who were guiding them in their learning and research. It was told that the valedictory session of the project would be the next day. They were finding it difficult to accept that the project had ended. One among them had announced that, that night they were going to have 'cultural' programmes. They went for their dinner; most of them had a bath and came fresh to the hall by nine o' clock in the evening. They occupied the podium. They arranged the chairs so that they can have enough space for dancing. The stage protruding into the class, the podium, the table, their pens, white board markers and everything has become their musical instrument. Jose Peter, a resource person of the project, also joined the team that played music. They started singing songs, beginning with film songs, and then the *adivasi* songs. The *adivasi* songs are always accompanied with dances. By the end of the project, they had written six songs based on their field learning. All the six songs and their traditional songs were sung with dance. All of them were dancing. As the time went, the speed and rhythm of their dances got accelerated. It was already midnight, but there was no sign of them stopping the song. The songs and dances were in the full swing. They were not getting tired. The tireless involvement and spontaneity of their song, dance and their enthusiasm did not allow us to stop the dance though it was already past midnight. Surprised over their persistence in dancing so long, a PUP wanted to announce that everybody should go to sleep. Seeing at their enthusiasm, the PUP gave up that idea. The songs and dances were continuing with no sign of their merriment ending. The PUP called an RAP and asked why was that they were not getting tired. The RAP said that they dance because they were sad. This was also unlike that one would expect from the *vandavasi*. The NAP added that they were sad because the project was coming to an end. Though the PUP was at a loss to understand how people could sing and dance when they are sad, he respected the participant's sentiments and their involvement with one another and the project. The NAP was asked how could one ask them at this point of time to go to their room and take rest? He said he can help and then vanished into the dancing participants. He initiated a new song for dance, which later he informed was the song they sing at the end of their community dancing. The dance ended, as the lead person coming out of the circle ritually, pointing out programme was ended. The programme came to end by one o clock post-midnight.

The next day was the final day of the project. They were all in a meditative and gloomy mood. They were evaluating the project one by one. Everyone was crying. It was deeply touching the PUPs. They also could not hide their emotions. All the participants including the PUPs were burst into tears overwhelmed by the charge of emotions. It was a great surprise to hear, until the end of the fourth phase that the RAPs were suspicious about the intention of KILA as well as the PUPs running a programme that is sincerely meant for their well-being. The PUPs never had a clue that most of them were suspecting the intentions behind the project. Some said that they were suspecting that, it was an effort to take away valuable information from them and sell it for money; and others were suspecting that The PUPs were trying to know more about them to exercise more governmental control over them and so on. They were confessing that because they were suspecting the intentions of the organisers they had only partly revealing the information they had collected though they had used this opportunity to work with their own people. Some confessed that had they know that the organisers were so much sincere they would have better involved in the project. Some of them expressed the financial difficulties they had to go under as they were spending their time for fieldwork and classroom sessions giving up their chance to earn for their family. Of course, a small honorarium was allocated for them to undertake their fieldwork. At every end of the course work, they used to receive the honorarium. As it was the last phase, there was no provision to provide them with honorarium within the amount budgeted. It was deeply hurting the organisers to send them empty-handed, to their families as the participants were attending the programme for six days in the last phase giving up their earnings as wages. Many of them came to the programme taking credit from their friends and relatives thinking that they would get the honorarium from the project. While confessing, they were blaming themselves for expecting money to work for themselves among their community. They were making it clear because of financial difficulties they could not work with the people as they were working previously during the *praxis* intervention project, even though it was a worthy endeavour to be carried on. The PUPs were overwhelmed with their commitment and truthfulness amidst their monitory poverty.

The PUPs started the exercise thinking that, they were sufficiently equipped to 'train' the *adivasis*. Moment after moment in their involvement with RAPs, the PUPs could realise that they are ill equipped and over dominated by their own biases. Their biases were dominating them even when they were willing to give them up. For example, The PUPs could observe that the *adivasis* unlike the usual 'mainstream' participants always expressed themselves with songs, dances and other cultural expressions. They hardly noticed the importance of the songs and dances in their life despite they could see its overwhelming presence in their everyday classroom experience with them. Until the end of the project, they have never asked them to explore its significance in their life. All that the PUPs had in their mind was health, education, environment, economy, history, land use, development, gender, decentralisation and other things. They were pushing them to study something about education but nothing was coming forward from their field study. They gave the least importance to agriculture that had dominated their fieldwork, while the RAPs could convince their people the importance of food grain storage and in this front, the RAPs could make practical improvement. The PUPs were expecting them to report what they were doing in the field; but though they did not report everything they were fully immersed in working with the hamlet people. It came as a surprise to the PUPs that the people were overwhelmingly practising food grain cultivation as they could notice the change only when they visited RAPs field locations. The persons who appeared less active in the classroom sessions were actually more active in their fieldwork.

The PUPs were trying to 'teach' them gender justice and gender politics. Though the RAPs heard everything the PUPs had to say patiently they were coming up with the importance of looking at gender beyond identity politics. The RAPs were teaching the PUPs the importance of being '*enas.*' They were also aware that '*ena*' culture is vanishing. Within the *ena* perspective, the pairs are not individuated into two persons. However, the *ena* relationship by now has become a 'zombie category.' The PUPs were telling them how important the land right for women is for the gender empowerment. The RAPs were coming back with field understanding, how alienating property rights are especially in the case of gender relations. The PUPs were talking about the importance of labour and labour rights. The RAPs were teaching the PUPs back with data from the field how alienating the experience of labour is. Yet, they resign to their labourer status, as there are no other choices left. The PUPs were telling them the decentralisation initiative could be an opportunity to express their collective action; the RAPs were informing the PUPs that it was just yet another mechanical practice having no spirit of the community life.

In the classroom discussions on preserving water resources, the PUPs and EEs always had the rivers in their mind. River assumes importance as a water resource as the middle class culture informed them so. However, for the *adivasis* the *uravu* is more significant water resource than the river. For some reasons the earlier generations had shown interest in settling down around the *uravu*s rather than on the riverbeds. When the IIRPs and RAPs were talking of the depleting water resources, they were actually talking about the depletion of *uravu*s, around which their hamlets are located. Only towards the end of the project the PUPs learnt that *uravu*s are considered as a purer water resource than the rivers. *Adivasis* were never a community that practised irrigated agriculture. For them, water is mainly meant for drinking. Hence, *uravu*s were more of a significant source of water than the rivers. When *uravu*s dries up the entire hamlet face the problem of acute drinking water shortage that could only be poorly replaced by the bore-wells and hand pumps. As the PUPs and EEs were dominated by their cultural bias of considering only the rivers as water resource, they were less effective in discussing water resources. RAPs were speaking but the PUPs were hearing only what were familiar to them. These are a few of the instances the PUPs could recognise where their cultural biases were overpowering them. There could be many such biases that they could never notice.

For PUPs, the ecology and environment are simply the landscapes, water flows, soil fertility, and trees and so on. This is how they were trained to view the environment culturally. They could understand after many interactions that *adivasis* are not looking at the environment as the PUPs were looking at them. For the *adivasis*, especially for the elderly among them, the environment does not seem to be a physical, geological or topological object alone; it has something to do with their existence and self-definition. A participants' observation gives a glimpse of their worldview:

> There was plenty of water in the rivers. There was plenty of food and everything we needed though there were no modern amenities. Water, food, forest, community life, and everything were our wealth, (*sothu*) Just within 30-35 years, though the modern amenities were introduced, but the wealth (*sothu*) has been eroded by 'development.'

It is an extension of themselves. When the PUPs speak of the environment as something physical, it does not appeal the RAPs. Still the 'zombie ideals' dominate their mind. Their songs and dances also incorporate the environment as the part of their existence. This feeling of the environment guides the way in which they use their land resources. The incident of J resisting the clearance of plant over the surface of hilly landscapes looking from the perspectives of honeybees, birds, insects and humans is an indicator of a different mind-set.

The PUPs never doubted that the RAPs were suspicious of the PUPs' intention of running the project. It is only during the final evaluation session almost all the RAPs were saying that only from the fourth month of the project they started trusting the PUPs intentions. The mainstream bias that the *adivasis* are naïve unsuspecting *is* in fact misplaced. They were judicious in trusting the mainstream. They are even judicious in not resisting the extremely violent mainstream and the state despite they have less agreement with what is being done to them. It was a new knowledge that they were alert fully cautious about the project undertakers and their intensions. Being cautious and not giving, even a clue that they are cautious is something came as the greatest of all surprises to the PUPs.

From our experience it can be said that the *praxis* intervention is an action research as well as its reverse: a research action. It is a research action as it involves the interpretation of one's own life-world; it is an action research as it involves research into action i.e., research leading to action: knowledgeable action. The fieldwork has instantiated both. The research action and the action research in *praxis* intervention help the participants in take care of themselves. The *praxis* intervention action instantiated here is not a full-fledged case of *praxis* intervention but only a test case.

5 CONCLUSION: TOWARDS A PRAXIS MODEL OF SOCIAL WORK PRACTICE

In this chapter, we attempt to locate the *Praxis* Intervention in the current schemata of social work practice. To understand the present schema of social work we explore the definitions given to it, its concerns, its modes of practices, and its critiques. We explore the alternatives for the mainstream practice of social work and examine whether *praxis* intervention could offer an alternative method. The implications of *praxis* intervention, its extension possibilities and its limits are explored towards the end of the chapter. The chapter ends with a discussion and a plea for further researches in this direction.

Social Work Defined (?)

The social work having a history of uncertainty and constantly changing identities makes it 'notoriously' difficult endeavour to pinpoint what forms a professional social work practice [Munday 1996:7]. In this regard, Catherine McDonald views:

Social work has always been a difficult entity to pin down precisely. It encompasses an extremely diverse set of activities (for example casework, case management, counselling, group work, community development, policy development, advocacy, and activism) undertaken in diverse contexts (including hospitals, community correction offices, youth shelters, aged care settings, child welfare departments, juvenile correction facilities, local communities, local government authorities, schools, and so forth). Whatever the activity undertaken and in whichever context, social workers mediate between institutions and individuals, in particular between the state and the people it governs. The range of activities social workers undertake, the multiplicity of locations in which they practice, and the variety of techniques they deploy are held together by a collectively articulated commitment to individual and social well being and justice. The diversity of practices organized under the rubric of 'social work' can accommodate the differences, ambiguities, and contradictions that inevitably arise in the pursuit of these commitments.[127]

According to the International Association of Schools of Social Work (IASSW), the social work is a profession, which in its various forms, addresses the multiple, complex transactions between people and their environments [IAASW 2002: 9; Ramsay 1999]. The mission of Social work according to IASSW is 'to enable all people to develop their full potential, enrich their lives and prevent dysfunction.' The 'professional' social work is focused on the problem solving and change. As such, social workers are change agents in society and in lives of the individuals, families and communities they serve. The Social work is an interrelated system of values[128], theory[129] and practice' [Ibid]. The International Federation of Social Work [IFSW] after years of research with extensive review of literature adopted a version of social work definition in its general meeting held at Montreal, Canada on 25 July 2000 stating:

---

[127] McDonald 2003:124

128 In explaining Social Work values, the IASSW newsletter points out, 'Social work grew out of democratic ideals, and its values are based on respect for the equality, worth and dignity of all people. Since its beginnings over a century ago, the social work practice has focussed on meeting the human needs and developing human potential. Human rights and social justice serve as the motivation and justification for social work action. In solidarity with those who are disadvantaged, the profession strives to alleviate poverty and to liberate vulnerable and oppressed people in order to promote social inclusion. Social work values are embodied in the professions' national and international codes of ethics.' [IAASW 2002: 9]

129 The IASSW newsletter states, 'The social work profession draws on theories of human development and behaviour and social systems to analyse complex situations and to facilitate individual, organisational, social and cultural change' [Ibid].

The social work profession promotes social change, problem solving in human relationships, and the empowerment and liberation of people to enhance well-being. Utilizing theories of human behaviour and social systems, social work intervenes at the points where people interact with their environments. Principles of human rights and social justice are fundamental to social work.

The broad definitions given to social work such as above lack both in precision and exactness as it hardly captures what social work is from what it is not.

The difficulty in defining what constitutes social work has much to do with the profession's formative history. Historically the social work as a profession is a response to the depleted human condition, consequent to the 'industrial revolution' [Shanin 1998; Ramsay 1998]. Social work as a voluntary service is said to have begun with the sympathy expressed by the socialite women who wanted to do some 'good works'. The 'Social' in social work meant the "facelessness" of the poor who were destined to be consumers of the charity work of the socialites. The 'work' in social work initially meant the 'work' that involves in 'aiding the indigent' [Wooster 2002]. In its origin, social work as a practice emerged owing to socialite commitment to Christian morality rather than its obligation to social problems and its effects on individuals. It is only since 1970's poverty, unemployment, poor housing, homelessness and other such 'secular- social' issues were the focal points of social work practice partly as a resultant of the economic crisis followed by the shooting prices of the oil [Grimwood et al. 1995: 35, 39].

The Social Work Concerns

The major concerns of Social work had been the lessening of the effects of poverty, social exclusion, hunger, illness or disability, homelessness, the frailty of old age, family breakdowns, domestic violence, mental illness, environmental damage, inequality, unemployment, injustice or violence, child abuse, learning difficulties: in fact with issues related to the 'quality of life' of individuals, groups and communities [Lyons 1999: 10, 46; Davis 2002]. According to Ramon the Social Work Profession today, stands in majority of its practices to restore its client's ability to act independently within the given social context [Ramon 1991]. Lyons remarks that Social Work is mostly concerned with:

> amelioration of social problems, and support and empowerment for the individuals, families, groups and communities affected by them; with advocacy and negotiation about policies and practices … and sometimes with intervention aimed at reconciliation between individuals and groups.

IASSW deliberating on the social work concerns points out:

> Social work addresses the barriers, inequities and injustices that exist in society. It responds to crisis and emergencies as well as to everyday personal and social problems. Social work utilises variety of skills, techniques and activities consistent with its holistic focus on persons and their environments. Social work interventions range from primarily person focussed psychological processes to involvement in social policy and planning and development. These include counselling, clinical social work, group work, social pedagogical work and family treatment and therapy as well as efforts to help people obtain services and resources in the community. Interventions also include agency administration, community organisation, and engaging in social political action to impact social policy and economic development.'[130]

Since the social work has its origin in the socialite work practiced in era of the 'industrial revolution,' the clientele of social work had traditionally been the factory workers. These days, the clientele of the practice consists of broken families, abused children, abused women, destitute, physically or mentally challenged, persons affected by the natural, social or cultural disasters, marginalized,

---

[130]   IAASW 2002: 9

unemployed and the emotionally disoriented. Social work assistance is also sought as a paid service by the people under medical treatment, psychiatric treatment, correctional administration, deviation control, socialisation of children and so on.

The mode of Social work Practice

Social work being a practice bereft of academic rigour and professional autonomy, the issues themselves mutually related, had always been carried out by the dominant paradigms characterising the ages it had passed through. It has been identified that there has been three broad periods in the 'development' of social work: as a moral enterprise, as a therapeutic endeavour and finally as a managerial project [Gregory and Halloway 2005: 35, 37]. Within the managerial schema of social work practice, the model presently popular in community social work, intended to 'empower' people concerned, is Participatory Rural Appraisal [PRA] and its varieties. It has been claimed the PRA methods provide participatory methods for data extraction for planning [Oxaal and Baden 1997; Uphoff 2001: 35]. PRA is presented as a set of participatory tools that 'enables rural poor to influence the research agenda, thus leading to an increased capacity to act in their own interest' [Koning 1995]. Being critical of the claims made by the PRA professionals that PRA essentially empowers the poor, Rosemary McGee comments, "In any case, participatory approaches do not necessarily empower, and are not by definition non-extractive" [2001: 85].

One recent forms of PRA promoted by World Bank, in which the social work skills are sought, is Participatory Poverty Assessment [PPA] in which the toolkits of PRA are used to promote self assessment of poverty to be addressed through projects meant for poverty eradication. The PPA is presented as "primarily a research project directed at improving policy analysis" [Attwood and May 1998: 121]. The PPA is designed to be an instrument of planning that integrates the qualitative data participatorily collected with the quantitative data already collected to 'manage' poverty from the centres of governance.

[Chambers 2001:26-28; Uphoff 2001: 33-37].

Another argument forwarded to re-invent social work profession is called "The Evidence Based Social Work Practice" [Moren and Blom 2003; Mullen 1978; Mullen 2002]. The idea of 'evidence based' work is taken from the field of clinical practices in medicine[131]. [Sackett et al. 1996: 71; Sackett et al. 2000; Mullen 2002]. The method emphasized the generation of evidence through empirical research and on the dissemination of such evidence to enable practitioners to incorporate it in practice. In principle, this means that the social work should follow empirically proven knowledge and method regarding the intervention and its effects on the clients. The underlying assumption is that there exist permanent and empirically observable regularities between the problems faced by the clients and the specific intervention; and finding out the relation with empirical studies would contribute to the knowledge base of the intervening profession. Once the relationship is found all that is necessary is to develop a 'package' of social work practice that could be administered with the systems of management meant for that. It is taken to be similar to the practice of finding the relationship between a medical treatment and its effect. In this approach the social problems and its manifestations are treated as if the society is an object similar to a sick body requiring treatment.

Malcom Payne notes that there are three 'general perspective' on social work: individualist reformist, socialist collectivist and reflexive therapeutic [Payne 1996:2]. According to him, social

---

[131] It has been observed that even in the medical field the 'off the peg solutions' of the evidence based medical practice has not met with success in handling complex cases. According to Page and Hamer: What is clear, however, is that approaches to practice change that are more easily categorized and measured, such as the dissemination of research evidence or the use of clinical audit cycles, have met with relatively little success despite their widespread promotion and substantial resources. The reason for this is most likely to be found in their failure to recognize the complexity of practice settings. Practice development, on the other hand, as defined here, is an approach which explicitly recognizes and seeks to match this complexity. [Page and Hamer 2002: 4-5, 15].

work contains the element of these perspectives in different degrees with one or another being influential at different times [Lymbery 2001:371]. Taking a cue from Payne's classification of Social work Martin Davis claims that in the present day the practice of social work shows more of a tendency of 'individualist reformist' subsumed under a 'general theory of maintenance' [Davies 1994: 54]. It has been pointed that the 'profession' had even been a handy tool for 'social engineering' in the regime of pre-war Nazi Germany [Lyons 1999].

Critique of Social Work Practice

Any field of activity that claims to be a profession is expected to have a coherent body of theory and practical skill to apply the theoretical knowledge in a given context. Social work has problem in both these fronts [Parton 2000a]. It does not have a well developed theoretical base; it has no special skills to apply whatever little knowledge base it has. Hence, as the critics rightly point out that it is 'heavily under-theorised discipline and profession, less acknowledged as an academic discipline among academics, and less accepted as a profession among the established professions' [Shanin, 1998;   Toren 1972].

The 'professional practice' in social work these days just refers the practice of handling some prefixed varieties of problems with prefixed solutions and a set of mechanical procedures. Karen Healy and Gabrielle Meagher in their recent article complaint that the social work with the advent of managerialism is deeply fragmented and routinised, concomitantly reduced the opportunities for the profession to exercise creativity, reflexivity and discretion in direct practice and invite the profession to be re-professionalized [Healy and Meagher 2004: 244]. The social work, with its lack of theoretical body informing its practice and vice versa, destined it to remain a profession with no autonomy; neither capable of having academic autonomy nor an autonomy of its practice [Lymbery 2001a: 369; Giarchi and Lankshear 1998:27]. Some social work scholars remark that autonomy was never a serious possibility for social workers as the professionally autonomous social work practice never had a 'market' [Parry and Parry: 1979: 47]. There should be caution applied on the meaning of the word autonomy here. By the expressions 'loss' or 'lack' of 'autonomy' it is not meant 'autonomous decision making, unhindered by pressure from both managers and clients, may well be an ideal closely defended by public sector professionals' as some scholars take it to be[132]. Rather, the loss of autonomy of the academic / professional field is regretted. The loss of the academic/ professional autonomy of the field is implied by (a) the profession being succumbed to powers elsewhere and not the knowledge base that informs its practice and (b) the creation of a knowledge base to itself being bent to similar power equations rather than guided by scientific methods of knowledge production. In other words the loss of autonomy means that the guiding philosophy of social work practice is lost to some other fields like management or state craft [Bourdieu and Wacquant 1992: 177-178].

There are reasons internal to the social work profession for its loss of autonomy [Wilensky 1964:148; Healy 2001a] as also external to it[133]. The reason according to Nigel Parton is, 'social work does not have a core theoretical knowledge base, and that there is a hole at the centre of the enterprise' [134]; and the external one is the increasing claim over people and their resources for 'governmentality' [Foucault 1979] and 'profit' as desired by the fields of statecraft and market. In other words, it is not the social workers' power over its clienteles and their employers but the field of social work being succumbed to *'marketocracy'*[135] that is regretted [Noble 2004:293-299]. Each field

---

[132]   May and Buck 1998; Hall 1969; Johnson 1972: 77.

[133]   Fisher 1996; Fisher 1997; Shanin 1998; Dominelli, 1997; Ife, 1997; Rees, 1997

[134]   Parton 1994: 30

[135]   Madhu: The logic of capital with the help of bureaucratised regulation could alienate work, social relations, relation with nature and speculative faculty of Human lives from themselves and commodify them systematically. Without the emergence of bureaucratic rationality the universalisation of division of

has its own premise. The premise of statecraft is to rule, and that of the market is to accumulate monetary profit; the premise of management is to manage and that of social work is to care. Not letting the field 'free' in its professional endeavour in pursuing its cherished values is its loss of autonomy. The loss of freedom could happen either through violent aggression or an imposition of ban on certain kinds of radical social works as it happened in the Nazi Germany and during the MeCarthian USA in 1950s and 60s [Zahl 2003; Andrews 2001] or through imposing or stealthily replacing a field's value orientation with the another's and an *ideological assault* on the professional or academic values[136].

Social work is criticised for its being "'soft' yet repressive tool of the state. For the marginal populations, the social work functions as their defender and at times the organiser of their resistance (as well as, time and again, their only voice)" [Shanin 1998]. Many scholars have endorsed this view[137]. Samir Amin In this regard remarks:

> To wish naively, even with the best of intentions, for specific forms of "community development"-which, it will be claimed afterwards, were produced by the democratically expressed will of the communities in

---

labour would not have been possible. Bureaucratic rationality is formal tending to be universal, atemporal and hence by its nature it hardly relates to the rich and diverse everyday reality but rather stereotype and alienate human relation with themselves and with their social and natural environment. The bureaucratic rationality by its formal nature not just aids the alienating logic of capital but also replaces substance with form constraining the creative faculty of substantive rationality. Capital and bureaucracy reinforcing each other alienates human life from itself and from its relation with natural and social environment. The alliance between capital and bureaucratic rationality at the abstract level emerges as the alliance between bureaucracy of the governments and market forces entangling the expression of life in the public domain through politics. The age-old association of the rationality of the market and the bureaucracy culminates into the marriage of market and bureaucracy resulting in *marketocracy* [Madhu: 2003].

[136] Fisher 1996; Shanin 1998; Lymbery 2001: 374; Ransom and Stewart: 3; Clarke and Newman 1997:38; Larson 1977:184; Jones 2001: 552, 559.

[137] Bradon *et al.* 1995; Petras and Veltmeyer 2001: 121-2, 128-38; Morgan 1989:49; Beetham 1987:5.

question (the West Indians in the London suburbs, for example, or the North Africans in France, or the Blacks in the United States, etc.)-is to lock individuals inside these communities and to lock these communities inside the iron limits of the hierarchies that the system imposes. It is nothing less than a kind of apartheid that is not acknowledged as such… The argument advanced by the promoters of this model of "community development" appears to be both pragmatic ("do something for the dispossessed and the victims, who are gathered together in these communities") and democratic ("the communities are eager to assert themselves as such"). No doubt a lot of universalist talk has been and still is pure rhetoric, calling for no strategy for effective action to change the world, which would obviously mean considering concrete forms of struggle against the oppression suffered by this or that particular group. Agreed. But the oppression in question cannot be abolished if at the same time we give it a framework within which it can reproduce itself, even if in a milder form.

Being critical of using the participatory techniques for governmental purposes Uphoff also observes:

When we evaluate [participatory] methodologies … we need always to ask: for *what* purpose, or better, for *whose* purposes, will they be used? For academics for whom precision and elegance bring professional and personal rewards? For bureaucrats or policy-makers who need to make decisions about resource allocation? For the poor themselves, so that they understand their situation better and can act more effectively on their own behalf?[138]

Social work being reduced to an instrument of managerialism is a highly felt concern in the social work academia[139]. It has been broadly identified that social work has entered its third period

---

[138]   2001: 36

[139]   Jordan and Jordan 2000; Lymbery 2001a; Lorenz 2001; Jones 2001; McDonald 2003; Hatton 2000; Orme 2001; Healy 2001; Dominelli 1997; Ife 1997; Rees 1997; Adams 1998; Parton 2000a; Fook 2001; Ferguson

characterised my managerialism. The other two broad periods identified were those of moral social work and therapeutic social work. [Gregory and Halloway 2005: 37]. It has been observed that managerialism, 'evidence based social work enterprise' and the 'professional project' of the social work goes hand in hand [Meagher and Parton 2004: 10-11].

Managerialism is a set of beliefs and practices, that presumes better management alone would solve the social and economic problems; Under managerialism, the clients are customers; efficiency is cutting cost; social workers are 'staff' carrying out the managerial designs; professionals are employees; quality social work is that which complies with the pre-fixed standard. The complexity of the phenomenon 'social,' its status of being open to plethora of mindsets and multiple values people hold, cultural variations, varied contexts etc., are reduced here to a neat object responding to uniform treatment.

The practice of managerialism is well linked to the 'evidence based social work practice' wherein the management is not just a tool, rather the fundamental philosophy that overshadows the social work practice. The evidence-based practice is also 'result - based social work practice', wherein the results and means to achieve them are prefixed and standardised. The evidence based social work practice with its Humean premise "if x then y" neglects that the social world is 'open' and 'necessarily peopled' [Morén and Blom 2003]. It underestimates the complexity of the social world' [Rescher 1998] its dialectics, [Young 1981] and the fallibility of the fixed packaged solutions [Rescher 1998: 165]. The perspective is little humble in realizing that our purported scientistic knowledge about the social world is incomplete and potentially incorrect [Rescher 1998: 127]. In its over enthusiasm to make

2001; Pozzuto 2000

social world and social work practice manageable it simplifies complex social reality and expects the social world amenable to prefixed formulas. Its neglect of the folk reality, indexical settings, interactional process and multiple hermeneutics that is ordinarily found in the social settings amounts to becoming a mechanistic social work practice of un-care and unconcern. The world view of the evidence based managerial social work is too simplistic and can be explained in terms Herbert Simons' critique of administrative man:

> Administrative man recognises that the world he perceives is a drastically simplified model of the buzzing, blooming confusion that constitutes the real world. He is content with the gross simplification because he believes that the real world is mostly empty - that most of the facts of the real world have no great relevance to any particular situation he is facing and that most significant chains of causes and consequences are short and simple[140].

Working towards a prefixed agenda, is more of a tactics of governmentality [Foucault 1979] rather than that of the social work. The tactics of governmentality have the violence inbuilt in it as it trespasses into all aspects of life with 'judgementality'. Therefore, the evidence based social work or the result based social work is morally weak. The evidence based social work practice bases its epistemology on empiricism and logical positivism according to which the proper ground for knowledge is observation and experience of the world, rather than either abstract rational or introspective ideas, or unobservable causes and theoretical entities. Since empiricism itself is a theoretical stand, it cannot claim to be theory neutral[141]. More over, the process of selecting certain

---

[140] Quoted in Seeing Like State, Why Certain Schemes to Improve the Human Condition Have Failed, J.Scott, 1998, Yale University, p 45.

[141] Kuhn: What man sees depends both upon what he looks at and also upon what his previous visual-conceptual experiences has taught him to see [1962: 112].

values and not certain others to be fixed for empirical observation is itself theory laden of which unfortunately the empiricist would be hardly aware [Kuhn 1962:110,112,117,149]. The practice of ontology being reduced to epistemology, real reduced to actual in fact is an 'epistemic fallacy' [Bhaskar 1997:16; Bhaskar 2002:8-9].

It has been criticized that social work's adoption into the managerial schema and evidence-based project is part of its 'professional project'. In this regard McDonald comments:

> The idea of the professional project builds on the Weberian conception of society as an arena in which social entities compete for economic, social, and political rewards. In particular, it develops Weber's nomination of the occupational group, in some cases holding specific educational qualifications from which a living is derived, as one category of competitor. Such entities, in this case the professions, work to bring themselves into existence and to maintain or improve the groups' relative standing. In this way, the group pursues a *project*[142].

The professional project is political in the sense that it is fundamentally concerned with erecting boundaries that exert a distinction and create a border between insiders and outsiders [McDonald 1993; Larson 1977; Abbot 1988; Johnson 1972]. The professional project is a claim to a monopoly of competence. It is pointed out that the absorption of social work practice into the managerial schema is a win- win situation seen from the marketocratic need for social control and from the 'professional project' point of view of social work despite what is lost is the spirit of social work profession. The win-win schema in fact has removed the heart of the social work practice and replaced it with an automated machine.

---

[142]   2003: 126

Alternative Perspectives in Social Work

The present scenario of social work profession dominated by managerialism is countered by various critical perspectives [Dominelli, 1997; Ife, 1997; Rees, 1997]. The alternative perspectives give prominence to theory with a qualified understanding of theory as contemplative and systematic thinking in process. As the critical thinking is the guiding principle of the alternative practices, they can be collectively labelled as 'critical social work.'

Healy maintains that, the core mission of social work is promotion of social justice through social work practice and policymaking. Tracing the canon of critical social work since 1960's Healy is of the opinion that the threat for critical social work emerged more from the inadequacies within the tradition than from proponents of conservatism, economic rationalism and, more recently managerialism. For Healy critical social work refers to a broad range of practices that share: a recognition that large scale social processes, particularly those associated with class, race and gender, contribute fundamentally to the personal and social issues social workers encounter in their practice; the adoption of a self-reflexive and critical stance to the often contradictory effects of social work practice and social policies; a commitment to co-participatory rather than authoritarian practice relations; and working with and for oppressed populations to achieve social transformation [Healy 2001]

The canon of critical perspectives in social work was prevalent from the late 60s. Though one can find them still being practiced marginally in countering the racist, gender, economic and social discrimination in many of the countries, in the western world the conventional critical canon has come to demise. Some authors blame the unfriendly policy environment, the insensibility generally growing with the spread of mercantile neo-liberalism, neo-conservatism, economic rationalism and also the managerialism [Dominelli 1997; Ife 1997; Rees 1997]. It has been observed that social work in general has increasingly become a cold, passive, bureau profession of form-filling type[143]. For Ife, the deterioration of the critical perspective in social work is due to the social control functions of social work; the limited commitment of social workers to radical transformation and the lack of political sophistication of social workers [Ife 1997: 169]. Differing with Ife and others, Healy points out that more than the external threat or lack of commitment the internal threat from within the critical social work practice due to their unsophisticated claim to 'truth' following the vulgar varieties of Marxism, feminism, anti-racist and communitarian perspectives [Healy 2001; Fook 2002: 17].Their non-compromising position that sprung from their belief that their theoretical position explained the truth, Healy observes, in fact made dialogue impossible. The complex uncertain contextual dimensions of social work demanded a flexible and reflective interchanges between theory and practice rather than rigid truth claims [144]. He further argues that theories look unattractive to social workers as they are not immediately relevant to their practices. For them theory appeared at the best, as an intellectual curiosity, and at the worst, as authoritarian and esoteric[145]. Further, the conventional critical perspective claim that through rational thought and action people can change the way they live [Fay 1987:4] was also challenged from ethical foundations. It was commonly believed that a radical analysis will necessarily lead to actions that are ethical, socially just and progressive. Healy points out that such an assumption appears naïve to the inconstancies of human action [Healy 2001]. Indeed, history provides us with examples of the use of utopian theories, whether it is Marxism or Nazi ideology or the neo liberal utopia, to justify oppressive social practices[146]. In explicating the role of theory in the new critical

---

[143] Zahl 2003; Massey 1993: 195; Lymbery 2001a:374; Ransom and Stewart 1994:3; Clarke and Newman 1997:38; Laveridge 2002; Jones 2001; Jordan and Jordan 2000: 131

[144] Healy 2001; Fook, Ryan and Hawkins 2000; Parton and Marshall 1998; Leonard 2001.

[145] Healy 2000:1; Fawcett 1998; Featherstone and Fawcett 1995.

[146] Lyotard, 1984; Leonard, 1996:11; Penna 2004; Bourdieu 1999; Bourdieu 1998; Parton 2000b: 452

practice, Healy observes that the theory could serve only as a resource rather than a blue print for practice [Foucault 1991:84]. In this regard, Fook remarks that theory in a critical social work practice is essentially that the clients and the workers jointly or individually reflect upon in the practice of social work in progress on the issues of critical concern [Fook 1996; Fook 2001; Schon 1983].

For Richard Pozzuto 'Critical Social Work' has something to do with making the world we live in. We could consider creating the world "critical". Pozzuto further observes:

> It has to do with looking at something and not taking it solely as a given but also imagining what it could be. In this sense critical work is not work that duplicates the present but work that imagines possible alternative futures, and strives for them.[147]

For Rossiter, the questioning the innocence with which social work is taught and practiced is critical social work. To be a critical social worker from her point of view is to be deeply critical about the project of social work itself. The term 'critical social work' for her is only a euphemism for her suspicion of the very project [Rossiter 2001]. Social workers, she points out, are often involved in a 'messy' job of 'civilizing mission' that produces the 'other' in need of help, thereby sustaining the identity of the helper as good, innocent, and helpful. Such relations, she further adds, obscure the problem of power and privilege in the relations between helper and helped. Critical social work is maintenance of ethical vigilance of the work and its nature. It is the openness to the questions about the constitution of practice that helps us to 're-examine our value commitments' [Rossiter 2005]. A non-critical social work is a trespass for her. To make her point clearer she narrates an incident:

---

[147]   Pozzato: 2000

The example involves recently received money from the Ministry of Health to expand the Centre's outreach to Homeless people. One of the projects is to make sure that homeless people have health cards with which to access the regular health care system. I participated in a meeting with the Ministry of Health where officials were teaching us to use a computerized system for tracking how many health card applications had been made so that we could be "accountable'. The process of computerization necessitated creating a formal definition of a homeless person and slotting that definition into the computer software. Here is an example of the trespass of every initiative. In order to get health cards, a number of different and disparate people are turned into a category of sameness - the homeless. Only the creation of that category can get them the service they need. But the trespass is that people are inserted into a category through which their identity and personhood is marked by lack - they are "the homeless". The "homeless"- once non-existent in Toronto - are being created as an identity and my work to get health cards is part of that construction process. This is a trespass against the complex identities of people with housing problems.

In her later article she qualifies the critical social work as 'critical reflective practice' and defines it as:

> My view of critical reflective practice is that it must promote a "necessary distance" from practice in order to enable practitioners to understand the construction of practice, thus enhancing a kind of ethics – or freedom, in Foucault's terms [Foucault 1994:284] – which opens perspectives capable of addressing questions about social work, social justice and the place of the practitioner.[148]

Praxis Intervention as an alternative social work practice

The *Praxis* intervention carried out with the *adivasis* of Attappady is a test project. Here, the

---

[148] Rossiter 2005

term *praxis* connotes the reflexive potential of human beings in making sense of themselves and their environment. The term intervention in the phrase refers to human beings intervening with the constructed sociality around and their *habitus*. Social work is taken here as the imperative action carried on the social and the self from the nodal point where history, culture and moments of individual life meets [Rossiter 2005]. Acting upon the nodal point is pertinent as it is where the past through present to future, structure and agent, settled meanings, fresh sensuousness, also the other, and the self meet. It is an action research and research action characterized by interpretation of one's life-world in action and a research leading to knowledgeable action. It is a *praxis* intervention and a reverse *praxis* as it could act on both the *adivasi* participants and the project-organizing participants. It is a project of participant objectivation as it involved layers of participant objectivation; it is a participant objectivation exercise for the *adivasi* researchers, hamlet residents and the project undertakers as all the three kinds of participants reflectively and reflexively objectified themselves [Taylor and White 2000: 199].

The intervention could take the participants a long way from the initial chart they made in objectifying themselves [table 15 and 16]. The project could also bring significant changes in the project undertakers as they could realize their biases that blind folded them in understanding their practices and preferences. It had removed some of their presuppositions on gender relations, labour relations, and even that of their practice of social work.

For Healy, a critical social work should be self reflexive critical stand; for Fook, it should be a collaborative enquiry, for Pozzuto, it should be a critical work on the world around and for Rossiter, it should be a practice of self objectivation. In all these senses, the practice could meet the critical standards. Even to look from the evidence-based perspective, it could give evidences that the project of *praxis* intervention works.

The project objectified self, history, the present life-world and the future trends of the *adivasi* life. It is not the project undertakers but the *adivasi* participants themselves who interpreted their life-world. The project could initiate a process of gaining historical competence and for the first time in their life the *adivasi* participants wrote their history collectively. The *adivasi* participants did not just chronologically arranged what had happened to them rather they could interpret it. For example, they could trace the reasons for their ill-health through their research action and work on it through action research. The RAPs could interpret the changes brought into their gender relations and respond to their findings in their personal life. The RAPs could critically evaluate the futility of the formal politics and at the same time they could bring policy changes however minor, using their space within that.

The present venture is not to evaluate the project but to draw some generalizations from the specific experience. The project revealed, however poor people are how much so ever they were culturally, politically or socially deprived, so long as they can have a grip on their sensuousness they can draw resource from their *praxis* potential. It could also bring to light that oral history and its interpretations could be given at the community level which itself could be a tool to invoke their *praxis* potential. The method also proved that a combined research with the affected people works immediately on the people's mind. This opens up the possibility of undertaking a research *with* the marginalised instead of performing a research *on* them.

The theoretical assumption that it is possible to guide oneself and one's client community towards critical *praxis* suspending the otherwise dominant routine *praxis* is proved right in this experiment. The project could fix a reflexive eye on the social process of self-construction and the social construction.

Implications for Social Work Practice

The practice of *praxis* intervention for the social work could be extended to the social work situation such as helping people to help themselves. The *praxis* mode of social work depends on the sensibility that could be provoked in a given context: sensible towards one's own biography, historical locatedness, spatial positioning and the interaction setting. It could be a model for providing companionship to people in need of self-exploration. *Praxis* intervention as a practice can be carried on to the extent it is possible for people to take care of themselves and to the extent people require professional companionship of the social work practice. *Praxis* intervention practice requires the professionals and the client participants to be self-reflexive and self-critical. The model provides opportunity for the social worker to undertake a reflexive inward journey to get rid of biases that affect her practice. The context that is not suitable for self-reflexivity or self-criticism is not suitable for *praxis* intervention practice either.

The method could be fruitful in working with the marginalized people as marginalisation is usually a historical phenomenon. This would avoid people losing self-respect and dignity under the conditions of marginalisation. The method could be applied in other conditions of marginalisation such as working with people discriminated on the basis of gender. It can also serve as a model for opportunity scanning. The *praxis* intervention can be used as a method to initiate and implement participatory project provided the project has sufficient flexibility inbuilt for effecting a change from its pre-designs. A project management from *praxis* perspective should not have full-fledged blue print before hand, rather the projects should be flexible enough to wait till the participants themselves research and come out with a project plan. In the new practice, the experts could be facilitated to work with the participants. While a project is designed and carried out with this method, there should be options to change the course of project or even to suspend some projects according to the collective findings and evaluations of the collaborative research. Similarly the *praxis* method could be used in the planning process provided sufficient flexibility is allowed and reflexivity is tolerated. It has to be further tested whether the model works with socially, economically, and culturally heterogeneous set of people.

The *praxis* intervention practice has its implications for social work education. A social work education based on *praxis* model could shape the students and teachers self-reflexive, sensible. Through this method, it may be possible for students gaining theoretical and practical skills. However, the *praxis* model would be yielding better results if sufficient flexibility is maintained.

The *praxis* practice could also be extended to social work practice in the medical setting, AIDS care, psychiatric social work, management of juvenile delinquency, school social work, correctional administration practices in prison social work, gender related social work practice, geriatric social work, nursing, etc.

The *praxis* intervention model of social work may not be applicable in all the social work contexts. There are sections of people who cannot take care of themselves and hence require absolute external care. For example, persons suffering from progressive, irreversible diseases characterised by degeneration of the brain cells such as Alzheimer's disease would require complete external care. The *praxis* practice would be inappropriate for the people who do not need care. The approach could be helpful in accompanying people who can be helped to care for themselves. *Praxis* intervention practice is appropriate for working with the people who can be helped to care themselves with in a scale of caring (fig 11).

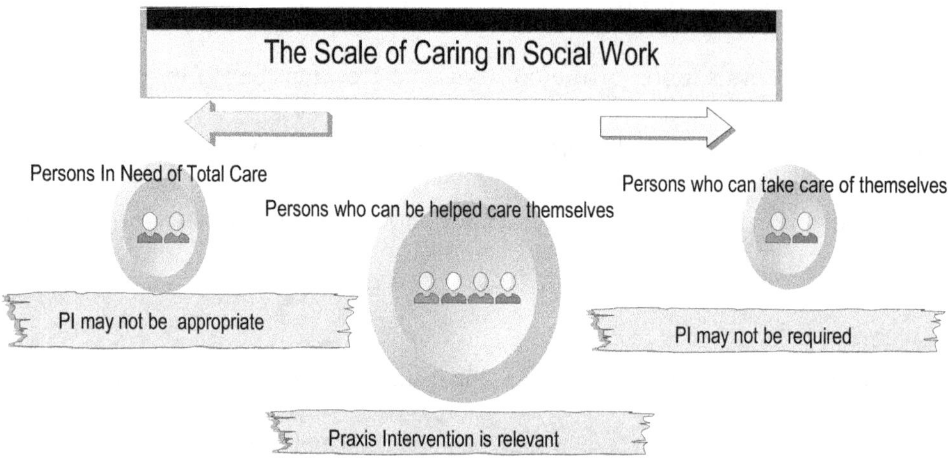

Figure 11 Scale of Care

Concluding Discussion

The thesis presented theoretical arguments from various fields of social sciences and related philosophical discussions on the possibility of provoking the *praxis* potential through an intervention strategy in the first chapter. There, we argued that the indeterminacy of meaning and the *praxis* potential human beings are endowed with could be resourceful in invoking human sensuousness towards creative *praxis*. We also argued that interpretation is action. In that chapter we were exploring the possibilities for *habitus praxis*. In the second chapter, we provided information of the fieldwork setting. The chapter gave a descriptive account of the location from which RAPs performed their fieldwork. In the third chapter, in an attempt to reflexively recapture the *praxis* intervention project we have critically explored the project. The present chapter has positioned the *praxis* model of social work within the critical schema of social work.

As the sufferings in the world increases, no doubt there should be institutions and methods facilitating people to overcome suffering. *Praxis* intervention is an initiative towards enriching the social work practice in its companionship with the sufferers. The *praxis* intervention project is one of the initial attempts in making this companionship fruitful.

The present world is fast transforming. The change happening is significantly social. People living in the world are expected to be spatially global and temporally futurised. Within the transforming world the social work field cannot afford to be static. The social work has to grapple with the transforming sociality. Social work has to converse in social theory and more to work on the social and the individuals affected. It requires continuous assessment of social theory and social science practice from the social work context. The social work can also offer vigilant critique of the social science perspectives from its practice environment.

The social is necessarily peopled and hence it is open ended. Therefore, no social intervention perspective can offer a complete closed precise prescription. In this thesis, a sample situation is dealt with – and a general framework for *praxis* intervention social work practice has been offered. For specific conditions new methods could be evolved to inform *praxis* intervention social work practice.

Though the perspective of *praxis* intervention sheds its doubts on empiricism it does not question the value of empirical approach to data collection and analysis. Retaining 'objective' approach to data collection for background knowledge that informs the facts of local history and local conditions that influence people's lives is necessary for a rigorous practice. In this regard objective research is important. Within the *praxis* method *etic* and *emic* approaches can be intermixed. The *emic* view proposes that reality is best understood in terms of the subjective meanings that people attach to their roles, relationships, material possessions, and the like. The *etic* view holds that reality is best viewed through the "optics" of concepts with cross-cultural relevance, like marriage or property or gender [Harris 1990: 48]. What emerges important in the *praxis* approach is not just the precise explanation of the social reality in accordance with the established practices in science rather the exact grasp of the relevant social reality akin to existing complex life patterns. Precision devoid of complexity appears more of a demand from the perspective of governmentality [Young 1981]. People living in their dialectical social context face-to-face with their interaction setting, with their competence in 'practical consciousness' and 'logic of *practice*' [Bourdieu 1990] and [Giddens 1986] coping with their life situation, in fact, are more capable of understanding their social reality in its complexity and exactness than a social scientist far removed from the local context. Hence, a *praxis* intervention practice requires being more akin to the exact complex life patterns and its assessment from the practical competence than to the precise theoretical or empirical findings. *Praxis* research is an intimate research practice that brings theory and methods of social science closer to people in its endeavour to accompanying them and not an alienating practice that intends only to extract information from them and present it devoid of complexities on behalf of managerial interests.

The thesis as a whole is an attempt to provide a *praxis* model of social work practice and initiate an informed debate in this direction.

However, caution should always applied in acceptance or rejection of models. Models necessarily simplify and the social is essentially complex. Thus, models inherently misrepresent. Modelling is the extension of the human potential to impose structure through abstraction. Hence, like the other solid human conceptions models too, despite solidifying abstractions, can lead to misrecognitions. Approaching social work, with the adequate cautions applied, with the *praxis* framework would be a fruitful exercise in enriching the caring profession.

APPENDICES

Appendix-1

<u>Classroom Phases ((Phases I, III, V and VII)</u>

Phase-I- (28th May to 1st June 2002) Social Construction of the '*adivasi*' social reality; History of the *adivasi* struggles; Development interventions with/for the *adivasi*s; Special Legal rights of the *adivasi*s; Environmental problems and the *adivasi* livelihood; Exploring local history; *Praxis* intervention with the *adivasi*s in their hamlet the idea and method; fieldwork guidance.

Phase-III. (1st July to 5th July 2002) Sharing Fieldwork experiences on: land utilisation patterns and its history; Landownership pattern and its history; exploring Myths; Exploring history of the hamlets; critical analysis of everyday life of the *adivasi*s men and women; exploring personal histories based on the data collected from the field; Comparing the collective life of the *adivasi*s in the past with the governmental/Non-governmental organisations/ development projects induced collectives; on the social action and fieldwork planning for the succeeding fieldwork phase.

Phase –V. (3rd Sept. to 7th Sept. 2002) Sharing Fieldwork experiences on the following: Problems affecting health; Environmental problems; Gender relations in everyday life; labour relations' assessment of development programmes; assessment of decentralisation initiative of the State Government; review of actions initiated and lessons learnt and fieldwork planning for the succeeding fieldwork phase.

Phase–VII. (5th Nov. to 10th Nov 2002) Sharing Fieldwork experiences on the following:

Further understandings on local history, ecology and the problems of women, education, health, hygiene, nutrition, agricultural practices, entrepreneurship, the present economic and social status as it is experienced in the day-to-day life; Discussion on actions undertaken, possible associations with decentralisation programmes, evaluating the *praxis* intervention practice, planning for future action. There was a practical session on using computers and a discussion on information technology.

Appendix -2

Fieldwork Phases. (Phases II, IV, and VI)

Phase-II. (2ⁿᵈ June to 30ᵗʰ June 2002) Exploring land use patterns walking with the owners of the land in their respective lands, observing the crops cultivated there, and probing into its use in the past; the agriculture practices adopted; plant protection and manuring methods, irrigation practices, etc, exploring life history of at least three members of a hamlet of which at least one being a woman; collecting the history of consumptions; probing into their labour status and so on.

Phase-IV. (6ᵗʰ July to 2ⁿᵈ Sept. 2002) Continuing the explorations in the earlier phase of the fieldwork with new questions posed from the classroom discussions; exploring the history of ecological environment; exploring the health status of the people; Exploration of water availability and its quality; enquiring into the education of the children; walking in group into the forests and observe; engage in active dialogue with the people and discussing their fieldwork observations and classroom discussions; finding a handful of volunteers to act on the problems they have identified.

Phase VI. (8ᵗʰ Sept. to 4ᵗʰ Nov. 2002) Continuing the explorations in the earlier phases of the fieldwork with new questions posed from the classroom discussions; Initiating people into agriculture practices and food storage at every home; starting action for clean drinking water; inviting discussions of just gender relations; introducing new experiments in agriculture practices; making people aware of their legal rights; making use of development and welfare initiatives of the state; countering the menace of alcoholism; questioning exploitative practices; and continuing with the tempo of the fieldwork and so on.

Appendix - 3

<u>Workshops</u>

I Workshop: 28th and 29th January 2002. Issues: Refinement of the draft proposal, identification of participants, identification of topics of enquiry.

The workshop began with Dr. Ponna Wignaraja's keynote address on "The Challenges of Decentralisation reforms and the pro-poor growth in South Asia- intervention through *praxis* and participatory development". He emphasised the urgency and need to learn from the ground. He cautioned. "It would be too late if we do not start learning from the ground. It is already a 'history' that Kerala was a model of development. Now there are discussions going on the underlying streams of failure of Kerala Model. Tomorrow it will be labelled as a failure case. When it is blamed as failure, the 'Technical Assistance' from the west would follow. The western experts who cannot understand the human warmth and caring prevailing at the ground among us, with their bookish knowledge and pseudo professionalism would recommend solutions that could only leave our status (especially that of the poor) further worsened off. With the imposition of the technical assistance from the western models of development, the state will lose control over its development process. This can be averted only if the state keenly listens to the voices from the ground. To act on the poverty condition, it is important that we listen to the poor. Listening to the poor is not putting our mind in their mouth using PRA, RRA or any other toolkits."

Dr. Wignaraja warned that, treating *adivasis* as *object* of service delivery system is dangerous, as this would inculcate dependency on the people and alienate them from their life.

Senior bureaucrats from the department of Tribal Development, Forest Department were also present in the workshop. They expressed the point of view from their parent departments. When the bureaucrats from the Tribal Development field emphasised the need for strengthening the *Ooru Kootams*[149] the spokes persons from the Forest department raised their concern about preservation of the forest resources should not be unattended while attempting to empower *tribal Ooru Kootams*. There were officials representing Eco-development Project[150] in the workshop. Their

---

[149] Assembly of tribal hamlets.
[150] Eco-Development Project is implemented at the Periyar Tiger Reserve forest at Idukki and Pathanamthitta districts of Kerala, with the funding assistance from the World bank.

emphasis was to promote the neighbour hood groups that could find out alternative means for their livelihood relying minimum on the forest resources. The votaries of 'Participatory Forest Management' expressed that any agenda of *tribal development* should have a component of enhancing the capacities of the *adivasis* in managing the forest resources in participation with the forest department. Some of the participants expressed that the main problem of underdevelopment or backwardness in the *tribal* community is not integrating them with the market mechanism. They were of the view that finding out market opportunities and training them in entrepreneurial skills would solve the problem. There was another section of observant who expressed that strengthening the *Grama* Panchayats and the decentralisation initiatives would bring about development for *adivasis*. In all these viewpoints there was an underlining message that 'development' is inevitable and it has to be brought to the *tribal* lives. The method suggested by them was 'participatory'. By participatory it was meant that the *tribals* should be organised into groups or *Oorukootams*, design implement projects of their development as it is guided by the bureaucracy or experts; here the *tribals* participate in selecting beneficiaries, identifying project locations and co-operating with the government initiatives. Some participants were unhappy about the word 'intervention' in '*praxis intervention*'. They were of the opinion that *non-tribals* should not intervene in *tribal* life. Some observed that the "tribal culture and identity" is corroding and hence, any intervention should give priority to reinstating their cultural ethos. Some of the participants expressed their apprehension about the use of foreign words such as *habitus* or *praxis* being widely used in the workshop. When some took an extreme view that only Malayalam words to be used throughout the training, the others said even Malayalam is a foreign tongue as far as most of the *tribals* in Kerala are concerned.

Prof. Rajan Gurukkal[151], in his effort to bring clarity to the workshop, explained why it is useful and important to use the concepts of social thought used by the so-called social scientists. He warned that commonsense can misguide us in our social endeavours. He reminded us that romantically idealising any culture and identifying a section of people with cultural aspects of a historical period might be an unworthy exercise. It is important, not to deprive the historicity to any culture. It would be misguiding if we start thinking that any culture is essentially good or essentially bad. Every culture is bound to transform. Secondly, he mentioned that whether we like it or not,

---

[151] Dr. Rajan Gurukkal, is the professor and director of the School of Social Sciences, Mahatma Gandhi University, Kottayam, Kerala.

there is intervention on all our lives. Capitalist World System and its instruments always intervene in our lives. The intervention need not be always ethical. Non-intervention also can be unethical in such circumstances. Ethical and non-assuming   intervention need not be treated on par with the unethical interventions. Commenting on participation, participation within the reformist ideology may be just a tool of containment strategy. The participation, as a reflexive practice is radically different from the tool-kit approach of the reformists.

As the philosophical differences were still un-clarified the participants moved on to discuss specific issues such as:

1.   Discussion on the draft proposal of the *Praxis* Intervention Project (PIP).

2.   Selection Criteria of the Participants of the PIP.

3.   Identification of Resource persons.

4.   Training Modules.

5.   On documenting the PIP.

6.   Identification of research problems for the PIP participants.

7.   On overall conduct of the programme.

The outcome of the workshop was:

The draft proposal had not been revised. Rather the participants expressed their agreement with the programme. A field study before the initiation o the programme had been suggested. No decision on preparation of training module was suggested. No decision was made on documenting the *praxis* intervention project. The subject matter suggested was varied; the forest department officials wanted this to be a training programme on 'Participatory Forest Management'. There was a suggestion to inculcate skills of marketing. For some others it should be a programme on *Oorukootam* and decentralised planning. Some officials felt that such a programme should be used to propagate welfare schemes of the government. In the workshop it was decided to identify a small group of resource persons and discuss the issues further in-depth. It was suggested that the elected members, and *tribal* promoters have to be the participants. Some suggested that it would be of little use if the elected members were trained, as they would be unable to act on behalf of the *tribal* community, because they are merely party representatives.

II Workshop: 15ᵗʰ and 16ᵗʰ April 2002. Issues: On a workshop with elected *adivasi* representatives of the local bodies (Panchayats).

The initial plan was to have elected representatives and the government appointed "Tribal Promoters" to be the participants of the project. The tribal promoters are appointed in the *adivasi* hamlets by the government to function as the intermediaries between the government programmes and the *adivasi* hamlets. The 'tribal promoters' were appointed by the "Tribal Development Department." A letter was sent to the secretary, tribal development department, requesting him to send a batch of 'tribal promoters' to the *praxis* intervention project. There was no reply from the department. When the secretary was contacted over phone he expressed his (the department's) unwillingness to send 'tribal promoters' for the *praxis* intervention project. To discuss on selection of participants and other issues the II workshop was convened.

The key decisions of the workshop were:

1. To conduct a workshop with the elected representatives belonging to *adivasi* communities of Palakkad, Idukki and Wyanad districts to decide on the field location of *Praxis* intervention project.

2. The workshop should sharpen the Training Needs Assessment of *Praxis* Intervention Project [PIP].

3. The trainees have to be called 'researchers' rather than trainees.

4. It should not be just the researchers but the inhabitants of their respective hamlets also should participate in the PIP.

5. The hamlets selected for action research should be preferably the hamlets where the researchers reside, or the hamlets where the researchers can continue their action research even after the PIP is over.

6. It was suggested that the responsibility to organise the programme and conduct them should be with a "core team" headed by the course director [the present researcher].

7. To advise the core group an advisory team had also been suggested. The advisory group suggested consisted of eminent scholars of Kerala.

III Workshop: 24th to 26th April 2002. The participants of the workshop held on 24th and 25th were the elected *adivasi* representatives from the districts of Idukki, Wyanad and Palakkad. The idea of *praxis* intervention was introduced to the participants of the workshop and the participants' response was collected. It was suggested that the *praxis* intervention project should cover all the three districts within a period of three years. It was also suggested that those who received training in the earlier phase could serve as resource persons for the subsequent projects. It was suggested that each training programme of *Praxis* intervention should last for a minimum of 4.5 months. Decisions were taken regarding the participating *panchayats* in the first initiative of *praxis* intervention.

The participants opined that the *praxis* intervention project should focus on the issues such as land deprivation, stories of slave-like experience, difficulties in coping with modern developments, issues of illness, women's health issues, failed entrepreneurial initiatives, excess of bureaucracy, exploitation of funds allocated for *tribal* development, unmindful political party leadership, the increasing menace of arrack, disoriented family life, loss of control over the fate of their children, futility of developmental projects, personal sufferings and so on.

On 26th the outcome of the workshop with the elected representatives was discussed and further course of action discussed.

The suggestions of the workshop were:

1. To use of participatory techniques and games in facilitating learning.

2. To have a workshop with academicians and subject experts on the method of *praxis* intervention.

3. Instead of inviting people to give lectures on discreet topics, every day programmes should be around a theme. All resource persons to be invited should be well briefed of the nature of *praxis* intervention. Care should be taken in maintaining organic linkages between all the classroom sessions.

4. Care should be taken to develop informal and friendly relation with the participants.

5. All topics selected for discussion should be directly relevant for their life situation. The areas such as health, nutrition, food security and health, land usages, land rights, education,

water resource utilisation, ecology, historical interpretation of their present life situations, innovative agricultural technology, gender relations, learning from personal histories, exploring the nature and history of communitarian life etc., has to be covered.

6.   Exploring opportunities from the decentralised planning initiatives, governmental schemes, and other such topics also recommended to be included. It was also insisted that the classroom sessions should be well linked to the fieldwork.

7.   It was suggested that the programme has to be labelled as "¦ÆßÕÞØß ¼àÕßÄJßæa ÉáÈV ÈßVÎÄß: ²øá dÉÞíØØí §¿É¿W (Revitalising the life of the *Adivasi*s: A *Praxis* Intervention Approach") with the following objectives:

- Prepare the participants to reflexively evaluate their present socio-economic and political conditions of life, and to act upon restructuring it.

- Facilitate participants to find a political space in the decentralisation initiative of the state government.

- Enhance the intervention capability of the participants towards their own and their community *habitus praxis*.

IV Workshop: 5ᵗʰ May 2002. The participants of the workshop were experts in the fields of tribal development, action research, sociology, development economics, gender specialists and activism. The workshop was held to sharpen theoretical insight. The key opinions expressed by the participants of the workshop were:

1.   Poverty eradication programmes look at tribal poverty in terms of the roof, floor, toilet facilities, road access, wage earning and other indicators. There was an excessive importance given to manipulate indicators rather than bringing about real change in the *adivasi* life.

2.   Decentralisation is more of an instrument of party politics and bureaucratic practices rather than something to do with the lives of the people concerned. Unfortunately the decentralisation initiative is reduced into an exercise of participatory data extraction for the purpose of governance and management.

3. Party politics has an aversion towards non-party politics and hence the local politicians need not appreciate a political project like praxis intervention.

4. Hardly one finds the presence of organised non-party politics in the *Adivasi* hamlets. Organised politics of party and non-party varieties neglect actual everyday life situation of the people in the tribal hamlets. This is mainly because the people in the hamlets are taken for granted as objects of their respective political stand.

5. The errors in implementing 'Tribal Sub Plan' through the decentralised set up have been highlighted by the bureaucracy to take back the funds to the departments. In their political game for fund control, bureaucracy had won over elected bodies of decentralised governance. Instead of thinking on improving the life conditions of *adivasi*s the focus had always been having control over the tribal development funds

6. Land ownership pattern, land utilisation pattern the pattern of marginalisation in terms of power, wealth and knowledge should be given prominence in the *Praxis* intervention project.

7. The participants should be helped to understand the cultural and symbolic patterns of dominance and deprivation.

V Workshop: 27th May 2002. The participants were the core faculty members. This was held to fine-tune the classroom sessions. There were detailed discussions and debates on the issues of identity politics, development, well being, forms of capital, reflexivity, social construction, forms of capital, dealing with history and other crucial theoretical issues fundamental to the idea of *praxis* intervention.

VI Workshop: 25th June 2002. The field visit was undertaken by a team of faculties to Attappady to review the fieldwork progress was discussed. The content, method and management of the third phase were also discussed.

VII Workshop: 5-6th August.2002. A field visit was undertaken for two days on 4th and 5th of August 2002. This workshop was held to assess the progress of the *praxis* intervention project and to decide on the next classroom phase. There were also theoretical debates.

VIII Workshop: 25th October.2002 This was to discuss a field visit undertaken on 27th to 29th of

September 2002. During the field visit, the *adivasi* participants expressed their concern on the plans of Bhavani river diversion towards Marnnarkad. The issue of Bhavani river diversion and its consequences were discussed with expert guidance. The course of action for the next classroom phase was decided.

Appendix 4

The List of Adivasi Participants of the Praxis Intervention Project

Participant	Location
Allan	Tookkan Palayam
Bina	Guddayoor
Dasan Master	Vattalakki
Dineshan	Padavayal
Gomathi	Kottathara
Jayan	Chundappatty, Pudur
Kali	Kolappady
Kali Muthu	Mamana
Mallika	Kandiyoor, Jellippara
Mani	Kunjoor
Meenakshi	Kavundikkal
Moorthy	Padavayal
Murugan	Koravan Kandi
Murukesan	Nellipathy
Maruthy	Agali
Nanjan	Nakkupathi
Nanjan T	Pudur
Pappa	Koravan Kandi

Palanisami	Sholayoor
Ponni	Paloor
Prakasan	Oothukuzhi
Pushpa	Thadikkundu
Pushpavalli	Bommiyan Padi
Ramachandran	Kavindikkal
Rangan	Mettu Vazhi
Rangasamy	Chindakki-II
Renuka	Karuvara
Resi	Sholayoor
Raveendran	Sholayoor
Santhosh	Pudur
Selvan	Pudur
Shantha Mani	Vellamari
Suresh	Chindakki-I
Sudhakaran	Mele Chundappatti
Vellingiri	Agali

Appendix -5

The Resource Persons associated with the Praxis Intervention Project

Resource Person	Field
Binitha Thampi	Associate Professor in "Women and Development"
Dr. Brahmaputran	Expert in Health Sciences
Dinesan V	Sociologist, History Expert.
Dr. Ganesh K.N.	Reader in History, Eminent Historian
Gopala Krishnan	Expert in Local Administration
Prof. Jayaprakash Raghaviah	Professor in Finance
Prof. John M. Itty	Professor in Pedagogy
Jose Peter	Activist in adivasi Issues
Dr. Kunjaman	Professor in Development Economics.
Madhu. P	Researcher
Dr. Nampoothiri. DD	Professor in Sociology
Dr. Neezar Ahmed	Professor in Philosophy, Eminent Philosopher.
Adv. Padbanapan. PG	Legal Expert, Activist and a Practicing Lawyer.
Dr. Prabhu Das	Medical Officer, Pudur, Attappady
Dr. Raghava Warrior	Professor in History, Eminent Historian.
Dr. Raghu Nandanan V.R	Professor in Veterinary Science.

Prof. Rajan Gurukkal	Eminent Historian, Sociologist.
Raju C.K	Associate Professor in Information Technology
Dr. Raju S.	Economist, Historian and Sociologist
Dr. Ramakrishnan A.K.	Professor in Political Science
Dr. Ravi Raman	Associate Professor, Development Expert.
Roy Mathew	Expert in Agriculture Economics and Soil Micro-Organism.
Dr. Sathish Chandran Nair	Eminent Environmental Scientist, Renowned Environmental Activist
Shobha PV	Sociologist, Gender Relations expert
Dr. Sunny George	Associate Professor in Local Administration
Thomas K.M.	Activist in Dalit issues, Social Worker
Adv. Vijayamma	Legal Expert, Activist and a Practicing Lawyer.

Appendix- 6

Public Institutions at Attappady

Specialized Operational Area	Government/ public Institutions
Agriculture	Office of the Agri Asst Director, Agali Krishibhavans - 3 (one each at Agali, Pudur and Sholayur) Attappady Co-operative Farming Society, Agali Vatlakky Girijan Co-operative Farming Society, Dasannur
Sericulture	Serifed Sub centre, Agali
Animal Husbandry	Veterinary hospital, Agali Veterinary Dispensary - 2 (one each at Pudur, Sholayur)
ICDP Sub centers	8
Industry	Industrial Development Officer ST Industrial Co-op Societies – 4
Diary Development	Dairy extension officer, Agali Milk societies – 14 Milk chilling plant, Naikarpadi
Irrigation	Minor Irrigation Officer, Agali and Kottathara Attappady Valley Irrigation Project Officer, Agali
Soil Conservation	Asst Director Office 5
Rural Development	Block Officer, Agali Village extension officer –14
Tribal Development	Integrated Tribal Development Officer, Agali Tribal Extension Officers – 3
Health	Community Health Centre, Agali

	Primary Health Centre - 3 (Pudur, Vatlakky, Sholayur) IPP Sub Centre- 28 Homeo Dispensary-4 Ayurveda Dispensary-3
Education	Model Residential School, Mukkali High Schools 7 Upper Primary Schools 4 Lower Primary Schools 18 Hostels 13 (Scheduled Tribes 12, Scheduled Cast 1)
Social Welfare	ICDS Project Officer, Agali Anganawadi 12
Communication	Sub Post Office, Agali Branch Post Offices 13 Doordarsan Relay Station, Agali Telephone Exchange - 2
Electricity	KSEB Substation, Agali
Forest	Forest Range Officers – 2 Forest Stations 2
Banking Institutions	Nationalised Banks 4 Scheduled Banks 1 Co-operative banks 3
Public Works	PWD Office 2 PWD Rest House, Agali
Public Distribution	Ration shops – 39

Law and Order	Circle Inspector's Office, Agali
	Police Stations - 2 (Agali and Sholayur)
Miscellaneous	Sub Treasury, Agali
	Sub Registrar Office, Agali
	Excise Office, Agali
	Employment Bureau, Agali
	Asst. Wild Life Warden Officer (Silent Valley), Mukkali
	Attappady Hills Area Development Society, Agali
	Silent Valley Information Centre, Mukkali
	Co-operative Societies - 7 (ST - 6, SC - 1)
	Self Help Groups by Block – 127
	Neighbourhood groups by Kudumbashree – 355
	Arts and Sports Clubs – 59
	Social and Voluntary Organisations – 10
	Weekly Market Places (Chantha) -3

Appendix -7

Major development projects implemented at Attappady[152]

In 1998, the Integrated Rural Technology Centre conducted a study to evaluate the efforts at Attappady, as per the request of the AHADS project. The findings partly reveal the extent of failure of the government sponsored development initiatives in the various fields of 'development.'

1.   Projects of the Agriculture Department.

Increasing production and productivity using modern technical developments and by adopting a scientific approach had been the declared objective of the Agriculture Department while dealing with the issues at Attappady. Towards this objective, the department had started various initiatives like distributing seeds and saplings of coconut, areca nut, pepper, paddy, cashew and other vegetables. The department also contributed to construction, erection or procurement of pumps, pump-sets, farmhouse compost units, biogas plants, wells etc. During 1986 - 96, roughly Rs. 4 crore, has been spent on various agriculture development projects at Attappady, where the cultivable area is around 130 sq km.

The report suggests that, though this department has maintained records of all transactions involving distribution of benefits, there are many accusations. Most of such accusations point that the real beneficiaries never got anything. It was the 'proxies' that managed to stash away most of the public funds. There are also accusations that seeds and seedlings distributed were not fit for the areas at Attappady as was also the case with pumps, pump sets etc.

Though the report exposes the corrupt practices involved in implementing the project it does not delve in to the question of the relevance of the projects.

2.   Minor Irrigation Project

Minor irrigation department was set up at Attappady with a view to introduce schemes for better irrigational utilisation of water. It may be recalled that the streams of Bhavani and Siruvani flow through the landscape of Attappady. The total arable land comes to around 23500 hectares,

---

[152]   Adopted from P. Madhu. "Introduction to the Document" Document on Praxis Intervention [draft]. KILA, 2003. [Unpublished]

where around Rs 1.7 crore has been spent during the period 1986 - 96.

Madhava Menon Commission report cites, "Many weirs constructed were washed off and only the remnants of the construction are now left. The money spent on these schemes has gone waste due to substandard construction works. The money spent from CD funds for irrigation and lift irrigation has not been able to provide the irrigational facilities to the tribal lands to the extent envisaged in each scheme".

"Unfinished works, even after several years, lack of proper planning, implementation and monitoring etc forced many of the projects to be abandoned. That most of the projects were ill conceived are evident from their subsequent abandonment." so says the study report prepared by IRTC.

3.   Attappady Valley Irrigation Project (AVIP)

The main aim of AVIP had been to increase the irrigational facilities at Attappady, besides generating 3 MW of electric power utilising the stream of Siruvani. The project envisaged setting up of a dam at Chittoor for irrigating 4347 hectares of land. In 1970 the project estimated the cost at Rs 4.76 crore which is presently revised to Rs 110 crore. 114 families were evicted. Bushes and hedges alongside the stream were shaved off, which paved the way for massive soil erosion. Construction of canal was completed for just over 4 km. Around Rs 11 crores have been spent on this project, so far. The utility values of this project for *Adivasi*s whose cultivation are concentrated on hill slopes are deeply doubted.

4.   Animal Husbandry Projects

The people of Attappady attach a great deal of priority to domestic cattle. It is believed that during 1991-96, around Rs 10 crore had been spent on various projects related to animal husbandry. The main investments were made on distribution of domestic cattle like goats, cows, bulls, etc and a few breeds of rabbits and poultry.

IRTC study was critical on this activity, it is observed that, it was not suited to the traditional system of *Adivasi*s and these animals were not adaptable to the climatic condition of Attappady.

5.   Dairy development project

The claimed intentions of dairy development project were to eliminate nutrition related problems and to a limited extent, unemployment. Investments to the tune of Rs 15.86 lakh were made during 1992-97 towards development of modern dairy farms, construction of cattle-sheds, cultivation of cattle grass, distribution of cattle, financial support to dairy development societies etc.

6.   Fisheries Project

IRTC study on the department lists out that " The project aimed at schemes usually introduced in the coastal areas or plains. While Rs 1000 was allocated for fish-feeds, Rs 1.75 lakh was spent on the construction of concrete sides and Rs 8 lakh was spent on erecting a check-dam. The fisheries department had set its objective on introducing pisciculture, as a novel project."

7.   Sericulture

"Generating additional income and employment opportunities were some of the motives behind establishing SERIFED in 1989 at Attappady. Since the business couldn't generate enthusiasm and expected outcome, it was rejected," mentions the IRTC report.

8.   Forestry

Around 59.62% of the total area in Attappady is forest of which around 22.69% are in degradable state. During 1992-97, forest department introduced 'social forestry' spending Rs 6.57 crore. Apart from this, there were efforts through ITDP, World Bank, Rural Development Project etc aimed at forestation. "Even though huge sums have been spent, there were no significant tangible results", says the IRTC report.

9.   Soil Conservation

One of the large projects undertaken by the department in Kerala is at Attappady. The project involves preventing sedimentation in the dam constructed across the *Kunta* stream. The project had other goals as increasing productivity, employment opportunities etc. During 1967-97, around 26859 hectares of cultivable land has been brought under this scheme. Moreover 18437 weirs, 236 ponds, 268 water-harvesting structures and 74 Km or sidewalls have been constructed. Around Rs 12.95 crore have been spent on this scheme so far.

10.   Other Departments

To cut a long story short, there has been similar occasions in almost all the departments where investments or expenditure have been made, most of which have come under sharp criticism from various agencies through study reports or otherwise.

Appendix -8

Our Song

1

We, the *adivasi*s of Attappady Lived here for centuries

in harmony and happiness

Amidst plenty of fruits, tubers, leaves and fish

Fresh deer meet, honey and honour.

Thillele thele machan thillele thele

Thillele thele machan thillele thele

2

Never selfish, ever sharing,

Fearless, content and helping each other.

Slashing, burning trees on slopes,

We grew millets and cereals.

[Thillele thele…]

3

Revering wisdom, knowledge and thought,

Manookarar guided folks,

Submitting to love and care,

They sow seeds for all of us.

[Thillele thele…]

4

Obliging to righteousness,

Cereals and millets grew in abundance.

We had plenty of harvest

To eat and store till next season.

[Thillele thele…]

5

With abundance of food

Mutual love, care and concern

Confident and fearless we were

merrily lived with songs and dances.

[Thillele thele…]

6

Ignorant of the selfishness

Ignorant of discriminations

We lived together singing and dancing.

We were one, we were healthy,

[Thillele thele…]

7

Then there came one Moopil Nair,

Claimed that he had birthright on lands

He was collecting rent from us,

For allowing us to live and work.

[Thillele thele…]

8

He collected rent through *Moopans*

He established a few *moopans* too,

Later he said he owns the trees

Animals, shrubs, soil and water.

[Thillele thele…]

9

How can humans own all these?

He brought people to cut them off.

Not just trees he took away,

Also, rain, mist and water springs.

[Thillele thele…]

10

With loss of trees, mist and raindrops,

We lost all and sad we felt.

Then came alien men and women.

They built houses and had farms.

[Thillele thele…]

11

Lands were taken off from us

And sow their seeds as they desired

Drove away animals, and burnt trees

With no reverence to *neethi, nela.*

[Thillele thele…]

12

We were stopped from moving free.

We were stopped from slash and burn

We could not grow crops as before,

Our lands became infertile and stale.

[Thillele thele…]

13

We were starving and hungry.

We had no grain of food stored

We lost soil, water, fresh breeze

We lost respect, honour and prestige

[Thillele thele…]

14

We had lost trust, faith and confidence

Sickness followed, we suffered.

We were ill and in distress,

We had lost our land and prestige

[Thillele thele…]

15

We were made to work for them.

For stale food, torn cloths and for arrack

With this we lost our life, land and everything

Above all we lost *neethi*

[Thillele thele…]

16

Neethi was killed and Nela was nowhere.

With the loss of *neethi* and Neri

we have no life worth living

Let us try to bring back the *neethi*

[Thillele thele…]

17

With that we will come back to life.

Let us grow grains, cereals and millets

Let us grow green leaves and tubers.

Let us have our granaries full.

[Thillele thele…]

18

This would bring our confidence back

Health, honour, respect and cheer.

This would bring our confidence back

Health, honour, respect and cheer.

[Thillele thele…]

Appendix 9

List of cases registered in Attappady (Palakad Dist.) Area pertaining to atrocities on Adivasis

Sl. No.	Crime No.	Name	Offence	Place of occurrence	Date of occurrence
1	146/02	Vella, S/o Rangan	Murder	Pattanakkal	29-07-02
2	114/02	V.M. Gangadharan	Not clear	Naikkarppadi	01-06-02
3	15/98	Kanchi, S/o Mudiyan	Murder	Veettiyur	25-01-98
4	27/00	Murukesh, S/o Konan	Hanged to death	Kolappadika	24-01-02
5	24/98	Gathan, S/o Kadan	Murder	Narasimukku	06-02-98
6	22/02	Lakshmi, D/o Sivan	Not clear	Vallapatti	22-01-02
7	88/92	Konan	Murder	Pattimalam	03-03-92
8	94/92	Nanchi, D/o Bhapli	Murder	Kunnamchala	06-04-92
9	133/00	Ponni	Not clear	Agali	18-07-00
10	206/99	Velli, S/o Ayyappan	Hanged	Anakkallu	16-10-99
11	71/02	Sivan	Murder	Sholayoor	09-08-02
12	29/01	Gopalakrishnan	Hanged	Vechappathi	01-04-02
13	56/01	Valli, D/o Balan	Suicide	Uttukuzhi	17-09-01
14	94/00	Sivan, S/o Chellan	Not clear	Sholayoor	27-12-02
15	18/01	Kongara, S/o Nanchan	Not clear	Puliyappathi	05-04-01
16	37/02	Thamandan,S/oNanchan	Murder	N. Kadambara	23-04-02

17	2/02	Mari	Notclear	Kathirampathy	03-01-02
18	3/02	Lakshmi, W/o Maruthan	Hanged	Kottiyoorkunnu	4-01-02
19	12/02	Vellachi, W/o Galikan	Hanged	Thazhikakkuppady	14-01-02
20	20/02	Ushadevi	Murder	Agali	21-01-02
21	41/02	Nanchan	Hanged	Kolapppadika	2002
22	54/02	Maruthan	Not clear	Veettiyoor	03-03-02
23	7/02	Murukan, S/o Nanchan	Hanged	Gulikkadavu	25-03-02
24	110/02	Vellingiri, S/o Rangan	Not clear	Kararai	30-05-02
25	33/89	Karuppan	Murder	Gottiyarkkandi	2002
26	68/98	Rami, W/o Kongara	Not clear	Pazhayurmantha	05-09-98
27	34/01	Maruthan,S/o Bhussan	Not clear	Pettikkal	28-05-00
28	2/02	Murukan, S/o Chinnan	Not clear	Nallasinga	03-02-00
29	5/02	Nagamma, W/oKuppuswamy	Not clear	Chalayoor	06-01-02
30	9/02	Murukeshan, S/o Kala	Hanged	Palakayoor	09-01-00
31	11/02	Bokkan, S/o Rangan	Suicide	Kandiyoor	11-01-02
32	13/02	Kamalam,W/o Ponnan	Suicide	Karathoor	15-01-02
33	14/02	Sivan, S/o Kara	Not Clear	Meelai Chuttara	2002
34	51/02	Rangan,S/o Kadukan	Not clear	Padavayal	25-02-02
35	56/02	Selvan,S/o Wellingiri	Hanged	Konamkuthi	05-03-02
36	62/02	Kakki, S/o Maruthan	Suicide	Pattanakkallu	11-03-02
37	126/02	Maruthi, W/o Veeran	Hanged	Vadakottathata	02-07-02
38	130/02	Maruthi, W/o Vella	Suicide	Mukkai	07-07-02
39	131/02	Mani, S/o Raman	Suicide	Thazai Golikkadavu	11-07-02

40	132/02	Soman, S/o Sundran	Suicide	Cheerakkadavu	12-07-02
41	153/02	Rajan, S/o Maruthan	Not clear	Bhuthuvazhi	06-08-02
42	160/02	Shinoy, S/o Uarkey	Hanged	Kallamala	14-08-02
43	167/02	Arumukan,S/o Krishna Mutkaliyar	Suicide	Kollangaza-Agali	23-08-02
44	1988	Dossi,W/o Thamandan	Murder	Vannanthara	1988
45	1990	Rajamani	Hanged	Varagampady	1990
46	1993	Sivadasan	Murder	Pothuppady	1993
47	1996	Vellingiri	Murder	Thuva	1996
48	191/02	Vellingiri, S/o Murugan	Murder	Palakayur	23-09-02
49	2002	Rajan	Murder	S. Chavadiyur	10/ 2002
50	30/02	Chinnu D/o Veraswamy	Suicide	Agali	28-01-00
51	77/00	Sindhu D/oVelli	Rape	Anavai	17-07-00
52	89/00	Jyothimani,D/o Ranjan	Rape	Pothupady	17-08-00
53	130/92	P.K.Chinnan, S/o Kadodi (Vijaya)	Vijaya was raped	Pudur	1992
54	10/93	Mari,D/o Chathan	Rape	Anavai	1993
55	1/03	Vijayalakshmi	Rape	Kathalakkandi	1993
56		Pappa, D/o Ranjan	Rape	Kathirampathi	1993.
57	57/93	Mallika, D/o Maruthy	Rape	Gonchiyoor	
58		Ponni, W/o Murukan	Torture	Elachivazi	1994
59	65/96	Mani, S/o Maruthan	Torture	-------	15-3-96
60	65/96	Mari, S/o Rangan	Torture	-------	7-3-96
61	83/96	Raman, S/o Maruthan	Torture	Nellippathy	30-4-96
62	110/9	Raman, S/o Chellan	Suspicion on	Anakatty	25-11-96

	6		death of grandmother		
63	118/96	Santhi, W/o Sivakumar	Attempted to outrage the modesty of the complainant	Bhuthuvazhi	13-7-96
64	133/96	Rani, W/o Rangan	Destroying property	Chemmannur	7-8-96
65	159/96	Bhagavathy, W/o Kunchan	Abused by calling cast name and assaulted	Osathiyur	1-10-96
66	139/96	Resi, W/o Majeed	Trespassed into the shop and molested her	Agali	4-9-96
67	150/96	Ramachandran, S/o Thithunny	Torture	Chindakki	20-9-96
68	188/96	Bhagavathy, W/o Chinnan	Torture	Agali	26-11-96
69	191/96	Kali, S/o Kadan	Burning House	Bhuthavazhy	3-6-96
70	CA2/97	Manikandan, S/o Rajan	Police torture under custody	Kottathara	1997
71	87/97	Nanchi, W/o Bhaskar	Torture	Thannichodu	1997
72	103/97	Kali, W/o Nanchan	Torture		1997
73	107/97	Vellingiri, S/o Mani	Torture	Agali Melattoor	1997
74	113/97	Karuppu Swamy, S/o Resan	Attempt of murder	Pudur	1997
75	115/97	Karuppu Swamy, S/o Resan	Burning the house	Pudur	1997
76	139/97	Murukan, S/o Kali	Torture	Kallamala	1997

77	145/97	Ranga Swamy, S/o Gopalan	Torture	Chindakki	1997
78	150/97	Kakki, S/o Mari	Abused by calling caste name	Chindakki	21-9-96
79	87/93	Ponnan, S/o Ponnu Swami	Police Torture	Gonchiyur	1993
80	107/94	Pandiyan (Valli)	Rape case	Kathirampathy	1994
81	92/95	Rangi, D/o Resi			1995
82	103/96	Resi, W/o Gopalan	Rape	Kulukkur	1996
83	1990	Mannan, S/o Maruthan	Torture	Chavadiyur	1990
84		Pushpa, D/o Krishnan	Gang rape	Chundakulam	10-8-97
85		Maruthy	Rape	Kulukkur	11-9-96
86		Lakshmi, Bhagavathi, Rugmini	Torture	Pattimalam	1997
87	72/97	Valli, D/o Siva	Unwed mother	Karayoor	11-11-97
88	1/93	Smt. Vijayalakshmi	Rape	Sholayur	-------
89	--	Sri. Thamandan, Parappanthara	Physical assault	Shalayur	------
90	92/95	Rekha, D/o Bhasi	Insulted by calling her caste name	Sholayur	31-8-95 03-9-95
91	97/95	Krishna Moopan, S/o Siva Moopan	Polluted the water by pelting the corpse of a dog in the Siruvani River	Sholayur	6-9-95 7-9-95

			from where water in drawn.		
92	110/95	Maruthan, S/o Nagan	Wrongfully restrained and beating with hands	Sholayur	15-10-95 16-10-95
93	69/96	Maruthan, S/o Chellan	Assaulted the complainant and beat with hands.	Sholayur	6-8-96 8-8-96
94	99/96	Sri. Rankan , S/o Dason	Assaulted by beating with stick and abused him due to wordy quarrel	Sholayur	17-10-96 23-10-96
95	32/97	Mani, S/o Ponnu Swamy	Assaulted the complainant by beating due to previous enmity	Sholayur	14-6-97 17-6-97
96	40/97	Meenakshi, W/o Anaidan	Trespassed into the house assaulted molested and abused by calling caste names.	Sholayur	19-7-97 20-7-97
97	41/97	Rajan, S/o Vellingiri	Trespassed in the Iswara Estate and assaulted the complainant by stabling with knife.	Sholayur	22-7-97 24-7-97
98	47/97	Balan Keruyan, S/o Kutty	Assaulted the complainant and abused by calling names	Sholayur	14-8-97 14-8-97
99	52/97	Ponnan, S/o Kuppan	Wrongfully restrained the	Sholayur	23-8-97

			complainant and assaulted him with hands.		23-8-97
100	56/97	Ponnu Swamy, S/o Chathan Moopan	Assaulted the complainant by sticks due to previous enimity	Sholayur	29-8-97 29-8-97
101	60/97	Usha, D/o Sivaraman	Wrongfully restrained the complainant and robbed away one gold chain	Sholayur	7-9-97 9-9-97
102	62/97	Jadayan, S/o Mari	Assaulted the complainant by sticks and manhandled him due to previous enimity.	Sholayur	24-9-97 24-9-97
103	-----	Smt. Ponny, W/o Murukan	Physical Assault	Agali	----
104	170/95	Ranki, W/o Chellan	Assaulted by beating with hand, abused her by calling her caste name.	Agali	28-10-95
105	194/95	Chinnamaruthan, S/o Kadumooppan	Wrongfully confined and manhandled	Agali	16-11-95 23-12-95
106	---	Kuttipperukki, W/o Late Pokkan	Murder of her husband	Puduppariyaram	----
107	23/96	Vasantha, D/o Chami	Raped by three persons	----	-----
108	23/97	Sakunthala, D/o Subramanian	Rape	Padagiri	13-4-97 15-4 97

| 109 | 56/96 | Babu, S/o Nagan | Raped by non-tribal | Akamalavaram | 9-5-96 |

Source: http://jjwoodworld.port5.com/jananeethi/archives/muthanga.htm

REFERENCES

Abbot, Andrew. <u>The System of Professions</u>. Chicago: Chicago University Press, 1998.

Adamczewski, Zygmunt. "<u>Questions in Heidegger's Thought About Being</u>." <u>The Question of Being: East-West perspectives</u> Ed. Mervyn Sprung. Delhi: Sri Satguru, 1995.

Adams, Robert. "<u>Social Work Process</u>." <u>Social Work: Themes, Issues and Critical Debates</u> Eds. Robert Adams, Lena Dominelli and Malcolm Payne. London: Macmillan, 1998.

Ahmed, Nizar. "Reinventing the political." <u>Keraleeyam</u> 7. 3 (2005): 13-19.

Ahmed, Nizar. "Wellbeing" <u>Pachakkuthira (Malayalam)</u>:1.8, (2005): 22-30

Amin, Samir. "Imperialism and Globalization." <u>Monthly Review</u> 53. 2 (2001).

Archer, Margaret. "For Structure: its Reality, Properties and Powers: A Reply to Anthony King" <u>*Sociological Review*</u> 48 .3 (2000a): 464-72.

Archer, Margaret. <u>Being Human: The Problem of Human Agency</u>. Cambridge: Cambridge University Press, 2000b.

Archer, Margaret, Roy Bhaskar, Andrew Collier, Tony Lawson and Alan Norrie(ed.),<u>*Critical Realism: Essential Readings*</u> London: Routledge,1998.

Archer, Margratte. "Morphogenesis Versus Structuration: On Combining Structure and Action." <u>The British Journal of Sociology</u> 3. December 1982 (1982): 455-483.

Arednt, Henna. The Human Condition. London: The University of Chicago Press, 1958.

Aristotle. Politics. London: Penguin, 1990.

Attwood. H and May. J "Kicking down doors and lighting fires: the South African PPA". Whose voice? Participatory research and policy change. Eds. J. Holland, J. Blackburn. London: Intermediate Technology Publications, 1998

Atherton, Charles R and Kathleen A. Bolland. "Post Modernism: A Dangerous Illusion for Social Work." International Social Work 45. 4 (1998): 421-433.

Bannet, Eve Tavor. Structuralism and the Logic of Dissent. London: Macmillan Press, 1989.

Barker,R. The Social Work Dictionary. III ed. Washington DC: NASW Press, 1995.

Barry, Monica and Christine Hallett. (Eds.) "Social Exclusion and Social Work: Issues of Theory, Policy and Practice." Lyme Regis: Russell House Publishing, 1998.

Barthes, Roland. The Pleasure of Text. Ed. Miller, R. New York: Hill and Wang, 1975.

Barthes, Roland. Mythologies. Ed. Lavers, A. London: Paladin, 1972.

Bauman, Zygmunt. "Modernity and Ambivalence." The Polity Reader in Social theory. Cambridge: Polity press, 2002.

Bauman, Zygmunt. Memories of Class: The Pre-History and After-Life of Class. Boston: Routledge & Kegan Paul., 1982.

Beck, Ulrich and Elisabeth Beck. Individualization. New Delhi: Sage, 2002.

Berger, Peter L. and Thomas Luckmann. The Social Construction of Reality. London: Penguin Books, 1991.

Bernstein, Richard J. Praxis and Human Action; Contemporary Philosophies of Human Activity. Philadelphia: University of Pennsylvania Press, 1999.

BES [Bureau of Economics and Statistics]. Report on the Evaluation of Schemes Implemented in the Tribal Development Block, Attappady. Thiruvananthapuram: Bureau of Economics and

Statistics, Government of Kerala, 1977.

Bhaskar, Roy. From Science to Emancipation: Journeys Towards Mera-Reality a Philosophy for the Present. Alienation and the actuality of enlightenment. New Delhi: Sage, 2002.

Bhaskar, Roy. A Realist Theory of Science, 2nd edition, London: Verso. 1997

Bijoy, C R and K Ravi Raman. "Muthanga: The real story: Adivasi Movement to recover land". Economic and Political Weekly. (2003) May 2003

Bijoy, C.R, Indigenous Peoples' Rights in Kerala, Paper presented at Indigenous Rights in the Commonwealth Project South & South East Asia Regional Expert Meeting, New Delhi, India. 2002.

Borda, Orlando Fals. Knowledge and People's Power. New Delhi: Indian Social Institute, 1998.

Borda, Orlando Fals. "Participatory Action Research in Social Theory: Origins and Challenges." Handbook of Action Research: Participatory Inquiry and Practice Eds. Peter Reason and Hilary Bradbury. New Delhi: Sage, 2001. 27-37.

Boschee, Jerr. The Social Enterprise Sourcebook. Minnesota: The Institute for Social Entrepreneurs, 2001.

Bottomore, Thomas. B. Karl Marx, Early Writings. New York: McGraw-Hill, 1964.

Bottomore, Tom and et al., eds. A Dictionary of Marxist Thought. Second ed. New Delhi: Maya Blackwell, 2000.

Bourdieu, Pierre. "Participant Objectivation: The Huxley Medal Lecture." Journal of The Royal Anthropological Institute 9. 2 (2003): 281-294.

Bourdieu, Pierre. "Social Space and Symbolic Power." The Polity Reader in Social theory. Cambridge: Polity Press, 2002. 115-66.

Bourdieu, Pierre. Masculine Domination. Trans. smith. Stanford: Stanford University Press, 2001.

Bourdieu, Pierre. "The politics of protest" Socialist Review. 242, (2000)

Bourdieu, Pierre. <u>Acts of Resistance: Against the Tyranny of the Market</u>. Trans. Nice, R. New York: New Press, 1999.

Bourdieu, Pierre. <u>Utopia of Endless Exploitation: The Essence of Neoliberalism</u>. Le Monde Diplomatique. Available: http://www. monde-diplomatique.fr/en/1. 1998.

Bourdieu, Pierre. <u>The Rules of Art: Genesis and Structure of the Literary Field</u>. Stanford: Stanford University Press, 1996.

Bourdieu, Pierre. "<u>The Field of Cultural Production Or the Economic World Reversed</u>." <u>The field of Cultural Production: Essays on Art and Literature</u> Ed. Randal Johnson. Cambridge: Polity Press, 1993.

Bourdieu, Pierre and Loic Wacquant. <u>An Invitation to Reflexive Sociology</u>. Cambridge: Polity Press, 1992.

Bourdieu, Pierre. <u>The Logic of Practice</u>. Stanford: Stanford University Press, 1990.

Bourdieu, Pierre. <u>Homo Academicus</u>. Trans. Collier, P. Cambridge: Polity Press, 1988.

Bourdieu, Pierre. <u>Distinction: A Social Critique of the Judgement of Taste</u>. London: Routledge, 1984.

Bourdieu, Pierre. <u>Algeria 1960</u>. Cambridge: Cambridge University Press, 1979.

Bourdieu, Pierre. <u>Outline of a Theory of Practice</u>. Cambridge: Cambridge University Press, 1977.

Bourdieu, Pierre and et al. <u>The Weight of the World: Social Suffering in Contemporary Society</u>. Cambridge: Polity Press, 1999.

Bradley, James. W and Kurt C. Schaefer. <u>The uses and misuses of data and models: the mathematisation of the human sciences</u>. New Delhi: Sage, 1998.

Branson, Jan and Don Miller, eds. "<u>Pierre Bourdieu</u>." <u>Social Theory: A Guide to Central Thinkers</u>. New York: Allen and Unwin, 1991.

Brock, Karen. <u>An Introduction to Participatory Poverty Assessment</u>". Brighton: Institute of Development Studies, 2000.

Burkitt, Ian. Social Selves: Theories on the Social Formation of Personality. London: Sage, 1991.

Butler, Judith. Gender Trouble: Feminism and the subversion of Identity, London: Routledge, 1990

Calhoun, Craig. "Pierre Bourdieu, the Centrality of the Social, and the Possibility of Politics." Available: http//: www.nyu.edu/ classes/ Calhoun/theory/paper_on_Bourdieu2 (2002).

Calhoun, Craig. "Putting the Sociologist in the Sociology of Culture; the Self-Reflexive Scholarship of Pierre Bourdieu and Raymond Williams." Contemporary Sociology 19. 4 (1990): 500-505.

Carig, Gary. "Poverty Social Work and Social Justice." British Journal of Social Work. (2002). 32: 669-682

Craig, Gary. "Unlucky for Most." Community Care (2001).

Castoradis, Cornelius. The Imaginary Institution of Society. Trans. Balmey, K. Oxford: Polity Press, 1987.

CDG [Center for Democracy and Governance]. Decentralisation and Democratic Governance, Programming Hand Book. Center for Democracy and Governance. Available: http:/inside.usaid. gov/G/DG/, 2000

Chakravarthi, Sathindranath. "Praxis and Nature." Person and nature Ed. George F. McLean. Vol. 1. Washington DC: University Press of America, 2004.

Chambers, Robert. "The Best of Both Worlds?" Qualitative and Quantitative poverty appraisal: complementarities, tensions and the way forward. Cornell: Cornell University Press, 2001.

Clarke, John and Jane Newman. The Managerial State. London: Sage, 1997.

Collins, Randall. "Erving Goffman on Ritual and Solidarity in Social Life." The polity reader in Social Theory. New Delhi: Polity Press, 2002.

Cook, David. "Camera Negrida: Barthes' Panic Scene in the Postmodern Scene." The postmodern Scene Eds. Arthur Kroker and David Cook. Montreal: New World Perspectives, 2001.

Cooper, Barry. "Constructivism in Social Work: towards a Participative Practice viability." British Journal of Social Work 31 (2001): 721-738.

Coulshed, Veronica and Joan Orme. Social Work Practice: An Introduction. Houndmills: Macmillan, 1998.

Curran, Laura. "The Culture of Race, Class, and Poverty: The Emergence of a Cultural Discourse in Early Cold War Social Work (1946-1963)." Journal of Sociology and Social Welfare 2003. September (2003).

Dahl, Robert. "Can International Organizations Be Democratic? a Skeptic's View." In Democracy's Edges Eds. Ian Shapiro and Casiano Hacker-Cordon. Cambridge: Cambridge University Press, 1999. 19-36.

Davies, Mike. The Essential Social Worker. 3rd edition ed. Aldershot: Arena, 1994.

Davis, Martin ed. The Blackwell Companion to Social Work. II ed. Oxford: Blackwell, 2002.

De Silva, G.V.S and et al. Towards a Theory of Rural Development. Lahore: Progressive Publishers, 1998.

Desai, V. and R. Imrie. "The New Managerialism in Local Governance: North-South Dimensions." Third World Quarterly 19. 4 (1998): 635-650.

Dilthey, William. Introduction to the Human Sciences. 1923. Trans. Betanzos, R.J. London: Harvester, 1992.

Dominelli, Lena. Sociology for Social Work. London: Macmillan, 1997.

Durkheim, Emile. "The Division of Labour in Society.". London: Macmillan, 1964.

Durkheim, Emile. "Rules for the Observation of Social Facts." Mainstream and Critical Social theory; Cannons and critical discourses Ed. J.C.Alexanders. New Delhi: Sage, 2001.

Durkheim, Emile. Pragmatism and Sociology. Cambridge: Cambridge University Press, 1983.

Durkheim, Emile. Elementary Forms of the Religious Life. 1912. New York: Free Press, 1995.

Easton, Bt Loyd D and Guddat, eds. Writings of the Young Marx on Philosophy and Society. New York: Doubleday & Co, 1967.

Eikeland, Olav. "Action Research As the Hidden Curriculum of the Western Tradition." Handbook of Action Research: Participatory Inquiry and Practice Eds. Peter Reason and Hilary Bradbury. London: Sage, 2001. 145-56.

Elias, Norbert. The Civilizing Process. Oxford: Blackwell, 1994.

Elias, Norbert. "Knowledge and Power : An Interview By Peter Ludes." Society and Knowledge Eds. Volker Meja and Nico Stehr. London: Transaction, 1984.

Elias, Norbert. What Is Sociology. London: Hutchinson, 1978.

Escobar, Arturo. Encountering Development, Making and Unmaking of the Third World. New Jercy: Princeton University Press, 1996.

Fahlander, Fredrik. Archaeology As Science Fiction; Microarchaeology of the Unknown. Trans. Leuven, J.V. Göteborg: Kompendiet, Aida Trading AB, 2001.

Fawcett, Barbara. "Disability and Social Work: Application From Post Modernism, Post Structuralism and Feminism." British Journal of Social Work 28 (1998): 263-277.

Fay, B. Critical Social Science: Liberation and Its Limits. Ithaca: Cornell University Press, 1987.

Featherstone, Brid and Barbara Fawcett. "Oh No! Not More Isms!" Social Work education 14. 3 (1995): 25-43.

Feuerbach, Ludwig "Principles of the New Philosophy". Principles of the Philosophy of the Future. Trans. Zawar Hanfi, (1972). www.marxists.org, 2003.

Ferguson, Harry. "Social Work, Individualization and Life Politics." British Journal of Social Work 31 (2001): 41-55.

Feyerabend, Paul. Against Method. Minneapolis: University of Minnesota Press, 1970.

Fisher, M. "Research, Knowledge and Practice in Community Care." Issues in Social Work Education 17. 2 (1996): 17-30.

Fisher, Robert and Howard Karger. Social Work and Community in a Private World: Getting Out in Public. New York: Longman, 1997.

Fook, Jan. Social Work: Critical Theory and Practice. London: Sage, 2002.

Fook, Jan. "Linking Theory, Practice and Research." Critical Social Work 2. 1 (2001).

Fook, Jan, Martin Ryan and L Hawkins. Professional Expertise: Practice, Theory and Education for Working in Uncertainty. London: Whiting and Birch, 2000.

Fook, Jan. "Critical Reflectivity in Education and Practice." Transforming Social Work Practice: Postmodern Critical Perspectives Eds. Job Pease and Jan Fook. London: Routledge, 1999.

Fook, Jan. The Reflective Researcher. New South Wales: Allen and Unwin, 1996.

Foucault, Michel. The Birth of the Clinic: An Archeology of Medical Perceptions. Trans. Smith, S. New York: Vintage, 1994.

Foucault, Michel. "Of Other Spaces." Diacritics 16. 1 (1986): 22-27.

Foucault, Michel. "What Is Enlightenment?" The Foucault Reader Ed. Paul Rabinow. New York: Pantheon, 1985.

Foucault, Michel. Power/knowledge: Selected Interviews and Other Writings. New York: Pantheon, 1980.

Foucault, Michel. "Governmentality." Ideology and Consciousness 6 (1979): 5-26.

Freire, Paulo. Pedagogy of the Oppressed. New York: Continuum Publishing, 1980.

Frideres, James. "Participatory Research: An Illusionary Perspective." A World of Communities: Participatory Research Perspectives Ed. James Frideres. Toronto: Captus University Publications, 1992.

Friedlander, Peter. "Introduction: Theory, Method, and Oral History." The Emergence of a UAW Local, 1936-1939: A Study in Class and Culture. Pittsburgh: Pittsburgh University Press, 1975.

Gadamer, Hans- Georg. Truth and Method. Trans. Glen-Doepel. Second Edition ed. London: Shed & Ward, 1979.

Garfinkel, Herald. A Conception Of, and Experiments With, "Trust" As a Condition of Stable Concerted Actions in Motivation and Social Interaction,. Ed. Harvey, O.J. New York: Ranold Press, 1963.

Garfinkel, Herald. "Studies of the Routine Grounds of Everyday Activities." Studies in Ethnomethodology. Cambridge: Polity Press, 1984.

Geertz, Clifford. Local Knowledge. New York: Basic, 1983.

Giarchi, G. and Gloria Lankshear. "The Eclipse of Social Work in Europe." Social Work in Europe, 5. 3 (1998): 25-36.

Giddens, Anthony. "Structuralism, Post Structuralism and the Production of Culture." Social Theory Today Eds. Anthony Giddens and Jonathan. H. Turner. Cambridge: Polity press, 1987.

Giddens, Anthony. The Constitution of Society. Berkeley: University of California Press, 1986.

Goffman, Erving. "The Interaction Order." Mainstream and Critical Social Theory Ed. Jeffrey C. Alexander. Vol. III. New Delhi: Sage, 2001.

Goffman, Erving. Asylums. London: Penguin, 1991.

Goffman, Erving. Frame Analysis; an Essay on the Organisation of Experience. Boston:

Northeastern University Press, 1986.

Goffman, Erving. Interaction Ritual. Chicago: Aldine, 1967.

Goffman, Erving. Encounters: Two Studies in the Sociology of Interaction. Indianapolis: Bobbs-Merrill, 1961

Goffman, Erving. The Presentation of Self in Everyday Life. New York: Doubleday, 1959.

GOK. Decentralised Planning – Annual Plan 2003-2004 – Formulation and Implementation of Tribal Sub Plan (TSP) by Local Governments – Guidelines G.O.(MS)No. 54/2003/Plg. Dated, Thiruvananthapuram, 31 st May, 2003

GOK. Report of the Administrative Reforms Committee. Thiruvananthapuram: Government of Kerala, 2001

Gooby, Peter Taylor-. "Postmodernism and Social Policy: A Great Leap Backwards." Journal of Social policy 23 (1994).

Gouldner, Alwin W. Marxism and Critique in the Two Marxisms. New York: Oxford University Press, 1980.

Gouldner, Alwin W. The Coming Crisis of Western Sociology. New York: Basic, 1971.

Gramsci, Antonio. Selections From Political Writings, 1910-1920. Trans. Mathews, J. Ed. Hoare, Q. London: Lawrence and Wishart, 1977.

Gramsci, Antonio. Selections From the Prison Notebooks. Trans. Hoare, Q. and Smith, G.N. Eds. Hoare, Q. and Smith, G.N. London: Lawrence and Wishart, 1971.

Granovetter, Mark and Richard Swedberg. "Introduction to the Second Edition." The Sociology of Economic Life. Boulder: Westview Press, 2001.

Green, Bryan S. Knowing the Poor: A Case-Study in Textual Reality Construction. Boston: Routledge & Kegan Paul, 1983.

Greenwood, Ernest. "Social Science and Social Work: A Theory of Their Relationship." <u>Social Service Review</u> 29. 1 (1955): 21-33.

Gregory, Marilyn and Halloway. "Language and the shaping of Social Work." <u>British Journal of Social Work.</u> 35, (2005): 37-53

Grimwood, Cordelia, Evelyn houseman and Cynthia Ransley. "<u>Getting to Grips With Social Work.</u>". London: Open Learning Foundation, 1995.

Habermas, Jurgen. "From Kant to Hegel and Back Again -- the Move Towards Detranscendentalization." <u>European Journal of Philosophy</u> 7. 2 (1999): 129-157.

Habermas, Jürgen. <u>Between Facts and Norms: Contributions to a Discourse Theory of Law and Democracy</u>. Trans. Rehg, W. Cambridge, MA: MIT Press, 1996.

Habermas, Jürgen. <u>Knowledge and Human Interests</u>. Cambridge: Polity press, 1987

Habermas, Jürgen. <u>Theory of Communicative Action</u>. Vol. I. Boston: Beacon Press, 1984.

Habermas, J. <u>Knowledge and Human Interests; Theory and Practice; Communication and the Evolution of Society</u>. Trans. Shapiro, J.J. London: Heinemann, 1972.

Harris, Marvin. <u>Emics and Etics :the Insider/outsider Debate</u>. Ed. Thomas N. Headland; Kenneth.L; Marvin Harris. London: Sage, 1990.

Hegel, Georg W. F. "<u>Introductory Lectures on Aesthetics</u>." Trans. Bosanquet, B. London: Penguin, 1993.

Hall.R. <u>Occupations and the Social Structure</u>. New Jersey: Prentice-Hall, 1969.

Hamel, Jacques. "Sociology, Common Sense and Qualitative Methodology: The Position of Pierre Bourdieu and Alain Touraine Respecting Qualitative Methods." <u>British Journal of Sociology</u> 49. 1 (1998): 1-19.

Haron, John. <u>Experience and Method: An Enquiry Into the Concept of Experiential Research, Human Potential Research Project</u>. Guildford: University of Sydney, 1971.

Healy, Karen and Gabrielle Meagher. "The Reprofessionalisation of Social Work: collaborative approaches for achieving professional recognition." British Journal of Social Work. 34 (2004): 243-260.

Healy, Karen. "Reinventing Critical Social Work: Challenges From Practice, Context and Postmodernism." Critical Social Work 2. 2 (2001).

Healy, Karen. Social Work Practices: Contemporary Perspectives on Change. London: Sage, 2000.

Healy, Karen. "Conceptualising Constraint: Mouzelis, Archer and the Concept of Social Structure." Sociology 32. 3 (1998).

Heidegger, Martin. "The Fundamental Question of Metaphysics." Trans. Manheim, R. An Introduction to Metaphysics. Delhi: Motilal Banarsidass, 1999.

Held, David. "Democracy and Globalization." Reimagining Political Community: Studies in Cosmopolitan Democracy Eds. Daniele Archibug, Martin Kohler and David Held. Stanford: Stanford University Press, 2002.

Heller, Agnes. "Five Approaches to the phenomenon of Shame." Social Research 70. 4 (2003). 1015-30.

Heller, Agnes. "The Concept of the Politics Revisited." Political Theory Today 1976. Ed. David Held. Stanford: Stanford University Press, 1991. 331-43.

Heller, Agnes. "From Hermeneutics in Social Science to Hermeneutics of Social Science." Theory and Society 18. 3 (1989).

Heritage, John C. "Ethnomethodology." The social Theory Today Ed. Anthony GiddensandJonathanH. Turner. Cambridge: Polity Press, 1987.

Heron, John. "Transpersonal Co-Operative Inquiry." Handbook of Action Research: Participatory Inquiry and Practice Eds. Peter Reason and Hilary Bradbury. New Delhi: Sage, 2001. 333-9.

Heron, John. Co-Operative Inquiry: Research Into the Human Condition. London: Sage, 1996.

Heron, John. Experience and Method: An Enquiry Into the Concept of Experiential Research. Guildford: University of Sydney, 1971.

Hick, S. Social work in Canada, an introduction. Toronto: Thompson Educational Publishing Co., 2002.

Honneth Axel. The Struggle for Recognition: The Moral Grammar of Social Struggles, Trans. Joel Anderson. Cambridge: Polity, 1995.

Hotton, Kieron. "Social Work in Europe: Radical Traditions, Radical Futures?" Social Work in Europe 8. 1 (2000): 32-42.

Humphries, Beth. Critical Perspectives on Empowerment. London: Venture Press, 1996.

IASSW. "Historic Agreement on International Definition of Social Work." IASSW Newsletter 2002. 1 (2002).

Ife, Jim. "Localized Needs and a Globalized Economy: Bridging the Gap With Social Work Practice." Canadian Social Work Review 17 (2000).

Ife, Jim. Rethinking Social Work: Towards Critical Practice. Melbourne: Longman, 1997.

IRTC. Assesment of the Development Projects Carried on at Attappady. Palakkad: IRTC, 1998.

Joas, Hans. "Symbolic Interactionism." Social Theory today Eds. Anthony Giddens and Jonathan. H. Turner. Cambridge: Polity Press, 1987.

Johnson, Terry. Professions and Power. London: Macmillan, 1972.

Jones. Robert Alun Emile Durkheim: An Introduction to Four Major Works. New Delhi: Sage, 1986.

Jones, Chris. "Voices From the Front Line: State Social Workers and New Labour." British Journal of Social Work 31 (2001): 547-562.

Jordan, Bill. "Tough Love: Social Work, Social Exclusion, and the Third Way." British Journal of Social Work 31 (2001): 527-546.

Jordan, Bill and Charlie Jordan. <u>Social Work and the Third Way "Tough Love As Social Policy"</u>. London: Sage, 2000.

Kant, Immanuel. <u>What Is Enlightenment</u>. The Philosophy of Kant. Ed. Friedrich, C. New York: Modern Library, 1977.

Kant, Immanuel. <u>Kant: Political Writings</u>. Political Writings. Cambridge: Cambridge University Press, 1991.

Kapferer, Bruce. "<u>Forward</u>." <u>Creating Culture: Profiles in the Study of Culture</u> Ed. Astin-Broos. Sydney: Allen & Unwin, 1987. ix-xvii.

Kemmis, Stephen and Robin McTaggert. <u>The Action Research Planner</u>. Geelong: Deakin University Press, 1990.

KFRI [Kerala Forest research Institute]. <u>Studies on the Changing Pattern of Man -Forest Interactions and Its Implications on Ecology and Management</u>.: Kerala Forest research Institute, Thrissur, 1980.

Koning, Korrie de. "Participatory appraisal and education for empowerment?" <u>PLA Notes (24)</u> *(1995):* 34-37

Kuhn, Thomas. <u>The Structure of Scientific Revolutions</u>. Chicago: The University of Chicago Press, 1962.

Laragy, Carmel. "Social Workers in the Year 2000." <u>Asia-Pacific Journal of Social Work</u> 7. 1 (1997): 47-58.

Larson, Magali S. <u>The Rise of Professionalism: A Sociological Analysis</u>. Los Angeles: University of California Press, 1977.

Laveridge, Martin J. "Mac-Social Work: The Routinisation of Professional Activity." <u>Social Work</u> 38. 4 (2002): 354-362.

Lefebvre, Henri. <u>Everyday Life in the Modern World</u>. London: Allen Lane, 1976.

Lefebvre, Henri. "<u>Space: Social Product and Its Use Value</u>." <u>Critical Sociology: European</u>

Perspectives Ed. J.W. Freiberg. New York: Irvington Publishers, 1979.

Lefebvre, Henri. Critique of Everyday Life. London: Verso, 1991.

Lefebvre, Henri. "Reflections on the Politics of Space." Antipode 8. 2 (1976).

Lefebvre, Henri. The Production of Space. 1974. Trans. Smith, D. Oxford: Blackwell, 1994.

Leonard, Peter. "The Future of Critical Social Work in Uncertain Conditions." Critical Social Work 2. 1 (2001).

Leonard, Peter. "Postmodernism, Socialism and Social Welfare." Journal of Progressive Human Services 6. 2 (1995).

Leonard, Peter. Postmodern Welfare. New Delhi: Sage, 1997.

Levinas, Emmanuel. Totality and Infinity. Ed. Lingis, A. Pittsburgh: Duquense University Press, 1969.

Lewin, Kurt. "Action Research and Minority Problems." Journal of Social Issues 2 (1946): 34-46.

Lewin, Kurt. "Frontiers in Group Dynamics." Human Relations 1. 1 (1947a): 5-41.

Lewin, Kurt. "Frontiers in Group Dynamics ii." Human Relations 1. 2 (1947b): 143-154.

Lorenz, Walter. "Social Work Responses to New Labour in Continental European Countries, British Journal of Social Work." British Journal of Social Work 31 (2001): 595-609.

Lorenz, Walter. Social Work in a Changing Europe. London: Routledge, 1994.

Lyotard, Jean Francois. The Postmodern Condition: A Report on Knowledge. Trans. Massumi, G.B. Minneapolis: University of Minnesota Press., 1984.

Lymbery, Mark. "Social Work at the Crossroads." British Journal of Social Work 31 (2001).

Lynd, Helen M. On Shame and the Search for Identity. New York: Science Editions. 1961.

Lyons, Karen. International Social Work: Themes and Perspectives. Ashgate.: Aldershot, 1999.

MacMurray, John. The Self As Agent. London: Faber and Faber, 1957.

Madhu.P. "What Is Good Governance." KILA Magazine: 8-16. 2003

Markoviç, Mahilo. From Affluence to Praxis. Boston: Beacon Press, 1974.

Marcuse, Herbert. One Dimensional Man. Boston: Beacon Press, 1964.

Marx, Karl. "Theses on Feuerbach." Writings of the Young Marx on Philosophy and Society Ed. Loyd D. Easton and Kurt H. Guddat. New York, 1967. 400-2.

Marx, Karl. "Grundrisse." of Marxist Archieve: www.marxists.org, 2003.

Marx, Karl. The Eighteenth Brumaire of Louis Bonaparte. Moscow: Progress Publishers, 1977.

Marx, Karl. Preface to a Contribution to the Critique of Political Economy.: www. marxist.org, 2003.

Marx, Karl. The German Ideology.: www.marxist.org, 2003.

Massey, Andrew. Managing the Public Sector. Aldershot: Edward Elgar, 1993.

Mathur, PRG. Tribal Situation in Kerala. Trivandrum: Kerala History Society, 1977.

Mattaini, Mark. Knowledge for Practice. The Foundations of Social Work Practice: A Graduate Text. Eds. Meyer, C. and M.Mattaini. Washington DC: NASW Press, 1995.

May.T and M.Buck. "Power, Professionalism and Organisational Transformation." Sociological research online 3. 2 (1998).

McDonald, Catherine. "Forward Via the Past? Evidence-Based Practice As Strategy in Social Work." The Drawing Board: An Australian Review of Public Affairs 3. 3 (2003): 123-142.

McDonald, Catherine and A. Jones. "Reconstructing and Reconceptualising Social Work in the Emerging Milieu." Australian Social Work 53. 3 (2000).

McGee, Rosemary ed. Qualitative and Quantitative Poverty Appraisal Workshop: Some Reflexions and Responses. Cornell University, 2001.

McKernan, James. <u>Curriculum Action Research: A Handbook of Methods and Measures for the Reflective Practitioner</u>. II ed. London: Kogan Page, 1996.

McKernan, James. <u>Curriculum Action Research: a Handbook of Methods and resources for the Reflective Practitioner</u>. London: Kogan Page, 1991.

McKevitt, David. <u>Managing Core Public Services</u>. Oxford: Blackwell, 1998.

Mead, George Herbert. "<u>Interaction and Meaning</u>." <u>Mainstream and Critical Social Theory</u>. New Delhi: Sage, 2001.

Mead, George Herbert. "<u>Mind, Self, and Society</u>." <u>Mind, Self, and Society</u> Ed. C. W. Morris. Chicago: University of Chicago Press, 1934.

Meagher, Gabrille and Nigel Parton. "Modernising Social Work and the Ethics of Care." Social Work and Society. 2.1. (2004): 10-27.

Mehan, Hugh, et al. <u>Constructing School Success: The Consequences of Untracking Low-achieving Students</u>. Cambridge: Cambridge University Press, 1996.

Menon, Madhavan and et. a l. <u>Evaluation Report on ITDP, Attappady, Kirtards</u>. Calicut: KIRTARDS, 1982.

Merton, Robert.K. <u>Social theory and Social Science</u>. New York: Free Press, 1957.

Midgley, James. "Globalisation, Capitalism and Social Welfare: A Social Welfare Perspective." <u>Canadian Social Work, Special Issue: Social Work and Globalisation</u> 2. 1 (2000): 13-28.

Mills, Wright.C. <u>The Sociological Imagination</u>. 1949. New York: Oxford University Press, 2000.

Mokeri, Ramachandran. "Adivasi-Kurumba Corpses: On the Alienation of Culture, Performance and Development of the Adivasi -Kurumbas of Attapady." RESEARCH PROJECT THESIS. Centre for development studies, 2000.

Morén Stefan and Björn lom. "Explaining Human Change: *On Generative Mechanisms in Social* Work Practice" <u>Journal of Critical Realism</u>. 2.1, (2003)

Morgan, Gareth. <u>Creative Organisational Theory: A Resource Book</u>. London: Sage, 1989.

Morgan, Steve. "Managerialism and State Social Work in Britain." <u>The Hong Kong Journal of Social Work</u> 36. 1-2 (2002): 27-43.

Mukherji, Partha Nath. <u>Methodology in Social Research, Dilemmas and Perspectives</u>. New Delhi: Sage, 2000

Mullen, Edward J. <u>Evaluation for Practice</u>. 4th International Conference on Evaluation for Practice. Ed. Mullen, E.J. University of Tampere, Tampere, Finland, 2002.

Mullen, Edward J. "Construction of Personal Models for Effective Practice: A method for Utilizing Research Findings to Guide Social Interventions." <u>Journal of Social Service Research</u> 2. 1 (1978): 45-63.

Munday, Brain. "<u>Introduction: Definitions and Comparisons in European Social Care</u>." <u>Social Care in Europe</u> Eds. Brain Munday and Peter Ely. London: Prentice Hall, 1996.

Muraleedharan, P.K, S Sankar and K.C Chaco. <u>Studies on Human Ecology and Eco-Restoration of Attappady Valley</u>. Trichur: Kerala Institute of Forest Research, 1991.

Murphy, John. "The Voice of Memory: History, Autobiography and Oral Memory." <u>Historical Studies</u> 22 (1986): 157-175.

Massey, Andrew. <u>Managing the Public Sector</u>. Aldershot: Edward Elgar, 1993.

Nair, Sathish Chandran. <u>The Drying Bhavani, Waterless Attappady and the Volatile Cauvery</u>. Available: <u>www.narmada. org/sandrp</u>. 2002.

Nair, Sathish Chandran. <u>Long Term Conservation Potential of Natural Forests in the Southern Westernghats of Kerala.</u> New Delhi: MAB Committee, Department of Environment, Government of India, New Delhi, 1988.

Nash, Roy. "The Real Bourdieu: Euphemism and Truth in Theories of Reproduction." <u>Ace Papers</u>. 8 (2001): 54-69.

Noble, Carolyn. "Postmodern Thinking: Where is it taking social work?" Journal of Social Work. 4.3 (2004): 289-304.

Neumann, Erich. <u>The Origins and History of Consciousness,</u>. Bollingen Series XLII. Princeton: Princeton University Press, 1954.

Oliver, Kelly. "Witnessing and Testimony." <u>Parallax</u> 10. 1 (2004): 79-88.

Oliver, Kelly. <u>In Witnessing: Beyond Recognition</u>. Minneapolis: University of Minnesota Press, 2001.

Orme, Joan. "Regulation Or Fragmentation? Directions for Social Work Under New Labour." <u>British Journal of Social Work</u> 31 (2001): 611-624.

Oxaal, Zoa and Sarah Cook. "<u>Health and Poverty Gender Analysis</u>" Brighton: Institute of Development Studies, 1998.

Page, Steve and Susan Hamer. "Practice Development— Time to Realize The potential." <u>Practice Development in Health Care</u> 1.1 (2002).

Parry, N. and John Parry. "<u>Social Work, Professionalism and the State</u>." <u>Social Work, Welfare and the State</u> Eds. N. Parry and M. Rustin: C. Satyamurthi, London: Edward Arnold. 1979.

Patron, Nigel and Patrick O'Byrne. "What Do We Mean By Constructive Social Work?" <u>Critical Social Work</u> 2. 2 (2000a).

Patron, Nigel. "Some Thoughts on the Relationship Between Theory and Practice in and for Social Work." <u>British Journal of Social Work</u> 30 (2000b): 449-463.

Patron, Nigel. <u>Social Theory, Social Change and Social Work</u>. London: Routledge, 1996.

Patron, Nigel. ""Problematics of Government", (Post) Modern Social Work." <u>British Journal of Social Work</u> 24 (1994): 9-32.

Patron, Nigel and W Marshall. "<u>Postmodernism and Discourse Approaches to Social Work</u>." Social

Work: Themes, Issues and Critical Debates Ed. L. Dominelli and M. Payne R. Adams. Houndsmills: Macmillan, 1998. 240-9.

Payne, Malcolm. "Social Work Theories and Reflective Practice." Social Work: Themes, Issues and Critical Debates Eds. Robert Adams, Lena Dominelli and Malcolm Payne. London: Macmillan, 1998. 117-37.

Payne, Malcolm. What Is Professional Social Work?. Birmingham: Venture Press, 1996.

Pease, Bob and Jan Fook. Transforming Social Work Practice: Postmodern Critical Perspectives. London: Routledge, 1999.

Penna, Sue. "On the Perils of Applying Theory to Practice." Critical Social Work 4. 1 (2004).

Pile, Steve and Nigel Thrift. Mapping the subject: Geographies of cultural transformation. London: Routledge, 1996

Pozzuto, Richard. "Notes on a Possible Critical Social Work." Critical Social Work 1. 1 (2000).

Prabhakaran. G. "Dalit Girl Hostel for Sexual Exploitation." The Hindu Sunday/2 Jul. 2000a.

Prabhakaran. G. "Tribals Being Pushed to the Wall: Study." The Hindu Wednesday/16 Aug. 2000b.

Pretty, Jules N. Regenerating Agriculture, Policies and Practices for Sustainability and Self-Reliance. New Delhi: Vikas, 1995.

Probyn, Elspeth. Seeing the self: Gendered Positions in Culture Studies. London: Routledge, 1993.

Ramon, Shula. "Beyond Community Care: Normalisation and Integration Work." London: Mind Macmillan (1991).

Ramsay, Richard. "Is Social Work a Profession? a 21st Century Answer to a 20th Century Question." Canadian Association of Social Workers (CASW) (1998).

Ramsay, Richard. 'Toward a Common Paradigmatic Home: Social Work in the Twenty First Century ' Indian Journal of Social Work 60,(1999) :69 –86.

Ransom. S and J, Stewart. Management for the Public Domain. Basingstoke: Macmillan, 1994.

Reason, Peter and Hilary Bradbury. "Introduction: Inquiry and Participation in Search of a World Worthy of Human Aspiration." Handbook of Action Research: Participatory Inquiry and Practice Eds. Peter Reason and Hilary Bradbury. New Delhi: Sage, 2001. 1-14.

Reason, Peter and William R. Torbert. "Toward a Transformational Science: A Further Look at the Scientific Merits of Action Research." Concepts and Transformations 6. 1 (2001): 1-37.

Rees, Stuart. "The Fraud and the Fiction." The Human Costs of Managerialism Eds. Stuart Rees and Rodlev. Leichhardt: Pluto Press, 1997.

Rescher, Nicholas. Complexity: A Philosophical Overview. New Brunswick: Transaction Publishers, 1998.

Rossiter, Amy. "Discourse Analysis in Critical Social Work: from Apology to Question." Critical Social Work 6. 1 (2005).

Rossiter, Amy. "Innocence Lost and Suspicion Found: Do We Educate for or Against Social Work?." Critical Social Work 2. 1 (2001).

Rossiter, Amy. "A Perspective on Critical Social Work'." Journal of Prgoressive Human Services 7. 2 (1996): 23-41.

Ruch, Gillian. "From Triangle to Spiral: Reflective Practice in Social Work Education, Practice and Research." Social Work Education 21. 2 (2002).

Sackett, D. L, et al. . Evidence Based Medicine: How to Practice and Teach Ebm. 2nd Edition ed. New York: Churchill Livingstone, 2000.

Sartre, Jean -Paul. "The Dogmatic Dialectic and the Critical Dialectic." Trans. Sheridan-Smith, A. Critique of Dialectic Reason, 1960.

Sayer, Andrew. "Valuing Culture and Economy." Culture and economy after cultural turn Ed. Ray. Land A Sayer. London: Sage, 1999

Sayer, Andrew. Moral Economy. 2004/07/02. Web: http://www.comp. lancs.ac.uk/sociology. Department of Sociology, Lancaster University. Available: http://www.comp.lancs.ac.uk/sociology.

Sayer, Andrew. "Moral Economy and Political Economy." Studies in Political Economy 61 (2000): 79-104.

Sayer, Andrew. "What Are You Worth?: Why Class is an Embarrassing Subject" Sociological Research Online, 7.3., (2002).

Scheff, Thomas J. "Shame and the Social Bond: Applying the Part/Whole Approach to a Case Study." Sociological Theory. 18, 86-99, (2000).

Schön, Donald. The Reflective Practitioner. New York: Basic Books, 1983.

Schutz, Alfred. "Choosing Among the Projects of Action." Mainstream and Critical Social Theory 1962. Ed. Jeffrey C. Alexander. Vol. II. New Delhi: Sage, 2001. 332-55.

Schutz, Alfred. "Commonsense and Scientific Interpretations of Human Action." Collected Papers. Vol. 1. The Hague: Marttinus Nijhoff, 1962.

Schwandt, Thomas A. Dictionary of Qualitative Inquiry. Second ed. New Delhi: Sage, 2001.

Sen, Amatya. Inequality Re-Examined. 1992. New Delhi: Oxford University Press, 1999.

Sennett, Richard and Jonathan Cobb. The Hidden Injuries of Class. New York: Vintage Books, 1972.

Shanin, Teodor. "Placing Social Work Within Social Theory and and Political Practice." The interface between social Work and social Policy Ed. S. Ramon L. Birmingham: Venture press, 1998.

Shaw, Ian. "The Quality of Mercy: Management of Quality in the Personal and Social Services." The Politics of Quality in the Public Sector Eds. I. Kirkpatrick and L. M. Martinez. London: Routledge, 1995.

Sheffy, Rakefet. "Models and Habituses: Problems in the Idea of Cultural Repertoires." Canadian Review of Comparative Literature XXIV. 1 (1997).

Shotter, John. <u>Cultural Politics of Everyday Life: Social Construction and Knowing of the Third Kind</u>. Buckingham: Open University Press, 1993.

Sjoberg Gideon and Robert Nett. <u>A methodology for social research</u>. New Delhi: Rawat Publications, 1992

Smith, Adam. <u>The Theory of Moral Sentiments</u>. India polis: Liberty Press, 1969.

Soja, Edward. <u>Different Spaces; Interpreting the Spatial Organization of Societies</u>. Atlanta, 2001.

Soja, Edward. "<u>Planning·In/for Postmodernity</u>." <u>Space and Social Theory</u> Eds. Georges Benko and Ulf Strohmayer. Oxford: Blackwell, 1997. 236-50.

Soja, Edward. <u>Postmodern Geographies</u>. London: Verso, 1989.

Spirkin, Alexander. <u>Philosophy As a World View</u>. 2003/07/03. www.Marxist.org. Available: <u>www.marxists.org/en/archive</u> /spirkin/works/1983/dm/.

Struever, Nancy S. "The Study of Language and the Study of History." <u>Journal of Interdisciplinary History</u> 4 (1974).

Surendranath, C. "Whose Land Is It Anyway? Adivasi Land Struggle in Kerala Takes a Violent, Tragic Turn." <u>HumanScape</u>. 10.3 (2003)

Swedberg, Richard. "Bourdieu's Advocacy of the Concept of Interest and Its Role in Economic Sociology." <u>Economic Sociology News Letter</u> 4. 2 (2003): 2-6.

Taylor, Cox and S.White. <u>Practising Reflectivity in Health and Welfare: Making Knowledge</u>. Buckingham, UK: Open University Press, 2000.

Thompson, Paul. <u>The Voice of the Past: Oral History</u>. Oxford: oxford university press, 1978.

Toren, Nina. <u>Social Work: The Case of a Semi-Profession</u>. Beverly Hills: Sage, 1972.

Tosh, John. "<u>History By Word of Mouth</u>." <u>The Pursuit of History</u>. 2nd Edition ed, 1991. 221-7.

Touraine, Alain. "A Method for Studying Social Actors." <u>Journal of World System Research</u> VI. 3

(2000): 900-918.

Turner, Jonathan. H. <u>The Structure of Sociological Theory</u>. Jaipur: Rawat, 1995.

Uphoff, Norman. "Bridging quantitative-qualitative differences in poverty appraisal: self-critical thoughts on qualitative approaches". <u>Qualitative and Quantitative poverty appraisal: complementarities, tensions and the way forward.</u> Cornell: Cornell University Press, 2001.

Urry, John. "Duality of Structure: Some Critical Issues." <u>Theory, Culture, Society</u> 1 (1982): 100-106.

Van Krieken, Robert. "<u>Norbert Elias and Process Sociology.</u>" <u>The Handbook of Social Theory</u> Ed. George Ritzer & Barry Smart. London: Sage, 2001. 353-67.

Vijayanand, S. M. "<u>People's Participation in Participatory Development Programmes; a Case Study of Attappady Integrated Tribal Developmet Project</u>." M.Phil Thesis. Centre for development studies, Thiruvananthapuram, 1997.

Weber, Max. "<u>Formal Organisation.</u>" <u>Mainstream and Critical Social Theory</u> Ed. Jeffrey C. Alexander. Vol. I. New Delhi: Sage, 2001.

Weber, Max and et al. <u>Max Weber: Political Writings</u>. Cambridge Texts in History and Political Thoughts. Cambridge: Cambridge University Press, 1994.

Weber, Max. <u>Protestant Ethics and the Spirit of Capitalism</u>. London: George Allen and Unwin, 1976.

Weber, Max. <u>The Logical Problems of Historical Economics</u>. 1903. New York: Free Press, 1975.

Wignaraja, Ponna. <u>The Intervention Through Praxis and Participatory Development</u>. Kerala Institute of Local Administration, Thrissur: Kerala Institute of Local Administration, Thrissur, 2002.

Wignaraja, Ponna. "<u>Towards a New Praxis for Sustainable Development in South Asia.</u>" <u>The Challenge in South Asia: Development, Democracy and Regional Co-operation</u> Eds. Ponna Wignaraja and Akmal Hussain. New Delhi: Sage, 1989.

Wilensky. "The Professionalisation of Everyone?" <u>American Journal of Sociology</u> 70 (1964): 137-

158.

Williams, Suzanne, Seed, Janet and Mwau, Adelina. "Oxfam Gender Training Manual." Oxford: Oxfam, 1994

Wise, Sue. "Becoming a Feminist Social Worker." Feminist Praxis: Research, Theory and Epistemology in Feminist Sociology Ed. Liz Stanley. London: Routledge, 1990.

Wittgenstein, Ludwig. Philosophical Investigation. Trans. Anscombe, G. Oxford: Basil Blackwell, 1976.

Wooster, Martin Morse. "Who Put the Social in Social Work?" Women's Quarterly (Autumn 2002).

Woznicki, Andrew.N. "Nature of Human Praxis in Karl Marx." Person and nature Ed. George F. McLean. Vol. 1. Washington DC: University Press of America, 2004.

Yeo, Stephen. "The Politics of Community Publications." People's History and Socialist Theory, Ed. Raphael Samuel. London: Routledge, 1981.

Young.TR. "Sociology and Human Knowledge: Scientific Vs. Folk Methods." The American Sociologist 16. 2 (1981).

Zahl, Mari -Anne. "The Impact of Social Policies on the Formation of Social Work." BSU/IUC Journal of social work theory and practice. 5 (2003).

ABOUT THE AUTHOR

Dr Madhu Prabakaran is the proponent of the Praxis Intervention Methodology in Social Science Research